IRON AND STEEL

HENRY M. McKIVEN JR.

IRON

Class, Race, and Community in

AND

Birmingham, Alabama, 1875–1920

STEEL

The University of North Carolina Press | Chapel Hill & London

The paper in this book meets the guidelines for

permanence and durability of the Committee on

Production Guidelines for Book Longevity of

the Council on Library Resources.

Library of Congress Cataloging-in-Publication Data

McKiven, Henry M.   Iron and steel : class, race,

and community in Birmingham, Alabama, 1875–

1920 / by Henry M. McKiven, Jr.   p. cm.

Includes bibliographical references and index.

ISBN 0-8078-2188-8 (cloth: alk. paper).—

ISBN 0-8078-4524-8 (paper: alk. paper)

1. Iron and steel workers—Alabama—Birmingham—

History.   2. Afro-American iron and steel workers—

Alabama—Birmingham—History.   I. Title.

HD8039.I52U573   1995

331.7′669142′09761781—dc20   94-27198

                                          CIP

99 98 97 96 95   5 4 3 2 1

CONTENTS

TABLES AND MAPS

ILLUSTRATIONS

ACKNOWLEDGMENTS

A project of this sort would not be possible without the intellectual, moral, and financial support of many people and institutions. Other scholars took time out of busy schedules to read and critique chapters, friends offered encouragement at critical times, and several institutions came through with research assistance, grants, or jobs. It is indeed a pleasure to thank all who have contributed directly and indirectly to the research and writing of this book.

I owe my greatest intellectual debts to Don Harrison Doyle, David Carlton, and Crandall Shifflett. Professor Doyle went beyond the call of duty as the director of the dissertation from which the book has evolved. He not only carefully read very rough drafts of all chapters, but he also patiently responded to the many questions of an overly anxious graduate student. There were times, I am sure, when he wanted to give the whole thing up. He did not and for that I am deeply grateful. Though Professor Carlton's frank criticism of my arguments often angered me, he forced me to reexamine arguments and to either sharpen them or abandon some that did not work. I have over the years come to appreciate how much he has done to improve this book. Professor Shifflett supervised my initial inquiry into southern labor history when I was a graduate student at Virginia Tech. His ideas about labor and race relations in the South continue to influence my own. More important, he insisted that I was capable enough to make it in this profession.

When this work was in its earliest stages, I benefited greatly from the criticism and camaraderie of a number of fellow travelers at Vanderbilt University. Doug Flamming, Robert Hall, Robert Tracy McKenzie, Patricia Miletich, and Mary DeCredico all patiently listened to me as I held forth at meetings of the Southern Social History Group. Since then Doug, Robert, and Tracy have either read parts of this work or listened to it during lengthy phone calls. Larry Eldridge, who was with us at Vanderbilt, read the entire dissertation and provided detailed suggestions about reorganizing and rewriting. He has maintained his interest through every stage of the revision process. Thanks to all of these folks for their help and their friendship.

Parts of this book would not exist if not for the gracious cooperation of

Robert J. Norrell. When I began the project, he had already been working on Birmingham's history for several years. In the true spirit of intellectual endeavor, he shared with me fruits of his labors that were relevant to my own. He then read the results more than once and suggested revisions that have improved the final product. He has also supported me in other aspects of my professional life.

Robert Zieger read the manuscript several times for the press and provided detailed recommendations for revision. His insistence upon clarity of purpose helped tremendously. If any portion of this work remains unclear, it is the responsibility of the author alone.

Other scholars have contributed to the work more indirectly. Professors Derwyn McElroy and Donald Dodd at Auburn University in Montgomery tried to teach me that thinking was not just an involuntary reflex. J. Mills Thornton conducted a seminar at Vanderbilt that shaped my thinking about the ideology of white supremacy in southern history. Elizabeth Fox-Genovese, after hearing a conference paper I presented, took time from her busy schedule to write me a letter encouraging me to forge ahead at a time when I had profound doubts about the whole enterprise. Since then she has been willing to talk to me at any time about my work or other issues. George Daniels, chair of the Department of History at the University of South Alabama, has been a wise counsel and has made sure I received the time to complete the manuscript. Leonard Macaluso, a colleague and friend, has spent many hours listening to and criticizing my ideas about social relations. He directed me to a number of studies in French working-class history that have influenced several of my arguments. His questions about my theoretical assumptions have been enormously helpful. James White, director of creative writing at the University of South Alabama, read several chapters with an eye to clarity of expression. Though it may not always be evident, he has taught me much about clear writing. Lewis Bateman has followed this work since it was only a dissertation prospectus. He has patiently answered any questions I have asked, and his advice concerning the book and running has been invaluable.

Through the years of research in Birmingham, I came to rely upon the fine staff of the archives at the Birmingham Public Library. Marvin Whiting, the director of the archives, never failed to answer my many questions and continued to watch for material that might be relevant to my topic. Above all, he made the task of research in Birmingham a pleasant experience. Thanks also to Arthur Edge and Leann Barr at American Cast Iron Pipe Company for allowing me to see some critical company records.

A number of people outside the halls of academe contributed their friendship and understanding over the years. Dennis Long, Sandra Zelley, Sam Miletich, Cindy Bona, and Leslie Emmitt helped keep me grounded in reality, while letting me know that what I was doing had some merit.

Finally, I want to express my everlasting gratitude and devotion to my family. My wife's parents, James and Bobbie Tucker, have made life for us a little better during some lean times. My mother, Anne Higgins McKiven, has always insisted that I disregard naysayers and do what I set out to do. My wife, Julie Tucker McKiven, has never wavered in her commitment to me and to what I have tried to accomplish. There have been times when I wanted to quit, and, given the nature of this business, it would have been easy for her to let me. Yet, she remained firm and so shored up my will to stay the course. I will never be able to express adequately what that has meant to me. I hope she knows.

IRON AND STEEL

INTRODUCTION

In the years following the Civil War, some southerners wrote of the need to free the region from a dependence upon agriculture that, in their view, was a
key factor in the failure of the Confederacy. They called for development of
southern industries that would capitalize on the region's natural resources
and would provide a source of employment for its population. Industrialization, according to the vision, would provide the way for the South to redeem
itself and, in time, rise again to ascendancy in the nation.

New South boosters did not ignore the potential problems that an in-
dustrialized society would generate. Of particular concern were problems
they associated with the presence of an industrial working class. Antebellum defenders of southern institutions had frequently argued that only in an
agrarian society, and preferably one based on black slavery, could freedom
and equality for white men be preserved. They described industrial societies
in Europe and the northern United States that created large classes of men
dependent upon other men for their existence. Among the "wage slaves"
resentment festered until it exploded in periodic attacks on the employing
classes. Advocates of the New South did not deny the accuracy of this image
of industrialism. The South, they declared, could learn from the failures of
older industrial societies. The industrial order they envisioned would dis-
tinguish itself from the industrial North by providing means through which
white men would experience the prosperity and upward mobility that were
essential to harmony in a free labor society.

Birmingham was something of a testing ground for the "New South creed." The builders of the town imagined a society in which white men would join together on the basis of common interest in the pursuit of economic prosperity on the industrial frontier. They believed that an economy free of monopoly in a region that had yet to be developed offered the material conditions for the harmony between capital and labor that had become little more than myth in the aging industrial North. Reinforcing the bond between white labor and white capital was a shared devotion to the subordination of blacks. Birmingham's boosters articulated an ideology of white supremacy that acted as a "social leaven," transcending divisions of class within the superior race. Blacks would perform common labor, freeing white workers to achieve positions in society reserved for them only. Recognizing their interests in the maintenance of the racial order, white workingmen would assist in the control of the black laboring class.

Historians agree that the South's social order rested upon the system of racial control mandated by the ideology of white supremacy. They differ sharply, however, when it comes to explaining the social origins and consequences of Birmingham's system of race and class relations. With a few recent exceptions, historians have embraced the argument that employers and other dominant groups, fearing a unified working-class challenge to their hegemony, skillfully used the ideology of white supremacy to blind white workers to their long-term interest in uniting with black workers.[1] Workers might unite to challenge the authority of their employers but rarely were able to overcome the racial hostility their employers actively encouraged. A racially divided labor force, the argument typically concludes, enhanced employers' ability to control the entire working class.[2]

It is this view that informs the most influential study of working-class race relations in nineteenth- and early-twentieth-century Birmingham. In his article "Black Workers and Labor Unions in Birmingham, 1897–1904," Paul Worthman argues that historians have placed too much emphasis on the "racial hostility" of southern white workers. To correct this imbalance he presents evidence of widespread support among Birmingham unionists for interracial cooperation at the end of the nineteenth century. This enlightened philosophy of class solidarity, suggests Worthman, originated among white workers who had moved to Birmingham from the North and therefore were "less moved by appeals to racial solidarity." Advocates of interracial cooperation, working through the American Federation of Labor, the Alabama State Federation of Labor, and the Birmingham Trades Union Council, made substantial progress in their campaign to bridge racial divisions among workers. They failed, however, to overcome employer hostility to the labor movement, which rapidly declined in strength after 1904 in the wake of an effective open shop campaign. Worthman concludes that as a result of organized labor's decline "discrimination and racial hostility, no longer held in check by cross pressures from the state's labor movement, came to the fore among white workers." Employers could then continue to "use racial hostility to discipline the class antagonisms of the New South."[3]

Worthman's article fully dissects the racial policies of a few exceptional labor leaders. As he admits, most workers, organized and unorganized, opposed the labor movement's opening to blacks. Workers in the iron and steel plants of the city were particularly hostile toward proposals for cooperation with black laborers. As Herbert Hill has argued, the existence of such white attitudes poses a dilemma for historians like Worthman who believe that "the class struggle, joined by united workers, would in time resolve the persistent and ideologically vexing issue of race by rendering it irrelevant." Worthman briefly dismisses white workers' opposition to cooperation with blacks as less a product of racial prejudice than a case of skilled workers' traditional antagonism toward the unskilled. But the fact that unions specifically excluded blacks suggests that workers' racial attitudes were more central to the Birmingham story than Worthman indicates.[4] If white metal workers were as free of racial hostility as Worthman asserts, they would not have singled out blacks for exclusion from their trades and organizations. Worthman also fails to explain the reasons for the development of the particular pattern of race relations found in Birmingham's iron and steel plants. Why did the iron and steel industry not adopt an employment strategy that relied solely on whites and thereby avoid the race problem?

No one has yet fully explained the origins of Birmingham's racial division of work, particularly the role of white workers' organizations in creating it. Indeed, Gavin Wright asserts that, because labor unions were weak during the early history of Birmingham, they can be dismissed as a factor in the creation and perpetuation of workplace segregation. A more important factor, he contends, was that black workers had learned unskilled iron work before and during the Civil War, while white workers had always monopolized skilled work. Postbellum employers simply extended these prewar employment practices, according to Wright.[5]

Wright's point about the nature of the labor market is well taken, but his further point about the role of organized labor in perpetuating a segmented labor market is somewhat off the mark. He, like the studies on which his conclusions are based, devoted little attention to the early history of labor and race relations in Birmingham's iron industry. During this period white craftsmen played a key role in defining principles of industrial race relations that few whites, workers and nonworkers, union and nonunion, ever questioned. White workers and their employers created a caste system in Birmingham that reserved skilled jobs for the "superior race" and relegated blacks to the most menial jobs in the iron industry. The system that evolved reflected the interaction of whites' ideas about the capabilities of the "inferior race," labor market conditions peculiar to Birmingham and the iron and steel industry, and the socioeconomic interests of white capital and white labor.

Cooperation between white capital and white labor in the subordination of blacks has often been cited to support the argument that the ideology of white supremacy had the power to submerge class divisions. For example, Horace Mann Bond argued in the 1930s that the racial division of work produced the unification of white labor and white capital celebrated by Birmingham's civic elite. In a recent variation on this theme, Gary Kulik contends that one Birmingham furnace company restricted blacks to unskilled jobs to "prevent the development of class consciousness."[6]

Obvious racial division may, however, obscure sharp class differences within the dominant and the subordinate race.[7] This was the case in Birmingham. From the perspective of white workers, the caste system, and the ideology of white supremacy that supported it, was essential to the defense of their class interests.[8] Skilled whites never thought that their employers were so devoted to the ideology of white supremacy that they would not replace whites with blacks if it was in their interest to do so. The claims of craftsmen to authority on the shop floor included the right to protect themselves against potential violations of the racial division of work. To accomplish this end they established unions that excluded blacks and sought to prevent the development of a supply of skilled black labor that could be used to undermine their position. White skilled workers believed that their social and economic interests were inextricably linked to the maintenance of a rigid caste system.

The sphere of production in early Birmingham generated a well-defined occupational hierarchy based largely on race that workers extended into the community. In their neighborhoods, their recreational activities, their organizations, and their politics, workers defined distinct social identities. Skilled white workers lived in neighborhoods that those beneath them on the occupational ladder could not afford. Their ability to live in residential neighborhoods away from the smoke and grime of industrial plants conferred upon them a status higher than that of unskilled workers, particularly blacks. Within these neighborhoods working people built social and cultural institutions that reinforced divisions within the working class.

Despite the existence of an oppressive system of racial subordination, thousands of African Americans moved to Birmingham, seeking freedom from the harsh realities of life in the countryside. What they experienced in the "Magic City" was certainly far removed from the stories of opportunity and success told by labor recruiters, relatives, and friends. But they managed to build a thriving community that offered an escape from the isolation and, to a degree, the dangers of the rural South. Moreover, through informal and formal means, black workers achieved a measure of control over their lives at work. Black workers constantly challenged the racial oppression their employers and white workers perpetuated. At times they formed their own organizations to enforce their understanding of their rights; at other times they exploited white class divisions to secure jobs traditionally closed to them.

Black workers' struggles often proved to be futile, yet they persevered. And, during the first two decades of the twentieth century, they began to experience dramatic, though limited, improvements in their condition. Although Jim Crow segregation remained firmly entrenched, the system changed as Birmingham's economy evolved, becoming more flexible in some respects. Employers began to challenge white workers' control of racial lines in their plants, hiring blacks for jobs white workers claimed. Organized whites fought to maintain their control of the racial division of work but failed to develop an adequate response to the transformation of work that came with the production of steel in Birmingham. The growth of a white semiskilled worker population suspicious of labor unions hindered labor leaders' efforts to build the kind of consensus on the race issue that had been possible during the first two decades of Birmingham's history. The labor movement vacillated between a strategy of absolute racial exclusion and a strategy that would have controlled blacks through organization in separate labor unions. To most black workers the latter option was no better than the first, and they remained outside of, and hostile to, the organized labor movement.

The class and racial conflicts generated by the transformation of work could not be confined within the workplaces of the city. As part of an effort to create a more efficient and disciplined workforce, a number of employers began to extend their influence into workers' lives away from the plant. Many workers embraced this "welfare capitalism," because they received benefits denied them by other institutions. Others, fearing further erosion of their autonomy, resisted employer interference in their private lives. A large segment of the working class—African Americans, native-born whites, and immigrants from Europe—also opposed moral reformers who sought to restrict citizens' personal independence by imposing codes of behavior they defined. Many other white workers, however, saw moral reform as a way to regain control of their community, to defend it against a perceived black and immigrant threat their employers had helped create. This fragmentation extended into and helped shape working-class politics. White skilled workers found it increasingly difficult to assert the level of influence that had made them a political force during the first two decades of the city's existence.

I have attempted to unravel the complex connections between the racial and class struggles that shaped Birmingham's social and economic order without assigning priority to either race or class. During the period covered herein, Birmingham's workers revealed an understanding of their place in the world that always linked their position in the socioeconomic order to the circumstances of their birth. White iron and steel workers struggled to preserve a place in the economic, social, and political spheres they believed to be their birthright. Black iron and steel workers, on the other hand, struggled against a class and racial system that denied them opportunity and full equality as citizens because of the color of their skin. These conflicts of class and race forced constant reevaluation and revision of the ideology of white supremacy and the concept of community that Birmingham's founders and early settlers embraced. The industrial city that eventually emerged looked much different from the "workshop town" of boosters' dreams.

CHAPTER I

The Creation of Birmingham
and the Problem of Labor

Historians of Birmingham and the New South have devoted much attention to southern boosters' continuous, and sometimes quixotic, search for capital. Their overtures to some of the leading finance capitalists in America have been well documented and extensively analyzed. Lack of capital was, to be sure, a serious obstacle standing in the way of southern industrialization in the aftermath of the Civil War. But Birmingham's boosters were as concerned with the recruitment of labor, particularly white skilled labor, as they were with attracting investors. During the 1880s the number of metal-working shops increased from three to thirty-three, exhausting the local supply of skilled labor.[1] Employers and boosters therefore looked outside the state and the region for the craftsmen essential to the success of their experiment in community building.

In addressing the problem of labor, promoters and employers embraced an ideology that became a standard against which citizens of the community measured the reality they experienced. Civic leaders spoke and wrote of an industrial society in which white labor and white capital worked together as equals for the good of the community. This "natural harmony" in the South was reinforced by the subordination of the black workers who would serve all classes of whites. Shared economic interests combined with a common devotion to the ideology of white supremacy would transcend the class division that plagued industrial centers in the North and Europe.

Reality in Birmingham was, of course, far removed from the boosters'

7

vision of an ideal industrial town. As the "workshop town" so central to promoters' understanding of free labor ideology evolved into a large industrial city, the gap widened between what working people of both races expected and what they experienced. Conflict ensued as various groups defended their particular definition of the ideals that attracted them to the Magic City. Subsequent chapters will be concerned with that reality. This chapter sets the stage by examining the vision boosters articulated in an effort to attract white craftsmen to their new industrial frontier.

The establishment of Birmingham was the climax of a movement for economic modernization in Alabama that had its origins in the 1850s. Many of Birmingham's founding fathers had been leaders of this earlier movement. Frank Gilmer, James Withers Sloss, Daniel Troy, and John T. Milner, to name just a few, became interested in the industrial potential of Jefferson and surrounding counties after Michael Tuomey's surveys of the extensive iron and coal deposits there began to appear during the 1850s. They and others recognized that the red rocks of the hills of Jefferson County could be the foundation for enormous wealth rather than just a source of red dye for local farmers.[2]

Tuomey's discoveries sparked a minor boom in coal mining and iron making in some northern Alabama counties, but inadequate transportation facilities limited development. Men interested in developing the mineral district lobbied during the 1850s for state aid to extend railroads throughout the region. Despite considerable opposition, advocates of state aid did manage to secure some assistance. While political conflict continued over the state aid issue and over the routes various roads would take, 610 miles of track were added to Alabama's system in the 1850s.[3]

One of the railroads the state assisted was the Alabama Central Railroad, or the South and North. The owners of the South and North planned to build a line through the mineral district to serve the iron- and coal-producing center they hoped to build. In 1854 the state legislature appropriated $10,000 for the South and North's survey of a proposed route from Montgomery, through the heart of Jefferson County, to Decatur that would eventually extend north, connecting it with the Louisville and Nashville Railroad (L&N). The man given this assignment was a young engineer named John T. Milner. In his report Milner confirmed Tuomey's findings but emphasized that the potential of the mineral district could not be realized without improved transportation facilities.[4]

Apparently Milner was persuasive, for work on the South and North began in 1860 after the state advanced the company $663,135. By 1861 the road had crossed the Cahaba coal fields to Calera in Shelby County, just south of Jefferson County. After the start of the Civil War, Frank Gilmer, then owner of 75 percent of South and North stock, secured enough aid to extend the road to Shades Mountain, which overlooked Jones Valley, the future site of Birmingham.[5]

As Alabama's railroad network expanded into the mineral district, the number of blast furnaces and coal mines in the state increased sharply. South and North stockholders undertook one of the most ambitious of the new projects. Gilmer, Milner, Daniel Pratt, and other officers of the railroad combined resources and organized the Red Mountain Iron and Coal Company. Construction of the company's furnace at Oxmoor was underway when the Civil War began. At that point the fortunes of Red Mountain Iron and Coal and of the entire mineral district became linked to the Confederate government's need for munitions.

The Confederacy subsidized the completion of Red Mountain's furnaces and directly or indirectly assisted in the establishment of other furnaces and rolling mills in the region. One of these was W. S. McElwain's Cahaba Iron Works. McElwain, a machinist originally from New England, moved to Alabama after the Confederate government purchased the equipment of his Holly Springs, Mississippi, rolling mill and furnace. He used money from the sale to finance the building of the Cahaba works, which then sold most of its pig iron to the Confederate arsenal at Selma, Alabama.[6]

The largest of the Civil War iron makers was the Shelby Iron Company. Horace Ware, a native of Lynn, Massachusetts, established the company in the late 1840s. Ware's father had been involved in the iron trade in Massachusetts, New York, and North Carolina before moving his family to Shoals Creek in Bibb County, Alabama. The elder Ware erected several primitive forges in Bibb and Shelby counties with his son's assistance. Then, in the early 1840s, the younger Ware bought some timberland and other property in Shelby County that contained brown hematite iron ore and prepared for his own venture into the iron business. Ware's Shelby furnace produced pig iron for conversion into hollow ware, which Ware then exchanged with local farmers, merchants, and blacksmiths for produce and other goods. Ware earned little profit during his first decade or so in business.[7]

The Shelby company continued to operate on a modest scale until 1862 when it secured a Confederate contract. In order to meet the demands of the Confederate government, Ware needed to expand his facilities but lacked the skilled labor and the funds to do so. To solve the latter problem, he looked to John W. Lapsley of Selma and the Confederate government. Ware, Lapsley, and the company's board launched an expansion program that would enable the company to more fully exploit the new market created by the Confederacy's need for iron products. The Confederate government covered approximately half of the costs of this expansion as part of its program to aid companies producing weapons and supplies for the war effort. Lapsley brought in Giles Edwards, a Welsh iron master who had worked in the Pennsylvania and East Tennessee iron industries, to rebuild the Shelby furnaces; he also hired Hamilton T. Beggs, an experienced English foundryman. Under Edwards and Beggs the Shelby Company produced iron for the Confederacy until 1865 when Union troops destroyed its facilities.[8]

In the short term the war was a setback for Alabama's iron industry. Union raids destroyed furnaces, foundries, and railroads throughout the region. But the opportunity for profit during the war had attracted men with experience in iron making to the state. Many of them stayed in Alabama when the war was over to take advantage of mineral deposits that Robert Somers, a British visitor to the region in 1870, called "by far the most deeply interesting material fact on the American continent." McElwain, Edwards, Beggs, and Ware, among others, would play leading roles in the reconstruction of Alabama's iron industry.[9]

Essential to this revival was the completion of railroad lines begun before the war. The South and North resumed its construction with assistance from the state and from James Sloss, president of the Nashville and Decatur Railroad, and Albert Fink, general manager of the L&N. Both Sloss and Fink wanted for themselves and their companies a share of the great profits they thought would soon flow out of Jefferson and surrounding counties. When the South and North finally opened for traffic in 1872, it was integrated with the L&N and thereby linked the mineral district to markets beyond the South.[10]

Having bought land along the road in anticipation of its completion, Josiah Morris, Milner, and ten other investors organized the Elyton Land Company in 1870 "with the view to the location, laying off and effecting the building of a city."[11] Elyton Land began to promote the mineral district as the place where the building of the New South would begin. Its investors believed manufacturing would provide the means through which they and their fellow southerners would restore a society of opportunity. An article in De Bow's Review (1867) predicted that around furnaces and factories towns

Iron works at Ironton, one of the earliest post–Civil War iron works in Jefferson County, ca. 1870. Alabama State Department of Archives and History.

would grow "to which every needed service is sure to come from the neighborhood or from abroad." [12]

Northerners funded a number of early ventures in the iron business, establishing a long lasting relationship between the Birmingham district and northern investors. After the war, when southern capital resources were limited, men who wanted to rebuild destroyed plants or build new ones went north in search of capital. They secured some financial backing initially, but interest in Birmingham waned rapidly as the national economy began slipping in the mid-1870s. [13] The severe economic depression of those years, combined with a cholera epidemic, left the town, as one early resident put it, "practically a graveyard." [14]

Birmingham's fortunes began to improve by the end of the 1870s thanks to an upturn in the national economy, a shift to a less costly method of pig iron production, and the discovery of a rich source of fuel. Until 1876 iron foundries in the Birmingham district produced charcoal pig iron, which cost more to produce than coke pig iron. Birmingham iron was not, therefore, competitive in national markets. If coke could be used, the coal deposits of the district could be more fully exploited through increased production and reduced costs. To this end the Eureka Mining and Transportation Company, which was owned by Daniel Pratt's son-in-law, Henry F. DeBardeleben, and the Cooperative Experimental Coke and Iron Company began to experiment with the production of coke pig iron. In 1876 they demonstrated that coke iron could be produced in the Birmingham district. Their efforts, combined with James Shannon's development of a method for reducing the amount of lime in local ores so that iron would be less brittle and Truman Aldrich's discovery of extensive deposits of coking coal in the region, increased Birmingham's potential as an iron-producing center. Aldrich, DeBardeleben, and James Sloss formed the Pratt Coal and Coke Company in 1878 and began opening mines in the "Pratt seam" to fill what they hoped would be an expanding demand for high-quality coking coal.[15]

Pratt Coal and Coke, hoping to attract investors who would build companies and use its coal, joined with Elyton Land and the L&N in a renewed promotional campaign. Pratt Coal and Coke offered cheap coal to any iron-producing concern that located in the Birmingham district, while Elyton Land offered cheap land to anyone who would build furnaces, foundries, and rolling mills. For example, DeBardeleben offered W. B. Caldwell of Louisville, Kentucky, Pratt coal at $1.15 per ton for ten years if he would build the town's first rolling mills. After visiting the town Caldwell accepted the offer, and, in July 1880, the Birmingham Rolling Mill Company went into production.

To supply pig iron to the rolling mills and several foundries established the same year, DeBardeleben and T. T. Hillman built the "Alice" furnace on property provided by Elyton Land. Alice began production in November 1880. As demand for iron grew in the early 1880s, other furnaces were established. DeBardeleben suggested to Sloss that he build a furnace. In return, DeBardeleben offered Sloss Pratt coal at cost plus 10 percent for five years. After securing a similar deal for iron ore, Sloss left the Oxmoor Furnace Company and, with the financial backing of the L&N and other investors, built the Sloss Furnace Company.[16] In 1881 J. H. and W. H. Woodward organized the Woodward Iron Company and began constructing furnaces on a site twelve miles southwest of Birmingham. The Woodward furnaces went into blast in 1883. Two years later C. P. Williamson's company began producing pig iron in addition to foundry products. Williamson, a native of New Richmond, Ohio, and a former machinist for the New Albany and Chicago Railroad Company, migrated to Birmingham after leaving the U.S. Army at the conclusion of the Civil War. He was managing the Linn Iron Works between 1875 and 1879 when he established a small foundry that employed 150 men. Williamson expanded into furnace work in response to the sharply increased demand for pig iron as the town grew during the 1880s.[17]

Sloss, Williamson, and Woodward joined an expansion that severely strained the local supply of labor. Robert P. Porter, a reporter for the *Times* (London), visited Birmingham in 1883 and praised its potential. He added, however, that "less effective labor," among other factors, would retard the town's development. Early promoters and employers shared Porter's concern with "the labor problem." Alabama's commissioner of industrial resources, James L. Tait, equated a shortage of skilled labor with a shortage of capital in explaining the obstacles to full development of the state's mineral resources. He wrote in an 1871 report to the Governor that "there is no doubt that within the boundaries of Alabama we have mines of wealth in our mineral deposits about which there can be no controversy; but there is one thing we lack, and without which no natural resources however vast, and no lands however fertile can be of any avail; I mean the labor and the capital that must develop them." The *Birmingham Iron Age* made the same point more emphatically three years later when it declared that the "hope of our country is the industrious mechanic. Without them our country would be a desert waste."[18]

Birmingham's workforce would eventually be made up of a large percentage of blacks, but neither Tait nor the *Iron Age* considered blacks a solution to the labor shortage. They and many early employers and boosters doubted the reliability of black laborers in nonagricultural work and hoped to limit their employment in industry. Moreover, the iron industry in the 1870s was heavily reliant on highly skilled workers, most of whom happened to be white northerners. Promotional literature in the early years, therefore, emphasized the need to attract skilled white labor to the town. This demand for skilled whites had a profound impact on the ideology of industrial development defined by promoters in their speeches and writings. Boosters articulated a vision of an industrial society that placed the white craftsman at the center of the social order.

Birmingham's early employers were well acquainted with the region's labor problem. Many of them had been advocates of industrial development before the Civil War and had learned that few Alabamians wanted to spend their lives working for wages. One of the most powerful beliefs held by nineteenth-century Americans was that working for a wage entailed a restriction of their autonomy. During the antebellum years northerners had modified this idea as they rationalized the growth of a wage-earning class.

But in the South, where a majority of those who worked for others were enslaved, the fear of descent into the ranks of wage earners remained strong through much of the nineteenth century. A man's status as a citizen depended upon independent ownership of the land, which would provide the means of subsistence for him and his family. And in antebellum Alabama, a majority of white men owned their land. In Jefferson County 80 percent of the white male population possessed their own farms in 1850. As long as white men could own their land, industrial employers would have difficulty convincing them to take the jobs they offered.[19]

It is no wonder that during the repeated crises of the 1850s antinorthern propagandists manipulated and reinforced southern prejudices against wage labor. One of the recurrent themes of secessionist rhetoric was the need to defend the South from northern- and British-style industrial development. Secessionist orators described northern industrial cities as poverty-ridden cesspools of vice where men depended upon others for their livelihood. These "wage slaves" had little hope of achieving the economic independence most white southerners enjoyed. If the people wanted to see the future as it would be if northern radicals had their way, they need only look at the examples northern cities offered. Slavery would no longer exist, so white men would be forced to compete with blacks for land and jobs. Inevitably many whites would descend to the miserable status of the hireling to live a degraded life. Freedom would be stripped of all meaning under those circumstances, and the South would join the North as a battle ground between capital and labor, a fate slavery had allowed it to escape.[20]

In response to this anti-industrial rhetoric, economic modernizers offered the image of a South free of the abuses of the industrial North. The South, they argued, would never achieve its full potential until it abandoned what these men considered to be an unreasonable devotion to agriculture. Economic diversification became their cause. They believed that agriculture should be part of a completely self-sufficient, diversified, dynamic economy of ever increasing opportunity for the people. John Milner in 1859 wrote that the development of manufacturing would "bring [the people of Alabama] together in a community of interest—social, commercial, and political. It will open to their industry a new field for their energy and capital. . . . It will tend greatly to effect their commercial independence." As the region moved toward secession, men who shared Milner's sentiments were even more insistent upon the need for the South to become economically independent.[21]

Antebellum advocates of economic progress never overcame suspicions of what they were trying to do. Before and during the Civil War iron producers and finishers experienced persistent shortages of skilled and unskilled iron workers. Antebellum employers found that free men who were willing to work were unreliable and that northern workers with requisite skills were reluctant to move south. A number of antebellum industrialists experimented with the use of slave labor but found owners hesitant to rent them at a reasonable price, especially during the 1850s.[22]

During the war-induced expansion of the iron industry, labor supply continued to be a problem, albeit, one now compounded by competition from the Confederate army for able-bodied men. Shelby Iron was unable to meet the demands of the Confederacy in 1862 because it could not find enough skilled men to operate blast furnaces, puddling furnaces, and rolling mills. Andrew T. Jones, president of the company, urged the government to assign men to the Shelby works. After repeated requests, the government began to detail men to Alabama and, on October 11, 1863, exempted from military service men engaged "in the production and manufacture of iron." The government's policy eased the labor shortage for a time, but labor supply continued to be less than adequate.[23]

The defeat of the Confederacy provided advocates of industrialization with a new argument for their program. At war's end large sections of the South were utterly destitute. Fields had been left uncultivated for years, livestock had been destroyed, and farm implements had been ruined. There were reports of starvation in Alabama. Julius Greene, a resident of Jefferson County during the war, wrote that the northern army that swept through the county in 1865 "destroyed everything in the country." Milner toured Jefferson and other counties and reported "no fences, no hogs, no cattle, no agriculture, no nothing. Bald, barren, uncultivated, and washed spots are seen everywhere. The white people here all belong to the now superabundant [sic] non-producing class and will work nowhere in the fields. . . . A conquered people of the white race ruined by the results of a great war."[24]

Town builders in Birmingham cast themselves as saviors. They wanted to build factories that would, De Bow's Review thought, "exert upon the South that recreative influence which springs from the ability of a country to profitably employ its idle labor." Milner wrote that it was time to raise the South from the ashes of war through a program of economic modernization that would feature a vibrant, prosperous industrial sector. Those who built factories, declared the Birmingham Iron Age in 1876, served the people. They would "deliver" Alabamians "from a state of poverty and misery," and "raise" them to a "state of proud independence." One local booster wrote that the wrenching experience of Civil War and Reconstruction had a "silver lining" in that "it urged individuals of hope and courage to seek in the mining and manufacturing resources, lying in such untold prodigality at their hands, a diversity which would secure commercial connections and thus operate to work a reform in the public spirit to the ultimate liberation of the energies of the white people." Entrepreneurs were considered public benefactors for providing jobs for the destitute and leading the people from a desert of "confusion and fear" to the promised land of a "most enduring prosperity."[25]

Factories, boosters believed, would attract people to the South, for, as *De Bow's Review* put it, "workmen go to furnaces, mines and factories—they go where labor is bought." But the men trying to revive the iron industry in Alabama learned a different lesson. James L. Tait, Alabama's commissioner of industrial resources, reported in 1871 that owners of foundries and furnaces could not find enough skilled and unskilled labor to man their plants. In an account of his travels through Jefferson County, Robert Somers remarked that in much of the mineral district "there [were] no negroes, little population of any kind." He concluded that this "absence of population," particularly men with skills required in the "industry to be pursued," could only be corrected through importation of labor. Little had changed when T. H. Aldrich arrived later in the 1870s. He reported to a U.S. Senate committee in 1883 that the lack of experienced industrial labor had retarded the growth of the Birmingham district.[26]

Alabamians' response to opportunities in the developing iron industry revealed continued fears that working for a wage entailed a loss of personal independence and status. Most whites still owned land and remained believers in the connection between property ownership and autonomy. Freedmen hoped to join the ranks of landowners, thereby achieving the autonomy they too believed was the essence of freedom. Neither group manifested much desire to march into the coal mine or the rolling mill, where, as they understood things, they would be subject to the control of others. Many of them suspected that promoters wanted to create privileged corporations that would use their economic power to deprive citizens of their liberty.[27]

Those interested in the economic development of the mineral district complained that this antipathy toward industrialization and wage labor slowed economic progress. Only by changing such attitudes would the labor problem be solved and the potential of Birmingham fulfilled, the *Birmingham Iron Age* argued. In 1878 J. L. M. Curry, an Alabamian and prominent advocate of industrialization, wrote that for "industrial reconstruction" to succeed, southerners must abandon some of their opinions, habits, and actions and learn the value of "productive work." Alabamians, he insisted, must learn that through hard work they could raise themselves out of the poverty enslaving them and contribute to the resurrection of southern civilization.[28]

But the reeducation of southerners would take time, and employers in Birmingham needed workers immediately. To fill their demand for labor, especially skilled labor, employers began looking to northern industrial centers. Migrants would meet short-term labor requirements and contribute to the long-term solution of the labor problem by teaching southern blacks and whites, as Mobile businessman Albert Danner explained, "the necessity and the value and the dignity of labor." Promoters and employers launched a publicity campaign designed to attract experienced white workers to Birmingham and to convince doubters among the native white population of the nobility of industrial labor. A common theme of their writings and speeches, particularly in the 1870s and 1880s, was their desire to create a society in which the abuses of industrialization would be eliminated. They described Birmingham as a place where labor and capital had an opportunity to build a social order in which the promises of the free labor ideology would be realized.[29]

At the heart of this vision of the free labor South was a promise of upward mobility in the Magic City. In dynamic, prosperous Birmingham, a white man of ability might start his working life as a wage earner but would soon advance to the status of independent craftsman or owner of one of the many manufacturing enterprises that the mineral wealth of the region could support. The industrial North, so the argument went, had, through a lack of vigilance, allowed conditions to develop in which a permanent class of wage laborers grew. Northern workingmen, especially skilled workingmen, faced degradation, wage slavery, and unemployment in a region that had sold its soul to the rulers of the large corporation. The South possessed untapped resources that would provide the means for the "busy" workingman to achieve wealth and status no longer available in older industrial regions. Boosters could point to C. P. Williamson and Hamilton Beggs as examples of what men could achieve. Both began their careers as molders in the North and moved south seeking new opportunities, and they eventually built Birmingham's first foundries. Promoters promised similar economic and social advancement on the southern industrial frontier to anyone willing to take a chance.[30]

Boosters devoted much attention to the ways in which Birmingham would avoid the problems that, in their view, plagued the North. Essential to maintaining a society of opportunity, they argued, was the prevention of the rise of monopoly power, a lesson they learned from observation of northern development. Editorial comment on northern strikes during 1877 made the consequences of concentration clear. The arrogance of corporations drunk with wealth and power, argued the *Birmingham Iron Age*, caused the turmoil that rocked the North in that troubled year. Corporations arbitrarily implemented policies that deprived men of their rights as citizens and their families of the necessities of life. Whole communities suffered as swaggering corporations attempted to reduce "the hard-working portion of the citizens" to the level of the wage slave. Monopolies, another paper asserted a few years later, were "creatures of a perversion of the law [and] have no moral right of existence, much less to compel the common people of the country to mildly submit to their insidious plundering." To prevent similar conditions in Alabama, wrote B. B. Lewis, the vice president of the Central Iron Works in Shelby County, the state legislature must abandon any policy that might foster monopolies.[31] He believed that an economy of small manufacturers guaranteed widespread prosperity and greater opportunity for advancement. Such conditions, Lewis insisted, were essential to maintenance of social order, for where the workingman had opportunities to become a capitalist, class harmony would prevail.[32]

A final and essential part of the ideology of Birmingham's founders and boosters emerged from their consideration of the problem of race. Unable to recruit enough white unskilled labor to meet demand, employers around Birmingham began in the late 1870s and early 1880s to rely on black labor, reinforcing the idea among whites that, in the South, industrial labor was reserved for the most degraded of the population.[33] Few white workers, northern or southern, skilled or unskilled, were likely to migrate to a place where the distinction between what they did for a living and what blacks did was unclear. The *National Labor Tribune* said as much in an 1889 essay on labor in the South. "Skilled workers," the *Tribune* warned southern employers, "would not work for long in a society where . . . labor was . . . looked upon as the connecting link between blacks and whites." The *Tribune* suggested that, if whites failed to establish their racial superiority at work, employers would use blacks to discipline them.[34]

Boosters and employers were sensitive to white misgivings about conditions in the South. They addressed these fears with a variation of the antebellum argument that black slavery guaranteed whites superior status in the socioeconomic order. The updated version of the argument split the workforce between whites, who would have unrestricted opportunity for advancement, and blacks, who would remain, for the most part, in the unskilled, menial positions whites considered appropriate for an inferior race. Boosters promised their audience that whites' control of the best jobs in industry would never be challenged. Promotional literature emphasized employers' commitment to the racial division of work. The Avondale Iron Works' literature assured readers that blacks performed only common labor, because the company did not "consider them reliable for higher grades of employment."[35]

To Birmingham's promoters a racial division of work was not only essential to the recruitment of skilled white workers, but it was also crucial to the maintenance of social order. A common interest in the defense of white domination, they thought, would reinforce the harmony that a common pursuit of economic prosperity supposedly ensured. Few whites in Birmingham would ever experience the degradation and exploitation that was the lot of the northern workingman, John Witherspoon Dubose, a leading booster, explained. Workers would therefore never become "dissatisfied and turbulent." The racial division of work, he wrote, "excites a sentiment of sympathy and equality on their [white workers'] part with the classes above them, and in this way becomes a wholesome social leven [sic]."[36]

By the end of the 1870s promoters' advertising campaigns and employers' own recruiting efforts began to attract men with needed skills to the Birmingham district. Newspapers, labor recruiters, and labor unions spread the message of Birmingham's promoters to iron-producing centers throughout the North and Midwest. Advertisements for skilled iron workers appeared regularly in the newspaper of the Amalgamated Association of Iron and Steel Workers (AAISW), the *National Labor Tribune*. At times the *Tribune* itself praised Birmingham as a place where puddlers, rollers, molders, heaters, and other skilled iron workers could join in the building of the "workshop town" and assume an honored and respected place in the community. The AAISW also provided more direct assistance to Birmingham employers. It informed workers of positions in Alabama and issued train tickets, purchased by Birmingham employers, to those who wished to move. In return for the cooperation of the AAISW, employers promised to employ only members of the union at rates of pay above those in Pittsburgh.[37]

Judging from the large proportion of nonsouthern skilled iron workers in the town between 1880 and 1900, this recruiting strategy was effective. Many early skilled workers learned their trades in the North and Midwest. D. H. Lloyd, for example, moved to the town from Aurora, Indiana, in the early 1880s. He left his job as a puddler in Aurora because he heard about pay rates in Birmingham that were higher than those in other parts of the country. Many men also migrated to Birmingham because their skills were no longer in great demand elsewhere. Since Birmingham's rolling mills and foundries manufactured only wrought and cast iron products, there remained a demand for men whose skills had been rendered obsolete by the technology of steel making.

For example, Sylvester Daly left England and settled in Pittsburgh, where he learned puddling at the Jones & Laughlin Iron and Steel Company. Finding it increasingly difficult to earn a living in Pittsburgh, he migrated to Birmingham in the late 1880s and went to work at the Birmingham Rolling Mill Company.[38] James Davis left Pittsburgh for the same reason Daly did. He first took a job as a puddler at an iron company in Niles, Ohio. After the company in Niles failed, Davis traveled to Birmingham and went to work for a rolling mill company. David U. Williams moved to Birmingham from south Chicago. He had learned puddling from his father after his family migrated to America from Wales in 1887. Upon completion of his training, he, like Davis, hoped to start his own puddling furnace but could not find a place in Chicago. He decided to move to Birmingham, where, in 1894, he went to work for the Birmingham Rolling Mill Company.[39]

Although nonsoutherners continued to be an important part of the skilled labor force in the nineteenth century, the proportion of the skilled population born in Alabama and the South increased significantly between 1880 and 1900. Three-fourths of a sample taken from the 1900 manuscript census had been born in the South; of the southerners, close to half were natives of Alabama. The rest of the sample consisted of men of northern and European birth. All but one of the European natives had been born in England, Wales, or Ireland.

Declining opportunities for whites in the hinterland of Birmingham no doubt contributed to much of the growth in the southern skilled population. Men facing poor economic conditions on farms migrated to cities where they could learn one of the crafts and, perhaps, improve their future prospects.[40] Not all of these southern-born craftsmen had migrated directly from nearby rural counties, however. Many of them had been born in Birmingham, the sons of northern or European natives who had migrated to Birmingham in the early 1880s. As the case of Hamilton Beggs and his sons illustrates, early skilled workers often passed their knowledge on to their sons, thereby reducing Birmingham's dependence on external sources of labor. Beggs, a molder and native of England, migrated to Chattanooga from Pennsylvania sometime during the 1850s. Shortly after the Civil War began he became the head founder for the Shelby Iron Company; by 1880 he had established his own foundry in Birmingham. During the next four years three of his sons, all of whom had been born in the South, joined their father's business as molders.[41]

So by the 1890s Birmingham had a well-established, largely self-reproducing, skilled white working class. Even so, the town failed to realize its boosters' dreams of a harmonious social order. The people of Birmingham were no more successful in their efforts to create this ideal world than the pioneers of America's industrial revolution had been. It soon became apparent that working people understood the promises that attracted them to the town in ways that often placed them at odds with their employers and each other.

CHAPTER 2

Skilled Work, White Workers

At the heart of Birmingham's social order was the relationship between capital and labor. The town's founders and promoters articulated an ideal of harmony between capital and labor that was dependent upon the unity of white skilled workingmen and white capital. In the 1880s white craftsmen moved to the city prepared to assume their rightful places at the center of the community. They expected to enter a community where they would be treated as equal members of a broadly defined producing class, which did not include black common laborers, or "wage slaves." Skilled workers' concept of white male equality rested upon work cultures they dominated. Through workplace organizations, craftsmen sought to defend the autonomy within the sphere of production that they believed set them apart from the powerless and dependent.[1]

Skilled workers' ideas about equality soon clashed with employers' understanding of the rights of property owners. Employers challenged skilled workers' power, arguing that labor organizations violated property owners' right to establish the terms of employment. They extended their defense of property to the right of a nonunion worker to sell his labor to whomever he pleased. Many skilled workers resisted what they considered a plot against their freedom. They initiated strikes to challenge employers' claims to absolute authority in their workplaces. The balance of power shifted back and forth throughout the 1880s and into the 1890s as workers and employers struggled to define their respective rights on the shop floor. Whether through craft unions or assemblies of the Knights of Labor, skilled workers forcefully denied that an employer possessed total authority on the shop floor. If employers had their way, workers insisted, the equality between capital and labor essential to social order and the commonweal would cease to exist.

For skilled men, work in Birmingham was much as it had been in the iron industry for many years. By the 1880s skilled iron workers no longer marketed what they produced, as had preindustrial artisans; however, they continued to organize the process of production. A nineteenth-century rolling mill, foundry, or machine shop consisted of a number of small workshops run by skilled workers. Craftsmen enjoyed considerable autonomy because they possessed the knowledge critical to production, a knowledge few men in the South possessed in the early 1880s.[2] The type of work performed by skilled workers set them apart from the dependent workers they called wage slaves.

Among the most skilled workers in nineteenth-century Birmingham were the men who kept its rolling mill companies operating. Rolling mills converted pig iron into semifinished wrought iron bars or plates, which metal-working shops then used in the production of finished goods. To produce iron a puddler, or boiler, with assistance from a helper, removed impurities from pig iron. Puddlers hired their own helpers, who were often relatives, and paid them from the earnings of the furnace. While assisting puddlers helpers learned the trade so they might someday operate their own furnace.[3]

Puddlers and helpers charged the furnace with approximately six hundred pounds of raw iron to start a "heat." Next the helper fired the furnace and melted the charge, which took about thirty minutes. At that point puddlers added iron oxide to the molten ore to cool the "bath" in order to oxidize phosphorous and sulphur. Throughout the process puddlers and their helpers stirred the charge with a hoe-like tool called a rabble. Stirring required considerable strength, since the charge thickened during boiling and the rabble used to stir it weighed twenty-five pounds.[4]

Puddlers monitored temperatures in the furnace closely. The temperature had to be lower early in the process to burn off the phosphorous and sulphur before the carbon. As the phosphorous and sulphur content of the ore decreased, the melting point of the metal increased. The puddler then instructed his helper to raise the temperature in the furnace to keep the charge molten. As the carbon began to oxidize, the charge began to boil.

During this critical "high boil" stage, the puddler and his helper alternately agitated the charge through a small hole in the furnace door to expose it to the action of the flames. The charge soon became pasty, so they had to work it more vigorously to weld the purified particles of iron together properly. When the puddling process was complete, puddler and helper broke the pasty mass into three or four balls weighing approximately 150 pounds each and removed them from the furnace. These "blooms" were then ready to be rolled into bar or plate iron.

A highly skilled occupation, puddling required considerable experience and good judgment. The puddler supervised his helper and laborers to ensure that they performed their jobs correctly and at the proper times. He had to be able to recognize through observation alone each stage of the puddling process so heat could be raised or lowered at the appropriate times. The work was physically demanding but was not continuous. After each stage in the puddling process, puddlers and their helpers rested and prepared for the next stage.[5]

Wrought iron blooms, or billets, from the puddling furnace went to a heater to be reheated before being rolled into bar or plate iron. Heaters' work did not entail heavy physical labor, but they were exposed to high temperatures and needed the regular periods of rest their work permitted. Each heater hired a helper, who assisted him in all aspects of his work.[6]

Once the bloom was at the right temperature, laborers transferred it to the rolling crew. Operation of a rolling machine required close cooperation between members of a crew under the supervision of the roller. To produce bar, plate, rails, and other shapes, rollers, helpers, and members of the crew, whom rollers hired and paid, manually passed blooms between two metal cylinders rotating in opposite directions. These "rolls" gripped the softened metal and reduced it to the desired shape. After the bloom passed through the machine, a "catcher" caught it and returned it to the front for another pass, if needed. A rolling machine crew might pass a bloom through the mill several times to reduce its cross section to the correct measurements. To increase productivity some Birmingham companies purchased three-high rolling machines, which allowed workers to pass metal through from both sides, thus eliminating the time consuming walk around the machine after each pass.

A second highly skilled group, molders and patternmakers, worked in the foundries of the city. Patternmakers produced precisely measured wooden or cast iron patterns for molds used in the manufacture of pipe, machine parts, stoves, and other metal products.[7] To produce the mold, molders and their helpers filled wood or cast iron patterns with sand, or loam. They first ensured that the sand was refractory and cohesive enough to withstand high temperatures, yet permeable enough to allow gases and steam generated in the mold to escape. To do this the molder or one of his assistants threw sheets of water on a pile of sand to make it more cohesive. Then a worker "cut" through the sand one shovel at a time to break up lumps. If the "sand cutter" left the sand too wet, steam produced during the casting would create "blowholes" in the finished product. If the sand was too dry, it would not hold together in the mold. The molder therefore tested the sand by squeezing a handful to see if it contained too much water. To test for dryness he pressed a lump of sand between his thumb and forefinger to make it break in the center. If the sand was not wet enough, it would crumble at the edges of the break.

Having prepared the sand, a molder "rammed" it into the pattern to make the mold, packing the sand tightly without making it so "hard" that gases and steam caught in the mold would create holes in the casting. If he left the sand too "soft," the mold surface would be weak and the molten metal would "wash out" the sand, leaving "sand holes" and "scabs" on the casting. Before casting molders and their helpers produced a "core" around which molten metal flowed. To make cores workers rammed sand into a core mold and then baked it. The core, like the mold, had to be strong enough to withstand high temperatures and permeable enough to allow gases to escape. After securing the core in the mold's "core seats," molders poured molten metal into the mold quickly and evenly.[8]

During the nineteenth century patternmakers and molders either performed each one of the steps in their exacting crafts themselves or directed the work of laborers who assisted them with some tasks. They were the most highly skilled workers in the foundry. Both crafts demanded a thorough knowledge of the properties of metals and judgment that could only be gained from years of experience. Failure to perform any stage in the molding process accurately would result in a flawed product and hours of wasted work.[9]

Rolling mills, foundries, furnaces, and many other establishments in Birmingham, employed machinists, who built and repaired the equipment used in production. Their work required a high level of technical knowledge and experience. While the trade was, perhaps, the most technologically advanced of the metal trades, nineteenth-century machinists still hand finished parts that relatively unsophisticated drill presses, lathes, and shapers produced only in rough form. From a blueprint they marked metal for the appropriate cuts, made the cuts, and, using files and scrapers, finished the part so that it fit the machine they were building. Like other metal tradesmen many machinists hired and paid their own helpers and apprentices.[10]

The critical role of metal tradesmen in the production process was the source of their ideas about their place in the social order. Skilled workers recognized that they produced the goods that generated prosperity. As the labor press repeatedly reminded the public, there would have been no major industry in Birmingham without the expertise of the skilled mechanic. "Capital is the child of labor," asserted the *Birmingham Weekly Review* in 1883, "and there would never have been a particle of capital in the world if labor had not created it." Before skilled workers moved to Birmingham, continued the paper, it was a struggling, disease-ridden town with an economy dependent upon a few furnaces and coal mines. People could look around them and see the rolling mills, stove foundries, machine shops, and other metal-working establishments skilled men created.[11]

Skilled workers thought of themselves as independent producers. This self-image flourished in a world of work divided into a multiplicity of units, each controlled by a craftsman. Independence at work distinguished metal tradesmen from laborers, most of whom were black, who carried out the orders of skilled workers. In the minds of craftsmen this independence also made them the equal of the men who owned the companies for which they worked.[12]

Though employers and civic leaders spoke often of their adherence to the ideals skilled metal workers embraced, the men who moved to Birmingham in the 1880s did not assume that employers would always be so deferential. Many of them moved to Alabama to escape employers' efforts to reduce them to "wage slaves." They hoped to build a world where they would once again be accorded the status they believed they deserved. To help accomplish this end skilled metal workers established institutions to protect the rights and authority at work that were so central to their concept of their place in the social order. While each organization enforced practices that reflected the peculiarities of individual trades, they all sought to defend workers' control of entry into the trade, the pace of work, and the compensation members would receive for their labor. The AAISW, which established a lodge at Birmingham's first rolling mill company in 1881 or 1882, provides an example of the way organizations tried to impose these values and protect the material interests of their members.[13]

Founded in 1876 in Pittsburgh, the AAISW unified three trade unions in the iron and steel industry: the United Sons of Vulcan (puddlers); the Associated Brotherhood of Iron and Steel Heaters, Rollers, and Roughers of the United States; and the Iron and Steel Roll Hands' Union (helpers and other semiskilled workers in rolling mills). Rolling mill workers organized lodges, which they modeled after the popular fraternal orders of the era. Secret passwords, ceremonies of initiation, and distinctive uniforms for special occasions fostered and reinforced a sense of brotherhood and common purpose.[14]

When the AAISW organized a mill it established the conditions under which its members would work and the method and amount of payment. AAISW contracts specified the amount of time it took to do a given job in the mill and the frequency with which the task would be performed each day. Puddlers in Birmingham worked six "heats" or "charges" a day. The length of time each heat took varied with the quality of the iron being used, but in the 1880s it generally took two to three hours per heat.[15]

The method of payment the AAISW established reflected rolling mill workers' producerist mentality. The lingering influence of the age of the independent artisan is demonstrated by the organization's adoption of a "sliding scale" method of compensation. Workers did not receive a wage; rather, the mill owner paid a "price" for the workers' product. Workers based this "price" on iron market conditions and the cost of production. The scale was tied to market performance and fluctuated with demand for semifinished iron products. In this way workers tried to ensure that employers alone did not determine the value of their labor; the free market would, in theory, dictate their "profits" just as it did those of their employers.[16]

In practice rolling mill workers attempted in various ways to guarantee that the "free" market worked in their favor. At times the AAISW reduced the number of heats in the workday to restrict output and maintain prices or to protect members from layoffs. Through a variety of restrictions, such as limits on the size of charges and the number of iron bars a roller produced in a shift, the AAISW sought to prevent employers from converting the sliding scale into an exploitative form of the piece rate. If a member violated these or any other work rules, two-thirds of his fellow lodge members could vote to suspend or expel him. A lodge that failed to punish violators could be fined for the first offense; a second offense might bring revocation of its charter.[17]

The AAISW and other organizations also sought to maintain prices and wages by controlling hiring in union mills. Craftsmen believed control of hiring was particularly important in Birmingham and the South, where they faced a potential threat from black workers. They had heard all the promises about white domination of skilled jobs but doubted that employers would forever resist the temptation to employ blacks to undercut the wages and privileges of white workingmen. Skilled whites had good reason to be concerned. After all, white coal miners faced competition with blacks as early as the 1870s. In 1881 the *Birmingham Iron Age* suggested that blacks could, with enough education, learn the skilled metal-working trades just as they had learned mining. A few years later Charles J. Hazard praised the abilities of black workers before a U.S. Senate committee. During the same hearings, Truman Aldrich reported that the "best labor [he] ever handled" was black labor. H. S. Chamberlain, an owner of a Chattanooga rolling mill company, confirmed the observations of Hazard and Aldrich; he had replaced skilled whites with blacks and found no difference in the quality of work.[18]

Such positive appraisals of black abilities revealed the limits of Birmingham employers' commitment to the ideology of white supremacy, argued the *National Labor Tribune*. Employers would not allow race loyalty to stand in the way of their pursuit of their own prosperity, the *Tribune* warned. They might at some time in the future follow the lead of the man from Chattanooga and others in the region and "throw out the white entirely, place mill work in the hands of the negro, and reduce wages to such a figure as will place the pay in European mills in bright contrast with that paid in this country." Black competition for white jobs, it concluded, meant "degraded labor, degraded workmen, a condition wholly foreign to republican institutions, and the subversion in fact, if not in name, of the constitutional guarantee of equality."[19]

Skilled white metal tradesmen relied on the traditional right to control access to their trades to counter the black threat. When they moved to Birmingham white craftsmen found few skilled black iron workers, and they intended to make sure this continued to be the case. They wanted to avoid the fate of white coal miners by preventing as much as possible the growth of a skilled black labor force. Iron workers hoped to institutionalize a split labor market that would protect them from employers' use of a divide-and-conquer strategy.[20] Some organizations specifically excluded blacks in their charters, while others did so in practice. The national AAISW did not officially prohibit black membership, but lodges in Birmingham did. Because the single rolling mill company in the city in the early 1880s hired only members of the union, no blacks could be found among the company's puddlers, rollers, and heaters. As other crafts formed organizations through the 1880s, they too prohibited black membership. When boilermakers formed Birmingham's first lodge of the Brotherhood of Boilermakers in 1889, they admitted only "white, free-born male citizens of some civilized country, twenty-one years of age . . . commanding the average rate of wages given in any well-regulated shop." Lodges of the Atlanta-based National Association of Machinists prohibited black membership as well.[21]

Union exclusion of blacks was not, of course, the sole reason for industrial segregation in Birmingham. Many employers expressed little confidence in blacks' ability to do skilled work, as we have seen. But much of what employers and promoters said about the race issue was in response to white workers' reluctance to work with a race of men they considered inferior. In other words, the racial policies employers and promoters articulated combined their own prejudices with their understanding of the prejudices of the white men who dominated skilled iron work. Thus, from the earliest days of Birmingham's existence, white skilled workers played a key role in shaping the town's system of industrial segregation. The organizations they created after arriving in the town further defined the system and offered to white workers a way to defend against employer violations of the racial status quo. White monopoly of the metal trades between 1880 and 1900 was in large part a testament to the effectiveness of unions' racial policies.[22]

Blacks certainly understood the role white workers and white-controlled unions played in their subordination. Jessie Claxton, a black carpenter in Birmingham, described white workers' racial attitudes for the Senate committee investigating relations between labor and capital in 1883. White workers, he reported, were more virulently racist than were more well-to-do whites. That was why, argued Claxton, union and nonunion whites did not employ black apprentices. He thought employers cooperated with their white workers because they feared they would lose white labor if they hired black craftsmen. The Reverend Isaiah Welsh explained that even organizations without specific rules prohibiting blacks "do practically exclude them," relegating them to "subordinate work."[23]

As the comments of Claxton and Welsh suggest, employers in Birmingham accepted the rules and practices of labor organizations during the years of relative prosperity in the early 1880s. Because they did so, harmony prevailed in relations between skilled iron workers and their employers. Letters from workers at Birmingham Rolling Mills to the *National Labor Tribune* praised conditions in the town and at the mills. Men wrote of the town's unlimited potential and the spirit of cooperation that existed between the AAISW and the company's management.[24] Judging from their descriptions, the social and economic order functioned much as the town's fathers had promised it would.

Daily life in the workplace soon began to generate discord, however. Despite rhetoric to the contrary, workers had established their unions because they had learned from experience that the economic system did not naturally generate harmony between capital and labor. Having seen employers seeking greater profits trample on the rights of skilled workers in other regions, they created organizations in Birmingham to protect themselves from the same fate. In the mid-1880s economic hard times brought to the town the class tension and conflict its founders had feared. Struggles between employers and workers revealed quite distinct and antagonistic ideas about how the socioeconomic order should function.

The trouble began at Birmingham Rolling Mills (BRM). In late May 1882 a committee representing workers in the puddling department complained to a company official named D. Reese about the poor quality of the iron ore the company supplied. Poorer grades of ore forced puddlers to work harder to produce wrought iron. The committee told Reese that they would not return to work until they received higher-quality iron ore.[25] With a supply of puddled iron stockpiled because of a slump in sales, Reese did not hesitate to relieve the men, an act of company "independence" that concerned all the company's skilled workers. Union officials feared that Reese's handling of the iron ore issue foreshadowed a company challenge to the power of the AAISW over the 1882 scale proposal. Still, they expressed confidence that differences between the company and the union could be settled amicably and that a new union scale would be signed in June.[26]

Their optimism proved to be misplaced. The mill closed for repairs in June, as was the practice at the time. When it reopened company officials rejected the AAISW's demands for an increase in prices over the preceding year. John D. Dwyer, representative of the company, explained to the local's scale committee that mill officials would not continue to pay the men a full dollar over prices being paid at Chattanooga. The company, he said, already paid more than it should by basing its scale on Pittsburgh rather than the Cincinnati prices, which governed the rest of the southern district.

Members of the AAISW protested an action that they believed violated the terms of the agreement that brought them to Birmingham. They reminded company officials that they had never agreed to work for Cincinnati prices. Men moved to Birmingham because the company offered a scale higher than Pittsburgh's, and they intended to hold the company to its original agreement. Skilled workers at BRM refused to return to work until the company signed a new scale for 1882. Business was slow, so the company filled orders from existing stock during the summer. Recognizing that they had limited leverage with the company, AAISW officials offered Dwyer a compromise. They would advise union members to end the strike if the company would agree to maintain the 1881 scale. Under this agreement, workers sacrificed a price increase for 1882 but still received prices above those paid at Chattanooga and Pittsburgh. Dwyer accepted the offer. AAISW members approved the plan as well and returned to work.[27]

Why Dwyer accepted the 1882 compromise is unclear. It is clear that company officials remained determined to lower wages to Pittsburgh rates at least. According to L. G. Pettyjohn, a puddler at BRM, the company used a slight depression in trade in 1882–83 to justify a reduction in Birmingham prices to Pittsburgh levels. The Birmingham lodge sent its scale committee to Louisville to meet with W. B. Caldwell, the owner of the company. The committee protested the rate reduction, emphasizing that the company had induced men to move to Birmingham with promises of rates above those paid at Pittsburgh. It assured Caldwell that members of the union understood the problems the company faced and wanted to reach an agreement fair to all. The committee therefore offered to accept a reduction to prices paid in Wheeling, West Virginia, which were slightly higher than those paid in Pittsburgh.

Rolling mill workers' continued insistence on prices higher than prices in Pittsburgh was more than a matter of principle. They argued that they could not work and live in Birmingham if they earned Pittsburgh prices. Unskilled help cost them 12 to 15 percent more than was paid elsewhere, they claimed. Low-quality iron and improperly cleaned coal forced puddlers and their helpers to tend fires almost continuously. During Birmingham's summers the heat around furnaces was almost unbearable, workers complained. After a hard day's work men went home to frontierlike living conditions. They paid high rents, unless they chose to live in one of the company's unplastered "shanties." Given such conditions, skilled rolling mill workers believed they should earn more than their counterparts in Pittsburgh.[28]

Caldwell thought differently, however. He refused to accept the committee's offer, insisting that the lodge accept the Pittsburgh scale. He argued that the cost of bar iron produced in Birmingham, at $45 per ton, was too high to be competitive with Pittsburgh and other places where skilled iron workers charged lower rates for their labor. To Caldwell and his managers it made no economic sense to continue to pay a premium for labor under such circumstances. Nothing that they said indicated any sympathy with the workers' argument that their compensation should take into account the harsh conditions with which they contended. The company would pay the same rates to workers as their competitors did.[29]

AAISW officials and members responded to Caldwell with scorn. They could not accept a policy that appeared to them to reduce men to nothing more than commodities. Workers understood that their compensation was tied to the market for their products but rejected the idea that the conditions under which they worked and lived should be ignored when determining a just price for their labor. The just price, they believed, was one that allowed skilled workingmen and their families to have more than the bare necessities of life. Because of the added expense of working and living in Birmingham, Pittsburgh rates would barely provide for workers' basic needs. Union leaders pointed out that Caldwell and his managers obviously wanted more than a subsistence living and charged higher prices than necessary for the company's products in order to support their standard of living. According to union officials, the cost of producing bar iron should have been $39 at the most, if pig iron was $17 per ton or less, as James Sloss had testified before a U.S. Senate committee. The price of Birmingham bar iron was too high, the union concluded, because Caldwell and his managers wanted more money for themselves. The men, L. G. Pettyjohn asserted, had tried to treat the company fairly but would not accept a reduction in pay so company officers could increase profits while workers struggled to make a living under adverse conditions. On July 1, 1883, the AAISW in Birmingham went on strike.[30]

Survival during the strike was of course difficult, but the strikers managed to get by with assistance from their union and sympathizers in the community. The AAISW paid workers $4.00 per week. Part of this money came from citizens who shared workers' outrage at Caldwell's intransigence. Other supporters helped the strikers by purchasing tickets to benefits that the union held to collect money for strikers' relief. Some merchants gave striking workers temporary jobs.[31]

The AAISW certainly needed as much community support as it could get, for it soon became apparent that the strike would be a lengthy one. As long as the iron market remained sluggish, the company could fill orders with existing stock, so it did not even respond to the strike for months. In late November leaders of the AAISW in Birmingham attempted to revive negotiations. They offered to accept a rate of $5.75 per ton for puddling and 5 percent above Pittsburgh rates for finishing mills. These prices, they contended, represented a tremendous sacrifice for the men when it cost them

20 percent more to live in Birmingham than in Pittsburgh. The company rejected the proposal. Caldwell and Dwyer could see no reason to pay workers in Birmingham more than men in the same jobs made in other cities.[32]

The stalemate continued through December. Then in early January 1884 the company moved to break the strike. An advertisement appeared in the January 12 issue of the *National Labor Tribune* offering rolling mill men work in Birmingham at Pittsburgh prices. Despite *Tribune* warnings to AAISW members to stay away, the company successfully recruited seventy men in Cleveland, Ohio, and transported them to Birmingham. When they reached the outskirts of town, the replacement workers moved to cars that carried them directly to the rolling mills, bypassing the city depot, where strikers would have had an opportunity to confront them. Later the strikebreakers did meet with representatives of the AAISW to hear their explanation of the strike. Afterward the newcomers appointed a committee to meet with mill officials and plead the strikers' case. They accomplished nothing, and all but six of the Cleveland group decided to respect the strike.[33]

This proved to be an empty victory for the AAISW, for the company found more "black sheep" in Cleveland, Cincinnati, and Chicago, where unemployment among iron workers was widespread. Michael Hanson, an iron worker in Chicago, explained in a letter to the *National Labor Tribune* that many men in the city had been unemployed for two years; to survive they had been working as common laborers. Though Hanson said that he and others like him would never accept the jobs of men fighting for their rights, many others desperately wanted to return to their crafts and grasped the opportunity to move to Birmingham.[34]

Obviously Caldwell and Dwyer imported strikebreakers because they hoped to return the plant to production at lower costs, but they also had a broader purpose in mind. By 1884 company officials had decided to free themselves from union control of hiring. As a local newspaper explained, the company had the right to "operate the mill with a crew of men of its own selection" free of interference from "an organization whose leader has his headquarters in Pennsylvania." Workingmen, the editorial declared, could join any organization they wanted but must not dictate to employers whom they could hire and must not deprive an individual of the right to work.[35]

Strikers continued their efforts to stop the importation of strikebreakers, but experienced little success. Fearing violence against the black sheep, the company hired a police force to escort them to and from work, preventing any contact between strikers and their replacements. Union members alleged that the company's private police arrested strikers without cause.

They charged that the company wanted to create the impression that union men, who had conducted themselves in a peaceful, lawful manner, were "incendiaries, cutthroats, and nose breakers." Union leaders conceded that some strikers thought they should abandon their policy of restraint for the more aggressive approach rolling mill spokesmen already attributed to them, but they had been able to convince members that violence would accomplish little.[36]

Yet the introduction of strikebreakers and private security forces did raise the level of tension, creating a potential for spontaneous violence, particularly in the public places of the city where strikebreakers and strikers mingled. At McGeever's and Brennan's saloon, a popular gathering place for rolling mill men after work, unemployed rolling mill workers expressed their bitterness and resentment toward the company in brawls with black sheep, the symbols of company tyranny.[37] Such incidents demonstrated workers' frustration after the company rejected repeated offers of compromise. When BRM first announced its intentions concerning the union scale, the AAISW approached the disagreement as one between equal partners. The union sought to settle differences over the division of the profit on the basis of mutual sacrifice for the good of all. But the company would not settle because it wanted more than wage or "price" concessions. By the spring of 1884 it had become apparent that Caldwell intended to establish his unquestioned authority on the shop floor. He and his managers would control hiring, wage levels, and working conditions. Their plan depended upon the successful employment of men they could dominate, so the black sheep naturally became the focus of strikers' hostility.[38]

Intimidation and appeals to their sense of independence as white men eventually convinced some strikebreakers to test the company's will. In the early summer of 1884 strikebreakers presented a union scale to Caldwell's managers. Confident of their ability to recruit skilled labor, company officials rejected the proposal. They then moved to eliminate all vestiges of worker power on the shop floor. Caldwell posted a set of rules all employees must obey if they wanted to keep their jobs. Caldwell's "iron clad," as workers called his rules, stated the philosophy that would henceforth govern relations between capital and labor in the mill. It left little doubt that a wide chasm had opened between the two antagonists in the year-old struggle.

Caldwell declared the mill nonunion but promised to pay the men Pittsburgh wages. If the AAISW in Pittsburgh failed to reach an agreement and struck, the men in Birmingham "must continue to work for the old scale until a new one is agreed upon and goes into effect." The iron clad then listed terms of employment. The management, it said, "demand and insist on each and every one in our employ being at his post of duty on time at each working day and attending to his business faithfully." Workers must give a one-week notice before quitting and at the end of the week "leave without attempting to create trouble of any kind or cause others to do so for him." Failure to obey this provision could mean forfeiture of any wages the company owed to the worker. The iron clad concluded with a demand that men "who cannot comply with these rules . . . stop work and leave the mill at once."

Many strikebreakers quit work after publication of the iron clad rather than suffer continued humiliation at the hands of the company. They and other strikers denounced the rules as a violation of their rights to determine the price at which they sold their labor and to establish the terms of their employment. Those two basic rights, they protested, distinguished them from dependent wage slaves. If men agreed to the iron clad, the strikers warned in a letter to the *National Labor Tribune*, they would lose the power to "prevent the management from using the whip, as was customary in this state before the first gun was fired at Fort Sumter in 1861." In a revealing expression of workers' linkage of their independence at work to their gender and racial identities, the strikers referred to "scabs" as "tools, formerly men," whose "black spots" would eventually become "so deep" that they would never be allowed to work in a "white mill." The company, they concluded, desired only men "in a position to sell [their] manhood"; it would hire no one "who has a spark of independence in his body."[39]

This response to the iron clad forcefully defined rolling mill workers' concept of equality and freedom. As free white men and the creators of capital, the workers claimed equality with BRM owners and the right to set the terms of their employment themselves. Under the iron clad skilled workers ceased to be equal and free. They descended into a dependent status suitable only for black men, and the ideology of white supremacy lost all meaning. Thus the strikers wrote of the darkening of white men who submitted to employers' rules. Only through resistance to such arbitrary and tyrannical authority could men preserve their "freedom and manhood."

But strikers' protests achieved no more than they had during the previous year. Caldwell took advantage of widespread unemployment among skilled iron workers to undermine union strength. Men needed jobs to survive, so they took the jobs available at BRM under the terms of the iron clad. For the next five years the company maintained the upper hand in relations with its workforce. During this period the AAISW's influence declined in Birmingham as it did across the nation.[40]

Many former AAISW members continued their struggle through the Knights of Labor. Knights organizers in Alabama called for producers to unify in a movement to prevent organized capital from imposing upon the people a system of class privilege that would mean the end of opportunity for self-employment and the general degradation of labor in society. If workingmen did not act, they would have to accept only what their "capitalist masters" wanted to give them. Their dependence, warned the organ of the Alabama Knights, the *Alabama Sentinel*, would have dire consequences. "The infamous doctrine that labor is only to receive what capitalism pleases to pay it and not what it is intrinsically worth," declared the *Sentinel*, "places the man with strong muscles but empty hands at the mercy of him, who, having monopolized all resources and closed all avenues to self-employment, amasses wealth by buying labor at a fraction of its value." The privileged class, warned a reader of the *Sentinel*, respected "neither the rights of a fellowman nor have the fear of God before their eyes to hold in check their wicked love of money and the exercise of the tyrannical power over the laboring element." Under such conditions, equality, the basis for harmony between capital and labor, could not survive.[41]

The Knights' analysis appealed to people growing increasingly resentful over wage cuts and assaults on their traditions in the workplace. During the mid-1880s the order in the Birmingham district and the state grew rapidly. Organizers had created fifteen local assemblies in and around Birmingham by the end of 1886; at the end of 1887 the Birmingham district remained the most well organized part of the state. Though the membership included skilled and unskilled workers, in "mixed" locals, skilled workers, with their long traditions of organization, usually dominated. The order welcomed blacks to its ranks, but black members typically formed assemblies separate from whites; in 1887 twenty-one black locals existed in the Birmingham area.[42]

On May 30, 1887, Birmingham's Knights proudly displayed their strength with a parade. An estimated nine thousand spectators looked on as thirty-nine assemblies marched through the streets. Marchers carried banners emblazoned with slogans that expressed the ideals of the order: "We seek to unite labor, capital, and honesty"; "Homes for the people are better then [*sic*] palaces for the rich"; "Labor and capital, parent and child, let justice rule between them"; "Labor creates wealth—the created should not dictate to the creator." Birmingham's Knights joined working people across the United States in demanding a humane economic system in which equality and harmony between capital and labor prevailed. They did not demand the destruction of capitalism. Rather, they demanded a capitalism that benefited all of the people, not just a select few.[43]

Birmingham's Knights did not encourage its members to engage in strikes or other forms of direct action against employers. Strikes, the Knights as an organization believed, might secure for workers short-term wage gains and even some control over their working lives, but they usually did nothing to bring down the true source of workers' oppression, a wage system that "places the laborer at the mercy of the employer."[44] Leaders of the Knights found the source of workers' exploitation in their separation from the means of production. Until workers regained control over the distribution of what they produced through ownership of the means of production, they argued, they would remain victims of the few who controlled productive property.[45] Through cooperation the Knights proposed to return ownership of productive property to workingmen, thereby eliminating the distinction between capital and labor.[46]

The ideals of the Knights of Labor were noble, but not all of its Birmingham members endorsed them. Birmingham assemblies continued to resort to the strike in disputes with their employers. In 1887, for example, owners of the Linn and Williamson foundries launched a campaign against organized molders. C. P. Williamson stated that his objective was to assert the right of employers to operate their plants free of interference from labor unions. Molders and other skilled workers at the two companies walked out and remained on strike for over a month. When they returned to work at the end of August, their organization remained in place.[47]

Despite such successes the Knights of Labor rapidly declined in strength. The strikes at Linn and Williamson exposed the strength of craft consciousness among metal tradesmen. Skilled iron workers never fully accepted the Knights' policy of organizing interracial unions of skilled and unskilled workers. This became clear when State Master Workman Nicholas Stack ordered skilled Knights to join a laborers' strike against the Linn and Williamson foundries in 1887. Craft assemblies denounced Stack and refused to support the strikers. Stack eventually managed to persuade many of the skilled workers at the two companies to stop working, but the episode left the Knights in Birmingham divided. The Cosmopolitan Assembly, the largest in the state, canceled its subscription to the Knights' newspaper and barred Stack from its meetings. After 1887 the Knights of Labor virtually disappeared from Birmingham.[48]

As the Knights faded, skilled workers revived their craft unions. With Birmingham's economy expanding during the late 1880s, the demand for skilled workers surged, and craftsmen regained some of the market power they had lost during the mid-1880s. They used their increased leverage with employers to reestablish their old craft organizations with their restrictive policies, racial and otherwise. The AAISW, for example, reemerged and resumed its earlier leadership in the district's union movement. Two new rolling mills had been built by 1889 in nearby Bessemer and Gate City, and management at both signed AAISW scales. From that foothold the union launched an effort to organize the remaining nonunion mill, BRM.[49] In January 1890 members of the Gate City and Bessemer lodges who had secured employment at BRM organized seventy-five other employees. Within a few days approximately two hundred workers, mostly puddlers, joined the union. The company, in keeping with the policies it had established in 1884, promptly discharged all union members and gave them a few weeks to renounce their union affiliation before nonunion men would be brought in to take their places.

The puddlers, unmoved by the threat, urged others to join them, and on January 27 four hundred men from the finishing department did. They formed a committee, which met with superintendent Dwyer to demand union recognition. Dwyer agreed to pay union scale and graciously conceded the right of the men to join other lodges of the AAISW, but he vowed to uphold the company's strict rules against unions. Before anyone went to work at the mills, he declared, they would have to agree to obey its rules and regulations. Dwyer then tried to recruit replacements for the strikers but had little success. Finally, in May the company reluctantly signed the AAISW scale.[50]

Other skilled metal workers joined newly formed unions of molders, boilermakers, machinists, and patternmakers. The International Iron Molders Union, the International Association of Machinists, the Patternmakers League, and the Brotherhood of Boilermakers all established locals in Birmingham. These organizations united with others in the Birmingham Trades Union Council, which coordinated the political and economic activities of the various organizations affiliated with it.

It was no coincidence that during the early 1890s May Day and Labor Day parades became major events in which the white community came together to celebrate workers' contributions to the building of the town. On parade days members of the craft unions donned their respective uniforms and marched with banners that reaffirmed their commitment as citizens to the commonweal. Through their work, marchers' banners proclaimed, craftsmen promoted the public good by creating prosperity for the entire community. On floats that union members constructed, workers displayed the skills so essential to the future prosperity of the town. Commentary in the local press captured the spirit of these events when it described them as festivals "of good cheer, and good will, in which all walks of life are asked to participate. The employer, the professional man, the merchant, the artisan, the wage earner all mingle together in a glorious holiday, glorious indeed where working men are enjoying the fruits of fair wages and good conditions." [51]

Inclusion of "artisan" here as a category apart from "wage earner" is revealing. Although skilled workers' relationship to the means of production placed them in the category of wage earner, they continued to embrace a vision rooted in another era. They did not believe that employers shared the same view of the world; the struggles of the 1880s had disabused most of that notion. Yet they continued to commit themselves to the creation of a society of equality and opportunity for the skilled white workingman. Those who marched undoubtedly understood that they faced more struggle before their ideals would become a reality.

CHAPTER 3

Unskilled Work, Black Workers

While Birmingham's skilled workers provided the technical knowledge essential to the establishment of the city's early industries, most of the jobs in those industries were low-paying, unskilled positions that required little more than physical strength and endurance. Before 1900 the proportion of iron and steel workers performing unskilled jobs remained near or above 50 percent.[1] Unskilled workers performed the dirtiest, heaviest, hottest, most dangerous tasks in the iron industry, at rates of pay barely above the subsistence level.

Birmingham's builders wanted to fill these jobs with whites. They thought blacks would work hard only if forced to do so. But during the 1880s not enough whites responded to appeals for labor to fill demand. So employers reluctantly looked to the black population of Alabama and surrounding states for their common laborers. Soon unskilled work became so identified with blacks that local whites began to describe such jobs as "nigger work."

Most African Americans who moved to Birmingham thought they could improve their lives, materially and otherwise. Their experience hardly fulfilled all of their hopes. The town's rigid system of industrial segregation severely restricted their opportunities. But the system was not so unyielding that black workers could not achieve some control over their working lives. Whites' commitment to a racial division of work allowed blacks such complete domination of certain jobs that they gained a degree of leverage in some sectors of the labor market. Black workers could and did exploit this monopoly, especially during boom times, to secure better wages and to define for themselves the terms of their employment. They daily challenged the power of white employers individually and informally. Employers frequently complained about black workers' absenteeism and their poor work habits. They expressed frustration at their inability to transform black workers into disciplined employees. Employers admitted that they had to adapt to the ways of black workers. At times blacks organized unions and collectively defended the rights they claimed in the workplace. Black unskilled workers clearly were not helpless victims of an oppressive system of segregation. They did not allow white employers to impose, without challenge, measures at the workplace that they, like white workers, equated with "wage slavery."

Few promoters of the Birmingham district in the 1870s included black laborers in their vision of a "workshop town," even as unskilled workers. Most embraced the myth that in the absence of the close supervision and discipline slavery provided blacks would not work. John Milner advised employers to limit their use of black workers and to distribute the few they did employ among white workers, who would control them.[2] Many employers shared Milner's preference for white workers but encountered difficulty finding enough of them to meet their needs. Despite hard times relatively few rural whites in the 1870s were ready to abandon their farms to go to work as common laborers in the mines and furnaces of Birmingham. Whites who did move sought other opportunities in agriculture.[3]

Milner and promoters of Birmingham thought they might be able to find white unskilled laborers outside of Alabama. They and employers of farm labor in the state eagerly sought white immigrants during the 1870s. Birmingham industrialists enlisted the aid of the legislature in their recruitment campaign. Jefferson county's state senators sought an increase in funding for Birmingham's educational system in 1872–73 because they thought better schools would attract white immigrants. Though this measure failed, other tactics were apparently more successful; by 1880, 40 percent of unskilled workers were whites, and half of them had been born in other states or countries.[4]

White immigration did not keep pace with demand for labor during the expansion of the 1880s, however. Birmingham's employers, therefore, hired more black laborers. They justified this extension of pre–Civil War employment patterns in the industry with appeals to prevailing ideas about the abilities of the races. John Lapsley, an owner of Shelby Iron, explained to a U.S.

Senate committee that as a race blacks were more suited for the physical demands of common labor than whites and had demonstrated their capacity for hard labor while previously working for his company as slaves. Naturally, when faced with labor shortages after the war, his company turned to men who had already proven themselves.[5] As John Ware, the son of Horace Ware, builder of Shelby Iron, wrote, "when [slaves] became free after the war, their knowledge of such work stood them well in hand, and they easily secured remunerative employment with furnace operators."[6] Truman Aldrich, one of the organizers of Pratt Coal and Coke, agreed with Ware's and Lapsley's appraisals of black abilities, though he complained about black laborers' inefficient work habits.[7]

But many employers and civic leaders remained doubtful about the long-term prospects of the district if they could not find an alternative to black labor. Into the 1880s and 1890s they continued to search for ways to attract white workers to Birmingham. Giles Edwards, superintendent of the Eureka Iron Works at Oxmoor, doubted that blacks would ever learn the discipline required of efficient industrial workers. He believed whites must replace blacks before Alabama's iron industry could flourish. Civic leaders agreed with Edwards. They were so concerned about the growth of the black laboring population that they launched a campaign in 1882 to raise capital for the building of a textile mill they hoped would attract white families to their town. If white men in the hill country knew that their wives and children could contribute to the family economy by working in a mill, they argued, they might be willing to accept low-paying, unskilled jobs in Birmingham. A group of investors created a company to build the mill but never built it, and the scheme died.[8]

Throughout the 1880s employers and civic leaders proposed other schemes for recruiting white workers, but most white Alabamians in the 1880s and 1890s were not yet desperate enough to take work they associated with blacks and therefore considered demeaning. Thus, as Birmingham industries expanded, employers continued to rely upon the state's black population for unskilled labor. Companies sent labor recruiters into the fields of the Black Belt to spread propaganda about the attractions of the Magic City. In time migration chains developed and became an important means of maintaining the black labor force. Labor agents contacted relatives and friends of men already working for the company they represented and provided train tickets to those willing to move. On many trips employees from the region accompanied recruiters.[9] Black residents of Birmingham advertised the attractions of the city through newspapers they distributed in their native counties. Natives of Marengo County, for example, published the *Christian Hope* to keep their relatives and former neighbors informed about their progress and to urge others to take advantage of what Birmingham had to offer. Black-operated "information bureaus" based in the city also publicized opportunities there and helped migrants find places to work and live when they arrived.[10]

Black Belt planters felt the impact of black migration to Birmingham and other places and took steps to stop it. During the 1870s the Ku Klux Klan threatened to use violence against freedmen who tried to leave plantations. Klansmen pursued emigrants and returned those they caught to the plantations they had abandoned. Plantation owners demanded state legislation to restrict black mobility, and the legislature responded with an 1879 law that imposed a state tax on labor recruiters.[11]

Black migration continued to be a problem for planters into the 1880s, a problem some observers attributed to increased demand for labor in the Birmingham district. Senator John Morgan warned Congress in 1883 that black migration out of the Black Belt would worsen a labor shortage in the region and drive up the cost of cotton production. "If industry in Alabama is to draw the labor from the cotton plantation continually by additional temptations," he said, "I do not see how we are to conduct our great agricultural enterprises." If labor continued to abandon agriculture for the mines and furnaces of the mineral district, he remarked, "I shall begin to believe after a while that it is more a curse than a blessing to have these great bestowments of coal and iron in the bosom of our state." Planters held meetings where they threatened to use violence against labor agents unless the state legislature aggressively moved to stop the exodus of black labor. The legislature again responded, passing a law that made the breaking of a sharecropping contract after acceptance of advances a criminal act.[12]

Intimidation, antienticement laws, and other statutes did little to stop blacks from moving if they chose to do so. From 1880 to 1900 the black population of Birmingham and surrounding Jefferson County grew from 5,053 to 56,334.[13] In 1880 approximately 60 percent of the unskilled workforce was black. Samples of unskilled iron workers reveal a sharp increase in the proportion of blacks during the 1880s to between 85 and 90 percent (see Table 3.1). By 1900, as Birmingham businessman N. F. Thompson explained to the U.S. Industrial Commission, whites in the city "regarded [black labor] as unskilled labor."[14]

Many of Birmingham's black workers may have left the Black Belt before entering sharecropping agreements and therefore were not subject to much

Table 3.1. Unskilled Iron Workers by Race (percentages)

	1880	1884	1888
White	42	22	12
Black	58	78	88
Total	100	100	100
Sample	113	82	130

Sources: The data for 1880 includes all iron and metal workers on the manuscript census schedule for Jefferson County. The data for 1884 and 1888 is based on samples of the population drawn from city directories for those years. For 1884, I included all iron workers from every other page of the city directory. In order to keep the size for 1888 approximately the same as for the other two years, I included iron workers from every fifth page of the directory.

of the legislation designed to govern the sharecropping system. Clearly, young single men were more likely to move than older married men. In 1880, 60 percent of black workers were under the age of thirty and 77 percent were under the age of thirty-five; less than 40 percent of them were married. A sample of black workers in 1900 reveals little change in the age structure— 59 percent were under thirty and 73 percent were under thirty-five—and almost half were unmarried. Anecdotal evidence from the period reinforces this statistical portrait. In his study of the Black Belt, W. E. B. Du Bois attributed a decline in the number of blacks between the ages of twenty and thirty to migration to towns and cities. Former slaves in Sumter County, Alabama, proudly told an interviewer for the Works Progress Administration about their children who had moved to Birmingham and other cities. Many of the migrants made their way to the city before they took on the responsibilities of marriage and family, burdens that might have restricted their choices. As a planter from the Tennessee Valley of Alabama remarked to the Industrial Commission in 1901, "Those who are unencumbered with families are disposed to seek the public works. They have gone off to the Mussel [*sic*] Shoals from my neighborhood and some have come down to Birmingham. . . . It is usually those that are encumbered with families that stay at home."[15]

Birmingham attracted young men for many reasons. Bored with the routine of life in rural Alabama, some men found the lure of Birmingham's social life irresistible. They could go there, find some work, and spend the money they made in the "Red Light," gambling, drinking, and consorting with practitioners of the oldest profession. For most, however, the recreational attractions of the Magic City were only incidental to their search for economic security and, for blacks, physical safety. Black tenants like Randolph Johnson, a former slave, heard the stories of jobs with regular paydays in cash and saw a possibility of escaping the poverty of the rural South. Robert Ransom Poole, Alabama's commissioner of agriculture, told the Industrial Commission that young blacks could go to Birmingham and work for a few months and be paid every couple of weeks or every month.[16] Tenant farmers or laborers had to wait a year for their pay, if they received any at all. The desire for freedom from debt and dependence on white landlords overcame black fears of arrest for leaving their farms.[17]

Of course, the experience of black migrants once they reached Birmingham fell far short of the promises they had heard or read. Blacks entered a town dominated by whites who deeply believed that their own freedom and opportunity for advancement depended upon restriction of black freedom and opportunity. Yet Birmingham did offer rural blacks a chance to advance beyond the miserable conditions they faced in the countryside, as Poole observed. This was certainly not much, but for thousands of blacks from Alabama and other southern states Birmingham offered enough of an improvement to keep them coming. What exactly could blacks hope to achieve? To answer that question we must go to the shops in which they labored.

Black men spent their working lives performing tasks that required considerable strength, stamina, and, in many cases, a willingness to risk personal safety.[18] Top fillers, virtually all of whom were black, worked at the top of the furnace, eighty to one hundred feet above the ground, distributing iron ore around the circumference of the furnace hopper. Working under conditions of extreme heat and always exposed to the elements, they risked asphyxiation from toxic gases as well as death from explosions or a fall.[19]

When molten iron reached the bottom of the hearth, African American laborers tapped the furnace. The casting crew drained the furnace four to six times within a twenty-four-hour period. It took six to eight men ten to sixty minutes to open the "cinder notch" through which the iron would pour. While they worked with hand drills and sledges to open the notch, the heat was so intense that the men at the notch had to be relieved every two to three minutes. Once the crew opened the notch, the molten iron flowed into a main runner from which a worker, using a long bar, directed it into channels cut into sand and arranged like "pigs suckling at the sow." The crew then closed the notch by placing a bar in the hole to chill the molten iron, making it solidify, or by ramming a ball of damp clay into the hole. In the meantime each channel, or runner, "led" the iron to a handmade sand mold.[20]

After the iron cooled, iron breakers, or iron carriers, used heavy sledge-hammers and crowbars to break the "pigs" from the "sow," the runner, and to break the iron left in the runner into manageable lengths. Workers considered the jobs of the iron breakers the heaviest and most disagreeable around the furnace. Men lifted and carried 100 to 125 pound iron bars across loose sand to railroad cars 200 to 250 times in a four- to six-hour period.[21] Their jobs were so physically taxing that few men could bear up under the strain. According to Edward Uehling, the inventor of the pig-casting machine, "the extraordinary muscular exertion required bars four-fifths of the laboring class" from iron breaking.[22]

Not all blacks worked as unskilled common laborers. Ore mining, like coal mining, was considered a skilled job and blacks dominated iron ore mining. By 1900 almost 80 percent of a sample of ore miners were black; a third of all black workers in the same sample mined ore for a living. Here again the origin of black dominance lay in the antebellum years when mine owners had relied upon slave labor.[23] Mine owners continued to hire blacks after the war, no doubt because they possessed required skills, and whites still did not want the jobs.

Experience was more essential in ore mining than any of the other jobs blacks held. Miners did not simply walk into a mine and start loading ore. First they had to set an explosive charge to "bring down" the rock that blocked access to the ore body. A knowledge of explosives was essential if this task was to be carried out correctly and safely. After blasting miners used picks to remove ore from the mine face. They then "sold" the ore to the company at a tonnage rate linked to the market price of pig iron. From their pay miners purchased most of the equipment—fuses, powder, dynamite—they needed for their work.[24]

Although African Americans possessed little formal authority on the shop floor, they found ways to impose their own ideas about work. They brought with them to Birmingham attitudes about work that often clashed with those of their employers. As slaves they had creatively resisted the work discipline planters desired.[25] In Birmingham they employed some of the same strategies to limit their bosses' power. Iron breakers, for instance, worked hard after a casting and then recovered while they waited for the the next casting. Often they extended their rest periods so that furnaces could not be tapped as frequently as their bosses might have liked. Many blacks sought jobs that permitted much individual autonomy, such as ore mining. As miners they decided for themselves how many cars of ore they would produce each day and experienced minimal company supervision. Few mining companies even tried to control the quality of ore that miners produced. They did, to be sure, find ways to deprive black miners of much of their profits. Still, miners enjoyed a great deal of control over their workday.[26]

Employers complained frequently about the independent habits of all of their black workers. James Sloss appeared before a committee of the U.S. Senate in 1883 and spoke at some length about the work ethic of black employees. They were not, he said, "disposed to settle down to regular systematic work." Blacks were "migratory by nature; love to change; today at work, and tomorrow away or idle. As long as they have a dollar in their pockets they feel independent and indisposed to work." An employer could threaten to discharge them, he continued, but would find that dismissal had "no terrors to them." While black laborers worked hard when given a task, they would not do so for extended periods. "They will not," complained Sloss, "hesitate to leave their work, even in emergencies, at any time, with or without excuse, to attend a circus, excursion, burial, etc., and it is almost impossible to keep a force at work at the furnaces after Saturday and until Monday, and not unfrequently they absent themselves until Tuesday or Wednesday and this is equally true of them after pay day."[27]

Racial stereotypes run through Sloss's remarks, but he did understand that something more than race explained workers' behavior. When asked if white labor would perform any better, he replied that because of their rural origins they too made poor industrial workers. John Lapsley thought that blacks' work habits reflected their inadequate understanding of free market capitalism. He attributed their work ethic to a disdain for accumulation of property and capital. If that flaw could be corrected, he believed, they might develop the discipline necessary to reap the fruits of the free enterprise system. He failed to explain just how this change would be brought about in a society based on the systematic restriction of economic opportunity for blacks.[28] Lapsley and Sloss wanted blacks to behave as if all of the supposed rewards of the free labor system were there for the taking.

Members of the black middle class agreed with employers' assessments of black work habits and lectured workers on the error of their ways. Citing themselves as examples, prominent blacks encouraged workers to improve their performances in the workplace and to curry the favor of their bosses to remove the stigma of black laziness. In 1902 the Negro Business League held a "negro workers' conference" at which Dr. W. R. Pettiford, president of the Alabama Penny Savings Bank and a leader of Birmingham's black middle class, urged laborers to be more reliable and efficient. If they failed to change their behavior, he warned, blacks would continue to receive low wages and would never be able to save money with which to purchase property and businesses. Embrace the work ethic of their employers, Pettiford assured the crowd, and rewards would surely follow. He elaborated these themes in a series of addresses he delivered to workers in late 1902. Pettiford complained to African American workers: you "too often leave your work . . . and the machinery of your company . . . has to be shut down." He concluded that blacks must alter their habits if they hoped to advance individually and collectively.[29]

Pettiford, Sloss, and Lapsley thought instruction in behavior appropriate to life in an urban-industrial society might improve the black workforce. Yet, before the early twentieth century, industrialists did not systematically try to instill in their common laborers the habits they preferred in an employee. They proposed solutions from time to time, such as the use of the educational system to alter workers' behavior, but did little to implement their ideas. Instead, they adjusted to the ways of the laborers. Employers hired more workers than necessary because they knew that many would not report to work on a given day. According to Sloss, he hired 560 men in October of 1882 to do work that required only 260. F. L. Wadsworth and T. T. Hillman, president and general manager, respectively, of the Alice Furnace Company, estimated in 1883 that for nine to ten months of the year only 12.5 percent of their employees worked full time; 25 percent worked fewer than ten days a month. At times employers, knowing their unskilled workers would not be present, closed down their plants completely. Most companies in the city shut down for a week or two during the Christmas season while black employees celebrated a holiday they and their ancestors had always received as slaves.[30]

Even if employers could have instilled discipline in all of their black workers, they would not have solved the problems of turnover and absenteeism. Certainly many migrants from the rural South lacked the work habits men like Sloss, Lapsley, Wadsworth, Hillman, and Pettiford desired. But the mobility of black unskilled workers was more than a consequence of inadequate preparation for life in the industrial world or a rejection of "capitalist values." Many black workers moved from job to job in search of better situations, taking advantage of tight labor markets, especially during the boom periods of the early and late 1880s and the early 1890s.[31] Wadsworth told U.S. Senate investigators that extensive building and high demand for labor contributed to his company's labor troubles; with plenty of jobs available, he implied, laborers tended to move around more. Tennessee Coal and Iron encountered the same problem after it moved into the district in 1886. President Nat Baxter reported to stockholders in 1888 that the building of four blast furnaces at the company's Ensley development had been delayed because of "some difficulty encountered during last summer in securing common labor, which was attributable to the great demand for such labor, created by the numerous new works and extraordinary amounts of railroad building that was being done in and around Birmingham." Having migrated to Birmingham to improve their economic condition and to secure a greater degree of personal autonomy, black workers used their leverage in the market to try to achieve both ends.[32]

The information available on workers' earnings and the cost of labor in Birmingham's nineteenth-century iron industry suggests that black workers derived material benefits from tight labor markets, at least within the limited sphere of unskilled work. In 1890 some iron carriers and top fillers earned as much as or more than highly skilled molders. Their pay approached that of furnace keepers, the highest-paid workers around a blast furnace, and was significantly higher than the wages of farm laborers. It appears that competition for the services of black workers drove up wages for some of the jobs blacks dominated.[33]

Black workers did not rely solely on informal and individual strategies to shape the conditions of their employment. Some participated in well-organized, collective efforts to defend rights they claimed in the workplace and to secure higher wages. In the late 1880s many blacks joined Knights of Labor assemblies.[34] After the collapse of the Knights, blacks continued to form their own labor organizations, sometimes with the blessing and co-operation of the American Federation of Labor (AFL), the Alabama Federation of Labor, and the Birmingham Trades Union Council.[35]

But the black commitment to long-term organization remained ambivalent at best. Whites controlled the labor movement in Birmingham and were more concerned with preventing black advancement than with promoting it. Black workers therefore tended to organize spontaneously and temporarily to address specific issues. In mid-June 1899, for example, a group of black iron ore miners met in the woods near Ishkooda, a mining camp outside of Birmingham, and decided to form a committee that would demand from the mining company an increase of 12½ cents per car and payment in cash. The company, a contractor for Tennessee Coal, Iron, and Railroad Company (TCI), paid the miners $.50 per two-ton car. At that rate a miner could earn $.90 to $1.50 per day. Miners paid $.50 a month to rent company houses and $.75 a month for insurance if single, $1.00 if married; the company gave them commissary checks for the balance of their wages. By paying miners in scrip the company forced them to pay unreasonably high prices for supplies they needed for their work and for their families' subsistence. In the end miners received little from a car of iron ore that the company would convert into $44 worth of iron.

When the committee met with company officials, the superintendent of the mine fired the committee members and all those associated with them and ordered them to vacate company houses. Rather than submit to the company's will, the disgruntled miners spread leaflets around the camp detailing their demands and urging miners still working to join in a strike. The company's response was quick and decisive. It enlisted black preachers and a black middle-class newspaper called the *Birmingham Hot Shots* in a campaign to educate non-strikers about the evils of unions and to show them that loyalty to their beneficent employers was in their best interest. In addition the company barred strikers from the Ishkooda church, which was on company land, and brought in sheriff's deputies to control alleged rioting. Deputies protected company officials who entered strikers' homes to evict them, arrested strikers for vagrancy and, in a few cases, adultery, and escorted strikebreakers to and from the mines. The presence of the deputies, combined with pressure from black leaders and the threat of eviction from company housing, probably convinced many nonstriking miners to remain at work. Whether strikebreakers worked because of company intimidation or because they disagreed with the strikers remains unclear. In any case enough miners continued to work to defeat strikers' efforts to hamper production at Ishkooda.[36]

A year after the conflict at Ishkooda, furnace workers at five of TCI's furnaces walked out after the company refused to grant demands for a 10 percent increase in wages, paydays every two weeks, and an end to a mandatory fee for a company doctor, who discriminated against black employees. Local newspapers reported that a thousand blacks under the leadership of a local of the Furnacemen's Union (AFL) joined the strike, completely shutting down two furnaces and causing delays at the others. A number of prominent whites in the community supported the strikers. White merchants were particularly sympathetic toward the furnace workers' cause. TCI's system of stores and its practice of paying workers irregularly and in company scrip deprived independent merchants of a portion of their potential market. Moreover the company store system had been a constant source of turmoil in the community. A group of merchants therefore urged TCI officials to accept the furnace workers' demands. Company negotiators conceded nothing. Because the depression of the 1890s had created a surplus of labor, the company easily found men to take the strikers' jobs and ended the strike on its own terms.[37]

At times conflict between unskilled workers and employers erupted when employers violated workers' rights. In Birmingham one of those "rights" was the freedom to leave a job and return to it in a few days or weeks. Employers found workers' irregular attendance disruptive, so in the fall of 1899 a superintendent at U.S. Cast Iron Pipe Company in Bessemer decided to instill more discipline in his unskilled workforce by dismissing those who left service without cause. The first test of the policy came when Jack Johnson, who had quit work on a Thursday, returned to the plant on the following Tuesday, expecting to resume his work as he always had after similar extended weekends. Much to Johnson's surprise the superintendent informed him that his place had been filled and that he was no longer in the company's employ. An outraged Johnson went to a representative of one of the remaining Knights of Labor assemblies and asked him to help force U.S. Pipe to respect his right to return to his job. The Knights formed a committee of furnace workers at the plant, which met with company officials to demand Johnson's reinstatement and recognition of the Knights as the furnace workers' organization. The superintendent refused to negotiate; the company, he told the committee, would deal with individuals only. A day later three hundred furnace workers failed to report to work, forcing the company to shut down.

Orders were down when the strike began, so U.S. Pipe shifted production to other facilities until more workers could be assembled. Two weeks later the company resumed operation with a force of 200 new employees. They proved to be as rebellious as the men they replaced. On their first day the strikebreakers entered the plant, went to their places, began to work, and then "with a whoop and a yell threw down their tools" in protest against the dismissal of four men "for failing to do their work properly." By the beginning of the following week U.S. Pipe had recruited 225 nonunion whites to fill the jobs, but conditions remained tense around the plant for the next month. According to newspaper reports, there were a number of shooting incidents between strikers and their replacements before conditions returned to normal. Jack Johnson and his supporters probably moved on to other jobs.[38]

Johnson and other blacks who moved to Birmingham hoped for a brighter future than that which lay before them if they remained on farms, working as tenants and sharecroppers, mired in a seemingly endless cycle of debt, poverty, and oppression. When they arrived in Birmingham they confronted a reality far removed from the stories of opportunity they had heard and read. But black laborers had migrated because they wanted to control their own lives as free and equal members of the community, and they struggled against imposing odds to achieve that goal. While their efforts left them short of their destination, they made enough progress to justify continuing the journey and the struggle.

CHAPTER 4

Life Away from Work, 1880–1900

Within the workplaces of Birmingham people identified with each other on the basis of their position within the system of production and their race. Skilled workers, most of whom were white, established a sharp line between themselves and unskilled workers, most of whom were black. They extended the distinctions of the workplace into the community and reinforced them. Away from work white skilled workers sought to build lives in accord with the status conferred by their work and their race. They lived in homes the unskilled, particularly unskilled blacks, could not afford and socialized with each other and the local middle class in institutions they helped build.

Inextricably linked to this process of self-definition was the humiliation of those excluded from the aristocracy of labor and race. The lives of black laborers when they left work were full of reminders of their subordination in all areas of life. Residing in the least-desirable neighborhoods, their families struggled to survive in substandard and often crowded dwellings. Yet African American workers joined other blacks in building community institutions where they experienced a measure of dignity and control over their collective and individual destinies.[1]

Essential to the development of working-class institutional life was the growth of residential areas populated primarily by workers and their families.[2] Before 1900 the city's industrial plants were located at its center, along a narrow band bordering the railroad tracks, which divided the city into north and south. Regardless of occupation or race, residents of the city lived and worked in an area measuring approximately two square miles. Working people in Birmingham tended to cluster in well-defined neighborhoods. Three factors contributed to a worker's decision about where to live. First, in the absence of a well-developed transit system, men had to live close to their place of employment. Second, workers lived where they could afford to pay the rent or purchase a house, so occupational status had a significant impact on residential patterns. And, finally, whites and blacks lived in separate neighborhoods.[3]

In the early years of the town's existence companies provided much of the housing available to workers. Robert P. Porter, a visitor to the town in 1884, reported that the population expanded more rapidly than the housing supply, driving the cost of dwellings beyond what many workers could afford or were willing to pay. To address the problem some companies built houses on their property and leased them at rates below the local market price. James Sloss told Porter that his furnace company built forty-eight frame houses for which he charged $4.00, $5.00, or $6.00 per month for one, two, and three rooms, respectively. Birmingham Rolling Mill Company provided separate residential areas for company officers and production workers.[4]

Unable to find affordable housing elsewhere, some skilled and unskilled workers occupied company quarters in the early 1880s. For many this was an unsatisfactory arrangement, however, and by the mid-1880s a number of company tenements stood vacant. At least one company, citing limited worker demand for company-owned quarters, sold its housing project. According to a company official, workers preferred higher-priced accommodations away from company property where they would not be subject to company regulation during their leisure hours.[5] Those workers in the city who continued to live in company housing were generally unskilled and black. All the residents of Sloss's houses in the 1888 city directory sample were black laborers; of the few workers who remained in BRM's quarters, all were laborers and only one was white.[6]

If most white and black workers sought housing in neighborhoods free of their employers' direct influence, they still lived near their workplaces because most walked to and from work.[7] Thus residential patterns emerged that reflected the occupational and racial divisions of the city's shops. Skilled white iron workers tended to live in preferred neighborhoods closest to their workplaces. For example, white employees at the Beggs Pipe Foundry, one of

Company housing at Ironton, ca. 1870. Note the contrast between the white buildings at left that housed company officials and the much smaller buildings in the right background that were provided for workers. Alabama State Department of Archives and History.

the first to be established in the city, lived between Third Avenue and Fifth Avenue North, only one or two blocks from the foundry. After the opening of BRM many of its white skilled employees resided in a three-block-long area along First and Second Avenues South, a block or two away from the mill. Over 50 percent of the population of some blocks in what came to be known as "rolling mill hill" consisted of rolling mill workers. (See Map 4.1.) The remaining residents of "rolling mill hill" were middle-class merchants and professionals. This residential pattern existed throughout the city.[8]

More striking than class or occupational division of the town's space was racial segregation. In the 1880s concentrations of blacks generally could be found on the fringes of the town. Blacks lived closer to whites than they would later, and blacks and whites often lived on the same streets. Spatial proximity should not be equated with spatial integration, however. If blacks lived on the same streets as whites, they did not live on the same blocks.

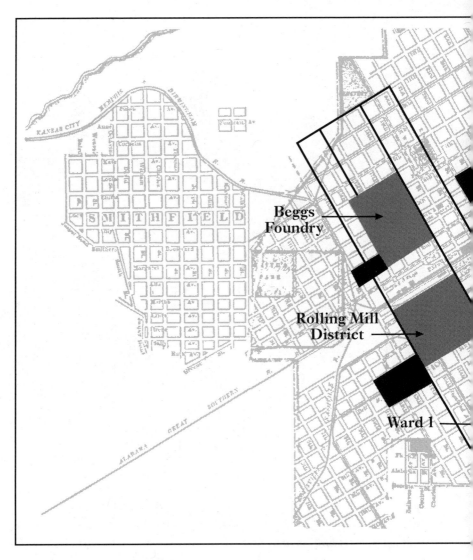

Map 4.1. Birmingham, 1883–1890

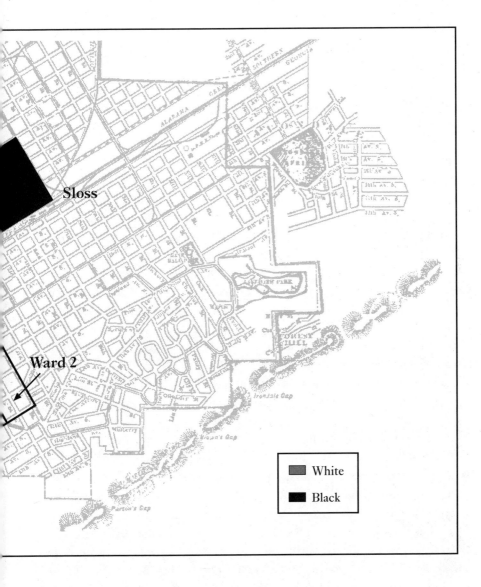

Sloss

Ward 2

White
Black

Blacks and whites lived near each other, but their worlds remained separate and unequal.[9]

A large proportion of Birmingham's workers rented rooms in the homes of others or in one of the city's many boardinghouses. Of all the iron workers in the 1880 census, 60 percent were boarders. Their average age was between twenty-six and twenty-seven, seven to nine years below the average for household heads, and most were twenty-nine years of age or younger. Men from all levels of the occupational hierarchy could be found among the boarding population. Almost 70 percent of skilled workers were boarders; 43 percent of all boarders were skilled.[10]

Boarding contributed significantly to the occupational and racial segregation of the city's space. Of black household heads with boarders, over half had boarders with the same occupation, laborer. Over 75 percent of skilled workers lived with other skilled workers, and none boarded in the household of an unskilled worker. Unskilled and semiskilled whites tended to live in the households of skilled workers; all of the helpers in the sample who were boarders lived with a skilled iron worker. Although it is impossible to know for sure, it appears that many white unskilled and semiskilled workers lived with the craftsmen for whom they worked.[11]

The proportion of boarders among iron and steel workers dropped sharply by 1900, particularly among skilled whites. This decline was one consequence of an expansion of the supply of housing that began in the late 1880s, in part because of the efforts of the Knights of Labor.[12] To provide affordable working-class housing at a time of soaring housing costs in Birmingham, a group of Birmingham Knights formed the Mutual Land and Improvement Company to purchase land for a community "where working men, no matter how hard they struggle for bread, may secure a home." The company bought thirty-seven acres of land south of Birmingham on the Alabama Great Southern Railroad, divided the property into 170 lots, and named the town Powderly. Each of the 120 company stockholders could buy a lot for $60, which could be paid in $1.00 weekly installments. For a minimum of $409—a price that could also be paid in installments—the company would build a house on a member's lot. A comparable house in Birmingham cost between $600 and $700. In addition to residences, the company planned to build schoolhouses, a town hall, a railroad station, and a cooperative store.[13]

Despite relatively low prices and favorable terms, only the most highly paid workers could afford houses in Powderly, and the town became an enclave for white craftsmen. At the end of the town's first year it had a population of two hundred, a school, a general merchandise store, a Knights of

Labor Hall, a free reading room, a railroad station, and a cigar store. Because the demand for lots in Powderly exceeded the number available, Emil Lesser, a Birmingham merchant and one of the founders of the Mutual Land and Improvement Company, formed the Beneficial Land and Improvement Company. Beneficial established another town, which it named Trevillick in honor of Knights lecturer Richard Trevillick.[14]

The building of Trevillick marked the Knights' final effort to solve the problem of working-class housing. By 1888–89 the Knights of Labor was in decline, and Birmingham's craft organizations lacked the commitment to the cooperative ideal that had been a driving force in the development of Powderly and Trevillick. Moreover men with greater financial resources than workers could muster began to recognize how profitable development of low-cost housing outside of Birmingham might be. After 1887 they directed the development of Birmingham's suburbs.

Built around industrial sites by many of the same men who promoted and developed Birmingham, the suburbs were miniature versions of the Magic City. For example, the Elyton Land Company, under the leadership of H. M. Caldwell, bought land east of Birmingham on which it built the Southern Rolling Mill Company and laid out the town of Avondale.[15] B. F. Roden, another Birmingham "pioneer," established the Avondale Land Company to sell the lots in Avondale to workers and merchants who expected to settle there. Roden also invested in the building of a rail line from Birmingham to Avondale to provide inexpensive and essential transportation between the two towns, thereby reducing the need for workers and others to settle within walking distance of their places of work.[16] As Caldwell and Roden hoped, relatively cheap housing and new jobs attracted mostly white workers to the town. By the late 1890s this process of suburb building had been repeated over and over so that industrial suburbs ringed the city.

During the same period a second more racially and occupationally homogeneous type of suburb emerged. These "residential suburbs" had no industrial base and were, as one study of Birmingham's development put it, "safely removed from the smoke and noise of Birmingham's expanding industries."[17] Developers designed some of them for the most wealthy of Birmingham's population and others for middle-class professionals and white skilled workers. An example of the latter was East Lake. Of the workers living in East Lake in 1898, most were skilled and white; only about 6 percent of the population was black.[18] Few blacks moved to the suburbs before the turn of the century, remaining instead in the areas at the center of the city that whites left behind.[19] (See Maps 4.1 and 4.2.)

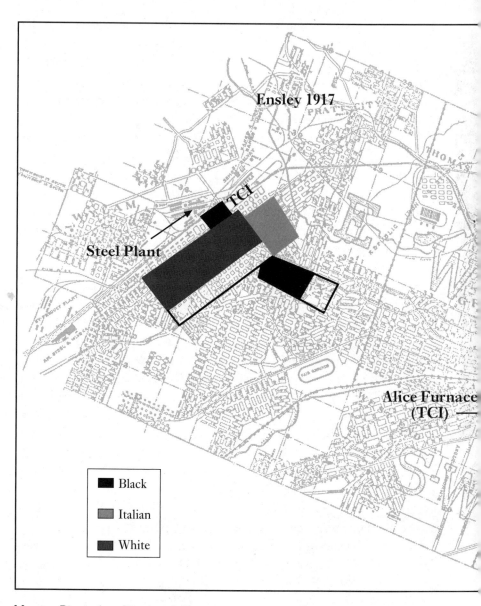

Map 4.2. Birmingham District, 1898–1917

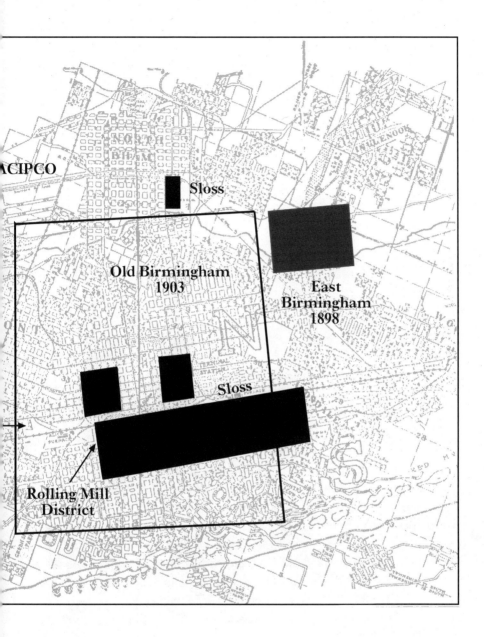

ACIPCO

Sloss

Old Birmingham
1903

East
Birmingham
1898

Sloss

Rolling Mill
District

Table 4.1. Household Structure, 1880 and 1900 [a] (percentages)

	1880		1900	
	White	Black	White	Black
Nuclear[b]	61	59	58	46
Extended	6	3	10	12
Augmented	24	19	23	16
Augmented-extended	6	3	3	5
Single	4	13	5	22
Total	101[c]	98	99	101
Sample	51	34	61	194

Source: Jefferson County Manuscript Census, 1880, 1900.

[a]Every household head who listed his occupation as an iron or metal worker in 1880 is included here. By 1900 the city was too large to include the entire universe, so I systematically sampled the population. From every fifteenth page of the manuscript census for Jefferson County, I took all household heads who were iron or steel workers or iron ore miners. I used a random number to select the first page.

[b]Household forms are defined as follows: nuclear—married couple with or without children or single parents with children at home; extended—nuclear households with relatives; augmented—nuclear households with lodgers; augmented-extended—nuclear households with lodgers and relatives; single—household head was unmarried, widower, or divorced with no children at home.

[c]Percentages may total slightly more or less than 100 because of rounding.

When workers entered their neighborhoods after work, they could see a physical expression of their status in the social order. Their neighbors were of the same race and occupational level. Their houses were monuments to their achievements or reminders of their failures or their oppression. When they entered their homes workers were again reminded of their places in society. The earning power of the household head, peculiarities of the dominant industry in the district, and the values working people brought with them to Birmingham determined the decisions families made concerning purchases, childbearing, and the contributions of family members to the household economy.[20]

Most workingmen's households from 1880 to 1900 consisted only of the head of household, his wife, and his children (nuclear household). Blacks and whites differed little in this respect. The striking difference between the two races reflected the dependence of the city upon single black unskilled laborers; the proportion of single black household heads was over three times that of whites (see Table 4.1).[21] Racial differences in household structure became even more pronounced by 1900, when 58 percent of white households and 46 percent of black households were nuclear.

Blacks and whites opened their homes to boarders and relatives through-out the life cycle of their households (see Table 4.1).[22] Alterations in house-hold structure tended to occur most often after financial burdens increased with the birth of children and, in many cases, the arrival of a needy rela-tive. This trend was particularly striking among black workers. Consider the cases of Andrew Philips and Thomas Green, both married black furnace workers with children. Philips's wife did not work outside the home, but she augmented his income by cooking and cleaning for two men who rented rooms in their house.[23] (See Table 4.2.) Green's household included a rela-tive and three children. He alone did not earn enough to make ends meet, so his wife assumed responsibility for the care of four boarders. Though household extension and augmentation was less prevalent among whites in all the sample years, reflecting the greater earning power of white household heads, many whites did open their homes to boarders and relatives. Hamil-ton Beggs, a molder and owner of Beggs Pipe Foundry, headed a household that included his wife, eight children, a boarder, and a relative.

These examples suggest that households were more likely to include boarders during the second and third stages of the life cycle when dependent children were most likely to be present.[24] Analysis of the household budgets of approximately two hundred Alabama iron workers at each stage of the life cycle further clarifies the relationship between the economic stresses on the household and household augmentation. The budget data confirms that the care of dependent children caused sharp increases in household expendi-tures. For unskilled workers in the sample, the birth of children meant that they would have very little money left at the end of the year or even went into debt to cover expenses. (See Table 4.3.) When facing such circum-stances, unskilled workers who owned or rented homes took in boarders. Skilled workers took in boarders for a different reason. With more money to spend, they could pay for higher-quality housing and evidently spent most of their yearly incomes to do so. If the arrival of children did not threaten skilled workers' economic survival, it did threaten their ability to maintain this standard of living. Thus skilled workers and their spouses often took in boarders so they could live comfortably while providing for the needs of children. While the share of total income boarders contributed to either skilled or unskilled households might not have been large, it certainly eased some of the economic burdens child rearing imposed. (See Table 4.4.)[25]

Wives and mothers rarely contributed to household income by working

Table 4.2. Household Structure by Age of Household Head, 1900
(percentages)

	Age Group				
	18–27	28–37	38–47	48–57	(N)
Nuclear					
White	61	57	73	44	(36)
Black	42	37	70	45	(88)
Extended					
White	16	9	9	0	(6)
Black	14	15	6	10	(24)
Augmented					
White	11	30	18	33	(14)
Black	9	21	15	20	(31)
Augmented-extended					
White	0	4	0	11	(2)
Black	2	6	0	5	(9)
Single					
White	11	0	0	11	(3)
Black	32	20	9	20	(42)
Total					
White	99	100	100	99	
Black	99	99	100	100	
Sample					
White	18	23	11	9	(61)
Black	64	76	34	20	(194)

Source: Jefferson County Manuscript Census, 1900.

outside the home. Opportunities for female employment outside the home were somewhat limited, since the iron industry did not hire women.[26] Women could have worked in other, less demanding occupations, especially after the building of a textile mill in the late 1890s, but none of the spouses of skilled, unskilled, white, black, or immigrant iron workers worked outside the home in 1880.[27] In 1900 no white spouse listed an occupation, and only 10 percent of black spouses did. Few of the black women who listed occupations worked outside the home; laundresses, the majority of black working women, took in wash. Those wives of black workers who did work outside the house-

Table 4.3. Mean Household Expenditures, Household Income, and Annual Balances by Age of Household Head

	Age Group			
	18–27	28–37	38–47	48–57
Unskilled and semiskilled[a]				
Children home		2.05	1.4	0.4
Expenditures	$476	$521	$488	$446
Annual income	488	538	482	452
Balance	12	17	−6	6
Skilled[b]				
Children home		2.3	2.2	
Expenditures	$638	$842	$1002	
Annual income	689	903	1060	
Balance	51	61	58	

Source: U.S. Department of Commerce and Labor, *Sixth Annual Report*.
[a]Sample comprised of 126 households.
[b]Sample comprised of 56 households. There were no skilled workers aged 48–57 who were household heads.

hold filled domestic jobs white women considered degrading.[28] The limited employment of wives outside of their households, despite increasing opportunities, suggests that working-class couples embraced survival strategies consistent with the idea that wives should be in the home performing domestic chores.

Families were more likely to look to children for income than to their mothers, especially if male children over the age of fourteen were present. Approximately one-fourth of the white and black households with children had at least one child working outside the home. As children entered the workforce during the second and third stages of the life cycle, employment of wives outside the household declined. Of the employed black women with children in the 1900 sample, only one had an employed child; the children of the others had not reached the age of fourteen, the age at which one-fifth to one-fourth of the employed children in the sample entered the workforce.[29]

Households, then, functioned as economic units. Household heads provided the greatest share of total income, but other household members contributed enough to get families through hard times or to enable them to do better than merely subsist. While the strategy a household might adopt at a particular time reflected rational economic calculation, widely shared be-

Table 4.4. Sources of Income by Age of Household Head
(percentages)

	Age Group			
	18–27	28–37	38–47	48–57
Unskilled and semiskilled[a]				
Father	94	88	89	86
Children	0	3	2	1
Proportion reporting income from children	0	9	9	1
Spouse	0	1	1	0
Proportion reporting income from spouse	0	6	3	0
Boarders	2	1	4	
Proportion reporting income from boarders	18	29	37	
Skilled[b]				
Father	95	94	95	
Children	0	4	1	
Proportion reporting income from children	0	17	11	
Spouse	0	0	2	
Proportion reporting income from spouse	0	0	1	
Boarders	1	0	2	
Proportion reporting income from boarders	20	3	1	

Source: U.S. Department of Commerce and Labor, *Sixth Annual Report*.
[a]Sample comprised of 126 households.
[b]Sample comprised of 56 households.

liefs about the proper role of wives and mothers limited the options people considered. If wives and mothers contributed to the household income, they usually did so in ways consistent with the idea that they should not work outside the home. In many cases children worked so mothers could concentrate on their household duties exclusively. Black and white households adopted such strategies. However, the increased employment of black women outside the household between 1880 and 1900 indicates that the poorest of Birmingham's iron workers found it increasingly difficult at the end of the nineteenth century to maintain culturally defined gender roles. Ideals seemed to be giving way to necessity.

The location of workers' homes and the circumstances of their lives could not be separated from their experience at work. Whites monopolized the best jobs and consequently enjoyed a higher standard of living than did black laborers. Workers further elaborated such distinctions in a variety of institutions and leisure activities. Fraternal orders, community celebrations, and saloons provided opportunities for workingmen to strengthen and reinforce the bonds of workplace and neighborhood.[30]

Workers' experiences as members of fraternal orders were particularly important in creating the bonds and in articulating the values that held social groups together. Many of Birmingham's workers joined a chapter of one of the fraternal and benevolent orders that existed in the town. In their lodges men celebrated the power of patriarchs in elaborate rituals featuring a theology that rejected "a feminized Christ the Redeemer" for the fearsome God of the Old Testament. Within this world of imagination, men reaffirmed "the primacy of masculine social organization."[31]

A man's status in nineteenth-century society depended in large part upon his control of dependents—wife and children.[32] His authority rested upon his ability to provide for dependents. Fraternal orders shored up this pillar of male dominance by providing a variety of benefits to members in times of illness and unemployment. Through dues payments members created a common fund, which the lodge used to provide assistance to needy members' families. On one occasion when a member of a Knights of Pythias lodge was unable to work because of sickness, the lodge paid a sickness benefit and provided school tuition for one of the man's children. Had he died the lodge would have paid for his burial. Through such benefits fraternal orders formalized and extended an ethic of mutual aid that had its origins in informal kinship networks. Members of lodges were "brothers" and like true brothers were expected to assist each other during hard times.[33]

Fraternalism served a broader social purpose as well. Nineteenth-century manuals emphasized the integrative purpose of fraternalism. One manual published by black Odd Fellows praised the organization for uniting "men of the most discordant opinions . . . in the bonds of brotherly love, affording by its frequent meetings, social intercourse." Another spoke of equality among members who joined together "beneath a common paternal roof."[34] Within fraternal orders men sought to escape the conflicts of the economic sphere and slip into a world where an ethic of mutuality governed relationships among men. Lodges were hierarchically organized, but the members distinguished their hierarchy of merit from the "artificial distinctions" industrial capitalism generated. An Odd Fellows manual instructed members to "disregard the factitious distinctions of rank and privilege which station confers, and judge of men by the only true standard, their *intellectual* and *moral character*."[35]

Judging from analysis of one surviving membership roll and lists of officers published in newspapers over several years, Birmingham's white associations sought to uphold this principle. White skilled workers belonged to most of Birmingham's fraternal associations, where they socialized with merchants, clerks, and some iron company officials. A lodge reflected the socioeconomic characteristics of the neighborhood in which it was located. In Avondale, for instance, all but two of the officers of the Odd Fellows chapter were from the large population of craftsmen who lived there. Other officers and members represented the clerical, managerial, and professional population of Avondale. Half of the officers and initiates who could be identified from a list published in 1893 worked for the same company.

Fraternal orders observed and reinforced prevailing racial etiquette. Blacks organized separate lodges of the same orders whites joined. By 1892 blacks had established lodges throughout the district. Exactly who joined black lodges is impossible to determine with the available evidence. But, given the dominance of industrial workers in the black population and the location of black Odd Fellows lodges in heavily industrial areas such as Pratt City and Bessemer, it appears that fraternal orders had become popular institutions among working- and middle-class blacks by the mid-1890s. Black associations actively assisted migrants in their search for jobs and places to live and, like the white associations, sponsored a variety of activities for members and their families.[36]

Regardless of race fraternal orders shared a commitment to the tenets of Victorian respectability. Odd Fellowship, said *The Odd-Fellow's Text-Book*, "teaches [men] to be good citizens; to be obedient to the civil power; to cultivate the social duties; to be good husbands, fathers, brothers, friends." In this way, and through the promotion of temperance, orders believed that they defended "the morals of the community." When a member violated the values of his order he could be disciplined. In July 1897 the members of Knights of Pythias Lodge 85 "tried" H. W. Eggler, a lodge officer, and William Wise after J. D. Gibson reported that they sold whiskey at their grocery stores. After hearing the arguments of the accuser and the accused, the other members found Eggler and Wise guilty and voted to suspend the two men from the lodge indefinitely.[37]

The sole voluntary association to which many workers belonged was their union. Unions in Birmingham during these years were not just workplace institutions. Union locals sponsored a variety of activities that brought the "brothers" and their families together, reinforcing relationships initially established in the workplace. In addition to providing assistance to families in need, especially during strikes, labor organizations sponsored picnics, balls, and other entertainments for members, their families, and the wider community. Regular socials featured singing, recitations, readings, dancing, and refreshments. Usually the activities promoted the cause of organized labor, as when A. C. Worsey read a piece entitled "The Objects of Labor Organizations" at an 1898 function of the AAISW. The rest of the program that night was less purposeful; David Williams recited a poem entitled "Gone with a Handsomer Man," and John G. Brown offered his rendition of "The Water Melon Shining on the Vine."[38]

Labor organizations often sponsored community celebrations on the Fourth of July and Labor Day. Merchants and shopkeepers closed their businesses, and large crowds of people gathered for these symbolic affirmations of the ideal of a white community of producers working together for the common good. Government officials, merchants, and the operators of small businesses participated in the processions, but both the Fourth of July and Labor Day were occasions for the celebration of workingmen as producers of society's prosperity. Parades expressed a communal ethos and dedication to the principle of equality between labor and capital. Union members donned the regalia of their respective trades and marched as units through the streets of the city, often preceded by floats on which craftsmen displayed their skills. After the parade people typically gathered at one of the local parks for a picnic, patriotic speeches, and lectures on the relationship between labor and capital. Then there would be balloon ascensions, parachute drops, and athletic contests before the day ended with a grand ball.[39]

Fraternal orders and other formal institutions were places where men defined their relationships to other men while paying homage to the tenets of Victorian respectability. Other, less formal settings allowed men to express certain social affinities while mocking Victorian ideals. One of those was the neighborhood saloon. In drinking establishments, as in fraternal orders and unions, men renewed the relationships that bound their social groups together. If the number of saloons is a measure of their popularity, then they were very popular indeed. In Birmingham during the late nineteenth century saloons flourished in almost every neighborhood.[40]

Obviously saloons provided a place for males to gather each day to drink. But, as one historian has argued, many saloons were "social clubs" that served more serious purposes. Men who worked and lived on or near "rolling mill hill" frequented the Rolling Mill Saloon, an establishment operated by a former puddler named Sylvester Daly.[41] During strikes workers assembled there to discuss strategy. Owners of drinking establishments supported striking workers by organizing campaigns for strikers' relief and acting as collection and distribution centers for donated food and money. If patrons needed assistance at other times, the neighborhood saloon owner often provided food or money to help men and their families get through hard times.

The social welfare function of the saloon was linked to its role as a center of political activity. By providing assistance to constituents politician–saloon owners attempted to secure voters' political loyalty. One of the most powerful political machines in Birmingham between 1880 and 1910 was based in the rolling mill district, with headquarters at the Rolling Mill Saloon. During election seasons men gathered there and at other such establishments for political club meetings, where they defined their positions on issues and listened to speeches.[42]

Saloons also catered to the baser instincts of men, particularly young single men. Rural males moved to the city not only to take advantage of economic opportunities but also to indulge in the "recreational" opportunities the city's red-light district offered. Conveniently many local prostitutes had their rooms above the saloons where their customers spent much of their free time. If a house of prostitution was not on the premises of a saloon, it was likely to be located not far away in one of many "boardinghouses." Saloon owners no doubt shared in the proceeds of "the business."[43]

Some citizens of Birmingham found the popularity of saloons and other forms of Sunday recreation among workers disturbing and a threat to social order.[44] In the mid-1880s moral reformers embarked upon a series of crusades to impose their ideas about proper Sabbath observance and to "overthrow the liquor traffic." Their activities sparked bitter conflict within the community as workers and their allies defended their right to decide for themselves how to use their leisure time. At times their struggle for their rights in the community paralleled their struggles for their rights at work.

Complaints about immorality and disregard for the Sabbath appeared in speeches and print in Birmingham from the time the first settlers arrived. It was not until 1887, however, that moral reformers mounted a well-organized campaign. Outraged by the decision of the Board of Aldermen to permit Sunday baseball, a crowd of about two hundred people gathered at the First Methodist Church to protest what they called "a bid for gambling, vice and law breaking." The Reverend Mr. Tyler, responding to local press reports that workers supported the board's decision, rejected the notion that workers needed Sunday amusement. He and others in attendance insisted

Saloons like this one (ca. 1890) were popular with Birmingham's workers. Birmingham Public Library.

that workers either observe the Sabbath by attending church or engage in productive labor at one of the city's industrial plants.[45]

If attendance at a baseball game on Sunday placed workers' souls in jeopardy, patronage of saloons before and after the game placed them at the very edge of the pit of hell, according to some reformers. Of all the evils moral reformers identified during these years, the saloon most aroused the fears of the righteous. In saloons men from all classes and races willfully and happily violated God's law and the teachings of Christ. Saloons provided tempting places for men to gather and spend money that should have gone to providing for their wives and children. Drunken men frequently participated in brawls, knifings, and shootings. Perhaps most shocking to Victorian sensibilities was the existence of widespread prostitution, a problem directly linked to the saloon menace. Poverty, crime, and even political corruption, reformers believed, could be traced to the saloon. The Birmingham Presbytery of the Cumberland Presbyterian Church defined the scope of the problem as advocates of moral reform understood it. It called on "all christians and lovers of humanity" to join the battle against "this foe of God and destroyer of property, happiness, and human life." The presbytery warned that the struggle would not be an easy one, for the saloon enjoyed the protection of the state and many prominent citizens. Such support allowed the "saloon business" to become "the worst curse with which church and state are afflicted." No other institution in society, the presbytery concluded, "destroys more lives, property, and happiness and produces more wretchedness and suffering in individuals and homes."[46]

Battles over Sunday observance and temperance caused divisions within the community that cut across class lines. At one extreme was a group of Methodist, Baptist, and Presbyterian ministers, aligned with the Women's Christian Temperance Union, which not only demanded increased attention to the instruction of the people in the evils of alcohol but also called for laws banning "desecration" of the Sabbath and close monitoring, if not complete prohibition, of liquor sales. A more moderate faction favored temperance and Sunday observance, but objected to the use of the law to force men to sober up. This group preferred moral suasion and sole reliance upon education. Although moderates left little doubt about their abhorrence of intemperance and the immorality it spawned, they frequently found themselves in alliance with saloon owners and their customers.

While workingmen could be found in all camps, skilled whites, the most articulate and politically influential members of the working class, tended to oppose Prohibition and Sunday closing laws. Their objection to both did not imply toleration of intemperance. On the contrary, their associations insisted upon temperance and scrupulous attention to one's responsibilities as head of household. At issue, as the labor press defined it, was the right of a largely middle- to upper-class group of moral reformers to impose their understanding of morality on others.[47]

The Board of Aldermen approved ordinances governing saloons and other Sunday activities during the late 1880s and 1890s, but city administrations in which the political machine based at the Rolling Mill Saloon had considerable influence did not enforce them. Ministers and others complained regularly about open defiance of statutes and in 1894 formed the United Ministers Conference (UMC) to force city government to strictly enforce existing ordinances. They demanded that brothels and saloons, which took "many a laboring man's wages and leave his family without bread," be closed on Sundays as the law required. The UMC received support from organizers of a Law and Order League, which had been formed in response to the violence associated with a miner's strike in the district and was dedicated to the destruction of unions. Both organizations blamed strike violence and other forms of disorder on the effects of alcohol, the support saloon owners extended to strikers, and the irresponsibility of union leaders.[48] Despite the election in 1894 of a mayor sympathetic to the reformers, the Law and Order League and the UMC failed to secure the level of saloon regulation they wanted. Government officials promised tighter saloon regulation and stricter enforcement of Sunday closing laws, but city administrations and the police department remained uncooperative.[49]

In their neighborhoods, households, and organizations, during their celebrations and their visits to saloons, workers further elaborated and reinforced solidarities and divisions firmly rooted in the sphere of production. A man's work and his race largely determined where he would live, what organizations he would join, and where he would have a drink. The fragmentation of the workplace shaped the community and struggles over citizens' autonomy within it. When confronted with what they considered to be threats to their rights, workers vigorously resisted, though they defined their interests in distinctive and conflicting ways.

Defense of their rights carried workers into the political arena, where they linked battles over authority outside of work to conflicts over authority on the shop floor. Workingmen believed that political power was essential to their status in the social and economic order. They thought, in other words, that without direct representation in town government they could not maintain their superiority, racial and otherwise, in any area of life.

CHAPTER 5

Workers and Politics, 1880–1894

To Birmingham's skilled white workers citizenship meant access to political power commensurate with their fundamental role as the creators of society's wealth. When Birmingham's early boosters recruited white skilled workers, they always linked economic status and race to prestige within the community. Skill and race set the craftsman apart from the mass of unskilled blacks and conferred upon him rights denied "wage slaves." Before 1894 skilled workers did indeed exercise substantial political power. Candidates for office eagerly sought their support and responded to their demands. Workingmen won election to city and county offices and held positions of leadership in the local Democratic Party. The rolling mill district emerged in the late 1880s and the 1890s as the center of working-class politics in the town. David Fox and Sylvester Daly, both former puddlers and members of the AAISW, built a powerful Democratic machine in the first ward. By 1892 Fox and Daly had expanded their base out of the first ward into working-class neighborhoods across the town through workingmen's political clubs. The voters rewarded them for their efforts in 1892 when they elected Fox to the mayor's office.

Fox and other candidates who sought votes among workers exploited conflicts generated by economic growth. Issues arose in the sphere of production that could not be contained within the workplaces of the city. Employers often injected these issues into the political system by seeking the protection of the state in conflicts with their workers. Workers then joined their fellow citizens to resist "corporate domination" of the "people's" legislature. They looked to the state when defending themselves against employer practices that they perceived to be violations of their rights as workers and citizens.[1] This is not to suggest, however, that workers agreed on the best way to address the problem. Some workers in the 1880s advocated cooperation with Republicans or abandonment of the two-party system, while others demanded loyalty to the Democratic Party. This division frequently followed racial lines. Blacks tended to support those who challenged the power of a Democratic Party that discouraged black voting and in 1888 prohibited black participation in its primaries. Opponents of the Fox-Daly machine in the 1890s openly appealed to black voters during their campaigns against "machine rule." White workers loyal to Fox resisted reform movements they considered to be efforts to deprive them of their rights as citizens and as white men. Class and racial conflict shaped the town's political culture.

When white workers migrated to Birmingham in the 1880s, they generally aligned with the Democratic Party, which controlled city politics. During the 1880s, however, a number of political movements arose to compete with Democrats for workers' loyalty. The local Republican Party and an independent political movement under the auspices of the Knights of Labor linked conflicts between workers and employers to corporate dominance of the Democratic Party and the state legislature.[2] As proof of the pernicious effect of this unholy alliance, they pointed to the convict lease system, exploitative company stores, and infrequent pay in company scrip. The Democratic state government, they charged, provided corporations in Jefferson County with convicts who competed with free miners and allowed them to impose the system of scrip payment that deprived miners of a fair return for their labor. Because miners did not receive their pay regularly in legal tender, they relied on credit from company stores to secure supplies necessary for their work. Company stores charged higher prices than private establishments in the district, raising miners' costs. Critics of the Democrats argued that the fight against such practices could not be limited to the workplace, because the corporations defended themselves through their influence in the state legislature.

All producers would eventually suffer from such corporate arrogance, the political reformers insisted. If corporations could use the state to advance its designs against the freedom of miners, they could use their political power against all of the people. Workers must not allow companies to use the state to extend their authority. If they did so, where might the abuses end? The reformers suggested that the practices of mining companies would spread across the district along with other state-supported schemes to restrict workers' freedom. And the threat did not end here. Merchants lost much of their natural market because of the commissary, the use of scrip, and the convict lease. Convict leasing filled Jefferson County with criminals who preyed upon the citizenry and posed a constant threat to the stability of the community. The people, reformers declared, must reclaim their state and local governments and end such practices.[3]

The reformers urged voters to rise above the spirit of political partisanship and vote for men who would return the government to the citizens. "Parties are not what is required at this time," an editorial in the *Labor Union* declared, urging citizens to vote instead for "men who will devote all their energies to the welfare of the toiling masses . . . men to represent you, men that will not be afraid to grapple with the convict question; men who will understand the duty of the hour." In 1886 the *Labor Union* endorsed Republican legislative candidates H. G. Sharit, a member of the Knights of Labor, and W. H. Hughes, a member of the Brotherhood of Locomotive Engineers, because they promised to work for abolition of convict leasing and for restriction of child labor. A "workingman's ticket" also challenged Democratic nominee A. O. Lane in Birmingham's mayoral and aldermanic elections the same year. The ticket reflected the broad definition of "workingman" then prevalent. A doctor named J. B. Luckie headed the slate; the aldermanic nominees included a proprietor of a clothing store, a roadmaster for the L&N Railroad, a dentist, a ticket agent at the L&N, and a grocer. Luckie promised to "prevent any class or corporations from invading the rights and privileges of another . . . [and] to advance the general and material interests of the city in every possible way."

The attempt of the "workingman's" or other candidates to harness resentment against the "corporations" in a challenge to Democratic hegemony proved to be ineffective. White skilled workers remained loyal to a local Democratic Party that welcomed them and included them at all levels of the party hierarchy. The Democratic mayoral candidate placed workingmen on his aldermanic ticket to represent wards with concentrations of white workers. Lane won the election with the support of white and black workingmen.[4]

After 1886 leaders of the Knights of Labor dropped the strategy of fusion with the Republican Party, a practice that made them vulnerable to Democratic charges that they wanted to revive "black" Reconstruction, and

inaugurated an independent political movement. They called for the unification of all producers in the United Labor Party (ULP). Drawing on antimonopolism, the labor theory of value, and republican notions of the public
good, spokesmen for the ULP demanded an end to class privilege and the
return of the people's legislatures to the people. Combining the nostrums of
Henry George with planks that addressed local issues, the ULP published a
platform that called for nationalization of railroads and transportation facilities, organization of production and distribution in the interest of producers,
land tenure based on use, abolition of convict leasing, prohibition of payment in anything other than legal tender, and biweekly paydays. The ULP
appealed to all elements of the community, including blacks, who, party
officials emphasized, were as subject to exploitation as whites. Few whites,
workers or otherwise, endorsed the ULP's attempt to remove racial barriers
in local politics. When the party held its state convention in September 1887,
it attracted little attention.[5]

Despite the failure of the ULP, the Knights of Labor tried again to organize a third party in the spring of 1888. C. W. Stewart used the columns of
the *Alabama Sentinel* to urge the producing classes to abandon established
parties. He charged that both Democrats and Republicans served monopo-
lists and their agents. "Man," he wrote, "has rights, natural rights, the gift
of his creator, and governments are established to protect the natural rights
of the individual. The next lesson is that it is not only the right, but the
duty of a free people to destroy old parties and create new ones whenever
the necessities of the case may require it." Stewart joined fellow Knights,
members of the Farmers' Alliance, and members of the Agricultural Wheel
in organizing the Labor Party of Alabama. Calling for an end to "class legislation," the Labor Party demanded shorter hours for workers; abolition of
convict leasing; prohibition of payment in scrip; state inspection of mines,
factories, and tenements; biweekly paydays; government ownership of railroad and communication systems; and adoption of the Australian ballot.
This new coalition also reached out to the black electorate; a number of
blacks participated in the Labor Party's organizing convention.[6]

Jefferson County's Labor Party nominated candidates for county and
state offices and appealed to the "producing classes" to vote for men who
would represent them and would restore harmony between capital and labor.
Democrats, they warned, would not address the problems that plagued their
community. Laborites pointed to John Milner's nomination for state senator
as an example of the Democrats' disdain for the commonweal. Since Milner

had employed convicts himself, he could hardly be expected to support a measure to abolish convict leasing.

Few people around Jefferson County defended the use of convicts in the mines or any of the other corporate abuses the Labor Party identified. The *Birmingham Daily News* denounced state government and its corporate clients for forcing the district to be "the dumping ground for all [the state's] moral filth and rottenness, the scene of constant outrages and of constant executions."[7] Milner and the Democrats did not expect to win elections by taking unpopular positions. Milner advocated reform of the convict system, and the other Democratic nominee for the state senate, R. G. Lowe, opposed convict leasing, company stores, and the scrip system.[8] Both men endorsed the efforts of Jefferson County's legislators to secure legislation that would correct these abuses.[9] The Labor Party therefore failed to convince the public that local Democrats were the tools of the corporations.[10]

Perhaps more damaging to the Labor Party's fortunes was its appeal to African Americans. Robert Warnock, who later emerged as a prominent member of a political faction based in the rolling mill district of Birmingham, toured the county charging that blacks dominated the Labor Party. To support his case he revealed that a Labor Party committee of seven blacks and six whites nominated W. A. Smith for sheriff. The *Alabama Sentinel* assured readers that whites controlled the Labor Party and urged them to disregard the Democrats' attempt to cloud the real issues of the campaign. Its efforts had no impact on the outcome of the election as white workers, according to the *Sentinel*, again stood firm with the Democratic Party.[11]

White workers' response to Democrats' racist appeals reflected their commitment to the subordination of blacks in the workplace and the community. Democratic candidates simply played to the fears of their constituency. Even if race had been no issue, the Labor Party offered workers nothing the Democrats did not offer. Democratic candidates responded to the demands of white workers, and workers held leadership positions in the party. So by the end of 1888 the Democratic Party had withstood challenges to its dominance and white workers remained loyal partisans.

City Democrats reinforced their hold on white workingmen when they banned blacks from party primaries, thereby making the party a white man's club and removing any doubts that might remain about its status as the defender of white supremacy. In addition the Democrats organized more thoroughly than before at the ward and neighborhood level. Building upon the organizational network of neighborhoods, party leaders in each ward formed

Democratic clubs. In Ward One (see Map 4.1), where much of the work-force at Birmingham Rolling Mills lived, Democratic leaders established the Workingmen's Democratic Social Club.[12]

Club meetings mixed politics and recreation. One gathering of the Workingmen's Democratic Social Club featured a string band that included among its repertoire "Dixie" and other "southern airs." Politics, though, was the primary reason for the club's existence. According to the consti-tution of the Workingmen's Democratic Social Club, it intended to spread the Democrats' doctrine: "Equal and exact justice to all, special privileges to none." Members vowed to vote as individuals in primaries but to unite as Democrats in contested general elections. They rejected third partyism, asserting their intention to work for the cause of workingmen through the Democratic Party.[13]

Workingmen's Democratic Social Clubs soon spread throughout the county and in the early 1890s became a powerful force in county and city politics. Local government officials and candidates for office eagerly sought honorary membership in the organization. Candidates appeared at meetings where members questioned them about their positions on important issues and communicated their concerns. The political club became an important means through which white workers shaped the agendas of state represen-tatives and city officials.

By 1892 skilled white workers had emerged as a powerful and orga-nized faction within the city Democratic Party. Sylvester Daly, a rolling mill puddler who became the proprietor of the Rolling Mill Saloon, and David Fox, a former puddler and member of the AAISW who operated a grocery store, built and led a working-class political "machine" in the rolling mill district with headquarters at Daly's saloon. From this base Daly and Fox began their climb to local political power. In 1890 they won election to the Board of Aldermen on the ticket of A. O. Lane. They then proceeded to consolidate their power within the party. By the end of 1891 Fox and Daly had secured control of the City Democratic Party Executive Committee.[14]

Early in 1892 Fox announced his candidacy for mayor and pressured the Democratic Executive Committee into holding an early primary in order to limit opposition. Daly and his Workingmen's Democratic Social Club backed Fox. Some leading Democrats, however, found Fox's politics dis-tasteful and denounced the plan for an early primary. They complained that his "machine" used unfair tactics to undermine the democratic process and to ensure its ascendancy. Anger over his actions revived a movement to defeat "machine" Democrats that had appeared two years earlier. Leaders of the antimachine faction (the Citizens' Reform Union, or Citizens) called for the nomination of a Citizens aldermanic ticket that would be independent of any individual who might be elected mayor. The *Birmingham News* promoted the plan as a way to weaken Fox's political machine and ensure that "the best men" won office. Fox's faction argued that the plan was based "upon the self-contradictory idea that a few men, in the name of the people, must protect the whole people from themselves."

Election day promised to be exciting. A few days before voters went to the polls, the *News* alleged that the Democratic Executive Committee had selected poll watchers and registrars who were loyal to Fox; these individuals would, the *News* warned, guarantee a Fox victory regardless of what the voters did. On election day Fox's opponents charged that his poll watchers stuffed ballot boxes and destroyed votes against their boss. In Ward Four South, they claimed, representatives of two candidates entered the polling place to supervise the activities of Fox's men. Fox's managers, objecting to the presence of representatives from the opposition, closed the voting boxes and promised to keep them closed until the men left. After a fistfight between Fox partisans and their challengers, voting resumed.[15]

Fox won, or stole, votes in all wards of the city, but he was strongest in Ward One North and Ward One South, winning 42 percent of his total vote in this section. Ward One, the home of Birmingham Rolling Mill, included within its boundaries (see Map 4.1) a large proportion of rolling mill workers. Much of the rest of Fox's support was concentrated in southern wards heavily populated with men who worked in the industries along the railroad lines that divided the northern and southern sections of the city. While he did well in northern wards, he either finished behind one of the other candidates or won by small margins.[16]

Men of working-class origin had held important positions, elective and appointive, in city government, but the election of Fox expressed most forcefully workers' political power. One rolling mill worker, writing to the *National Labor Tribune*, described Fox's triumph as a victory of the "labor associations." Judging from Fox's acceptance speech, some citizens feared that his constituency might push him to place restrictions on corporate interests that could hamper future economic growth. He assured his opponents that his followers had "no inclination to make war on capital or capitalists or corporations" because they understood that the community could not "get along without them." But, he added, he would not permit corporations to "claim privileges and immunities which would be detrimental to the rest of our people." His administration, Fox said, would "mete out equal and exact justice to all and special privileges to none." [17]

Several Citizens candidates challenged the election returns and threatened to run a candidate against Fox in the general election. The *Birmingham News* criticized Fox's tactics but still endorsed the Democratic nominee and urged others to do the same in the interest of party unity. The challenge failed, and the Citizens decided against a general election campaign. Fox took office in January 1893. He of course rewarded friends such as Sylvester Daly with patronage positions, but also sought to heal old wounds by bringing opponents into his administration. [18]

Fox's effort to reunify the city's Democratic Party, though, proved to be futile. During two stormy years as mayor he fought a well-organized attempt to deprive him of his power. Under the leadership of Rufus Rhodes, editor of the *Birmingham Daily News*, and downtown businessmen associated with the recently organized Commercial Club, the Citizens' Reform Union remained active after the election of 1892. The reformers demanded changes in the structure of government that would reduce the number of patronage jobs the mayor controlled, thereby eliminating many of the rewards that held political machines together. One important source of patronage was the police department. Mayors and aldermen selected the chief of police and officers, and usually filled the positions with their supporters. In late 1892 the *Daily News* announced its endorsement of a police commission bill designed to remove the police department from partisan politics. Reformers rallied behind a measure then before the state legislature that gave the county probate judge the power to appoint a five-member police commission. The legislature approved the bill, and Probate Judge M. T. Porter appointed the members of the commission. [19]

Mayor Fox publicly accused reformers of hiding their own political ambitions behind a cloud of homilies about serving the public interest. If the reformers had their way, he warned, they would deprive the people of control of their city's government. Raising the specter of corporate tyranny, he pointed out that Porter appointed to the police commission an officer of a street railway company. A man with such ties, Fox warned, could not be trusted to use the police force when necessary to protect the people from unspecified abuses by the corporation. With the approval of all but one alderman, Fox appointed a committee to prepare a new police commission bill. [20]

In the meantime the police commissioners appointed by Porter officially assumed office. But the commission possessed no power until the mayor and the Board of Aldermen adopted ordinances to govern its operation. Fox called a special meeting of the board to establish regulations requiring the commission to obtain the mayor's approval of all policemen hired and his permission to dismiss officers. In effect the mayor would continue to control the police department. The police commission disregarded Fox's ordinances and in March created its own police force; only Robert Warnock, a Fox loyalist who had secured an appointment to the commission, opposed the move.[21]

Birmingham, then, had two police forces in the spring of 1893. Declaring the police commission unconstitutional, Fox refused to swear in the officers and the chief it appointed. The commission filed suit in city court to force the mayor to obey state law and to remove Fox's chief of police, S. H. Norton, from office. At the same time the *Daily News* published two letters the mayor allegedly had written to Norton ordering him to ignore violations of Sunday drinking and gambling laws. Publication of these letters raised the struggle for the police commission to a high moral plane by linking it to ongoing agitation for stricter enforcement of Sunday closing laws. Order in the community, the reformers argued, would be restored when Fox rose above petty political concerns and permitted the police commission and its force to assume their duties.[22]

Fox did not deny that he wrote the letters. Instead he exposed the reformers' hypocrisy by arresting M. M. Boggan, a member of the police commission and prominent merchant, for illegal gambling and possession of a concealed weapon. Before his arrest, Boggan, the secretary of the police commission, had visited Fox to inform him of the commission's intention to take control of the police force. After the meeting concluded the angry mayor ordered policemen to the quarters of the Irish Democratic Club, where they found Boggan playing cards with several of Fox's political enemies. Boggan and the others appeared in recorder's court before city recorder and Fox ally W. P. McCrossin. McCrossin found them all guilty and fined each man $20.[23]

Throughout the controversy over control of the police force, Fox and his backers attempted to cast the movement for the police commission as part of a broader plan to concentrate power in the hands of a few men. Reformers portrayed themselves as battlers for clean government and public order. With the arrest of Boggan the mayor stripped away the moral veneer with which the reformers covered their attempt to alter the structure of political power in the city, and tapped an ever-present hostility toward special privilege. The men criticizing him for not enforcing the law, Fox explained, either used the issue to advance their own program or to deprive certain groups of entertainments in which the self-styled defenders of law and order indulged themselves.[24]

In the aftermath of the Boggan incident both sides in the conflict agreed to a truce while the state supreme court determined the constitutionality of the police commission. Fox reluctantly swore in the policemen the commission appointed. A few weeks later, the court ruled in favor of the commission but failed to define the relative powers of the commissioners and the mayor when it came to appointing and disciplining police officers and their superiors. Fox continued to claim the authority to approve the hiring or dismissal of policemen and reignited the controversy in early 1894.[25]

The police commission provided the issue around which opponents of the Fox machine mobilized another movement for "clean" government during the 1894 elections. Organized in the Municipal Democratic Club, reformers called for the election of a "business administration" that would run the city impartially and economically. In a statement of principles the Municipal Democratic Club demanded nonpartisan elections and vowed to eliminate the electoral fraud so prevalent in 1892. Municipal Democrats threatened to boycott any local primary or convention held before state primaries. Some members of the Municipal Democrats made preparations to run several nonpartisan Citizens' Reform Union candidates against the Democratic nominees for city offices. Like its companion organization the Citizens declared that its goal was to "secure and sustain faithful, honest and economical government in our midst by the enactment and earnest enforcement of proper and wholesome laws for the suppression of vice, disorder and crime of all grades, and to cultivate a healthy popular opinion and sentiment in favor of good morals."[26]

The Fox machine selected Robert Warnock as its candidate in the 1894 mayoral race. As the Municipal Democrats had anticipated the City Democratic Party Executive Committee, which remained under Fox's control, approved an early primary. The Citizens joined Municipal Democrats in protest against the early primary, and the two groups organized a boycott of the election. Members of the Democratic Executive Committee urged the people to disregard dissenters dedicated to the destruction of the Democracy, the party of the white man. Efforts to restore party unity before the June primary failed, however. The Municipal Democrats and the Citizens fulfilled their pledge to boycott the election, so Warnock faced no opposition in the primary.[27]

After the primary the Citizens and the Municipal Democrats announced the formation of a Citizens ticket, which would challenge Warnock and his aldermanic slate in the November general election. Though political division within the city did not strictly follow economic class lines, the election cannot be explained as solely a conflict over enforcement of laws governing morality. Since the mid-1880s reformers had employed moralistic rhetoric and had exploited fears of disorder to mobilize support for their positions and candidates. Many Fox loyalists, however, perceived the reform movement as an attempt to alter a system of government in which they had established a powerful presence. Few leaders of the reform movement had working-class backgrounds, and they described themselves as the "best element" in the city. In their attacks on Fox reformers tended to imply that his largely working-class constituency consisted of degraded men who were immoral lawbreakers. So what appeared to be a conflict over values was viewed by voters in class terms and exacerbated class tensions.

The Citizens nominated James Van Hoose for mayor. Van Hoose campaigned as a nonpartisan candidate committed to ending fraud in government and restoring moral order. He and his supporters placed a heavy emphasis on the enforcement of law and order, exploiting widespread concern with lawlessness in the aftermath of a violent miners' strike. "Law and order" leagues were formed by men who blamed strike-related violence on unions and workingmen's irresponsibility, moral laxity, and disrespect for property rights. They believed Daly and Fox, as representatives of workingmen, helped create an environment in which such evils could flourish.

Van Hoose's courting of the leagues as well as Republicans alienated many workingmen, organized and unorganized. To make matters even worse Van Hoose also solicited support from blacks. Warnock and the Democrats warned voters of the Citizens' antidemocratic tendencies and reintroduced the specter of "black" Reconstruction. On election day the rolling mill district remained in the Democratic column, and the candidates split the white vote across the city, but Van Hoose won almost all of the black vote and the election.[28]

The success of the Citizens in 1894 posed a serious threat to white working-class political influence. Clearly many prominent supporters of the Citizens tended to embrace a philosophy antagonistic toward organized workers and attacked institutions that provided white workingmen access to political power. Certainly many white workers perceived the campaign as a battle for their political survival. Failure in this struggle, they believed, would place them at the mercy of those who wanted to deprive them of their rights at home and at work, and white workingmen would lose the privileges bestowed upon them by their race and their role in the process of production. Labor leaders repeatedly warned workers against political apathy. They pleaded with them to use their votes to restore the people's government to the people, to replace men like Van Hoose with friends of workingmen. During the next ten years workingmen did win some elections. But organized workers found it increasingly difficult to mobilize a larger, more divided working class behind a political agenda. Political success would require a strategy that bridged divisions generated by profound changes in the nature of work during the next two decades.

CHAPTER 6

The Open Shop City

By the early 1890s, relations between iron workers and employers in Birmingham had reached a point of uneasy stability after years of conflict and tension. Skilled workers, through their organizations, enforced rules on the shop floor that reflected their sense of themselves as independent producers equal to the men who owned the plants in which they worked. It appeared that they had secured the right to determine the "price" they would receive for the product of their labor, to set the pace of their work, and to control access to their trades.

Relations of authority in the workshops, iron mills, and foundries of the nineteenth-century "workshop town" were rooted in an economy of relatively small enterprises that depended largely on workers' knowledge of production processes. Beginning in the late 1890s, economic expansion and technological change undermined the material foundations of skilled workers' power, creating conditions favorable to employers' imposition of their own ideas about authority in the workplace. In 1910 a worker provided clues to the nature of the change in a letter to the *Birmingham Labor Advocate*. He reminisced about his arrival in Birmingham when "every employee knew his employer." It was a small town, he remembered, where everyone lived near each other regardless of class position. The children of employers attended school with the children of workers. Employers and workers attended the same churches and shared in "each other's sorrow." Because the community was so close, labor and capital could settle their differences "amicably."

This harmonious society became a victim of its success, the writer explained. Seeing the potential for profit in Birmingham, "the foreign wealth" began to take over local enterprises. As the "foreigners" rose to power, the writer continued, the ties that had bound the old community together began to unravel. This happened because the new men "had no local self pride . . . belonged to other parts . . . were absolutely foreign to the traditions of our homes and everything that was common to the people of this district." Interested only in the profits men could produce, "they began to tighten down the screws a little tighter until they squeezed a little more of the sweets that belonged to us into their sugar bin."[1]

Clearly, the author romanticized the early years of Birmingham's history. Rarely had the kind of harmony he described ever existed in the city. But a transformation had begun in the writer's world, one so wrenching that it made the struggles of the early years appear insignificant. His use of the word "foreign" to describe the agents of change revealed more than some sort of localistic paranoia about outsiders. It denoted a number of developments that produced the conditions that the writer and his readers found so disturbing. "Foreign wealth" financed and supervised technological innovations which made possible steel production and modernization and expansion of machine shops and foundries. The city's industries relied more heavily on machines operated by semiskilled operatives than had the plants of the "workshop town." Large, fully integrated plants employing hundreds of workers, supervised by men whose primary concern was productivity, began to replace the small-scale, more personal shops the writer described. Between 1880 and 1920, the average number of employees per firm increased sharply. In 1880 the three iron establishments in Jefferson County employed an average of 66 workers. By 1900 four iron and steel companies averaged 2,040 wage earners, while sixteen foundries and machine shops averaged 873 wage earners. This growth continued during the first two decades of the twentieth century. In 1909 forty-one firms in iron and steel and foundry and machine shop products averaged 2,681 wage earners; by 1919 those figures had risen to sixty-two firms with an average of 4,708 wage earners.[2]

Increased use of machinery threatened craft union power in the workplace. Skilled workers had always exploited employers' dependence on their knowledge of production processes to secure their demands in the workplace. Machines reduced employers' reliance on skilled men and made it more difficult for the crafts to monopolize labor markets. By employing operatives who required considerably less training than craftsmen, employers expanded their potential labor supply. And since operatives could be replaced relatively easily, employers could impose their exclusive authority on the shop floor as long as they could prevent unions from controlling access to the new jobs. Employers sought to destroy union power by establishing open shops. Skilled workers vigorously resisted the open shop movement, attempting to extend the jurisdiction of their organizations to many of the new jobs technology created.

The battle over the open shop exposed deep divisions not only between organized labor and employers, but also between organized labor and unorganized semiskilled and unskilled workers, particularly black workers. The increased use of machine technology created thousands of new jobs that paid relatively well and conferred a degree of status on the men who held them. Advocates of the open shop appealed to men attracted to Birmingham by such opportunities. They told them that the closed shop limited their chances of improving their lives. To men who had probably experienced exclusion from jobs controlled by unions, the open shop made sense. Leaders of the open shop movement also looked to the state government and the courts for assistance in their struggle with organized labor. Courts repeatedly issued injunctions designed to hinder union efforts to prevent the employment of nonunion workers. The state legislature passed an antiboycott bill in 1903–4 that outlawed striker picketing in front of affected firms. Thanks to effective exploitation of worker division, the intervention of the state, and a favorable labor market between 1903 and 1917, employers were largely successful in their campaign against organized labor.

World War I seemed to change everything. Labor markets tightened and the federal government adopted policies supportive of the rights of unions. Organized labor in Birmingham seized the moment to try to end the era of the open shop. Labor leaders and union members learned, however, that the government was not interested in altering the status quo as it existed before the war. More critically, organized labor failed to bridge the divisions within Birmingham's working class that had always been essential to the success of those who opposed the labor movement. After the war, Birmingham remained an open shop city.

The single most important development in the city's economy during these years was the rise of the steel industry. As early as 1886, when Tennessee

Henderson Company, manufacturers of the first ton of steel produced in Birmingham in 1897. The process used by the company proved impractical, however. Birmingham Public Library.

Coal, Iron, and Railroad Company entered the district, industrialists and city promoters had touted steel as the key to Birmingham's future.[3] The iron produced in Birmingham, however, contained too much sulphur and phosphorous to be used in an acid steel-making process and too little phosphorous for use in the Bessemer process.[4]

Development of the basic open hearth method of steel making solved these problems, and in 1898 TCI built a steel plant in the new suburb of Ensley.[5] Steel produced in Ensley was not of high quality because of a lack of scrap iron and steel, which made up about one-third of an open hearth furnace's charge. Use of a combination of the Bessemer and open hearth processes—the duplex method—reduced the need for iron and steel scrap and improved the quality of steel produced.[6] Steel production continued to increase in Birmingham through the first two decades of the twentieth century, especially after U.S. Steel absorbed TCI. U.S. Steel expanded and improved the Ensley plant and added twelve conventional open hearth furnaces when it built its plant at Fairfield.[7]

The scale and pace of open hearth steel production dwarfed that of wrought iron production. The process began with the charging of the fur-

Henderson's first heat of steel. Center for Urban Affairs, University of Alabama in Birmingham.

nace. Alongside each open hearth furnace, approximately twenty feet above the ground, was the charging floor.[8] With charging machines, men picked up boxes of scrap and other materials, carried the boxes to the furnaces, and dumped them into the center of the hearth. After completing a heat, workers either tapped the furnace or tilted it to pour its contents into ladles. A crane carried the ladles to a position over the ingot molds so the steel could be poured into them. After the ingots cooled, men then stripped them from the mold and placed them in a soaking pit to be brought to a uniform temperature before going to the rolling mills for reduction into semifinished and finished shapes.[9]

Steel companies organized open hearth plants into groups of furnaces, each under the supervision of a melter. A first helper controlled each furnace within the group. His crew included second and third helpers, charging machine operators, ladlemen, ingot strippers, and common laborers. During the production process, a melter ensured that helpers collected samples, which he inspected for quality. He ordered additions to the initial charge until the metal met the specified grade.[10]

Production of open hearth steel did not depend as heavily upon the skill of

Open hearth building at TCI's Ensley plant, ca. 1899. Open hearth technology proved to be at least a partial solution to the problem of steel production in Birmingham. Birmingham Public Library.

individuals as did production of wrought iron. The jobs of melters and first helpers required extensive experience and knowledge of metallurgy but not the level of skill required of puddlers and their helpers. Charles Schwab, an officer with Carnegie Steel, estimated in 1902 that an agricultural worker of average intelligence could be trained for a melter's job in six to eight weeks; it would take the same individual two years to master the art of puddling. No longer did a worker stand at a furnace and stir molten metal. Open hearth workers spent more time supervising, monitoring temperature gauges, and collecting samples. Melters did not even make the final decision about the quality of a heat of steel; a chemist in a laboratory decided when a heat had reached its proper level of refinement.[11]

Less dependence upon human power made possible dramatic increases in production. Machines yielded levels of productivity unimaginable in iron rolling mills. The charging of a furnace by hand might take a puddler and his crew several hours, while one man using a Wellman charger could charge six to eight furnaces in one hour. Open hearth furnaces converted tons of iron into steel with limited human intervention. A crane operated by a single man transported loads that dozens of men would not have been able to move.[12]

Under the old sliding scale, a "tonnage man" might have benefited from higher levels of production. But employers took steps to separate pay rates from market prices for steel products. Arguing that capital investment in

Cranes carry a heat of molten steel to molds, ca. 1910. Harper Collection, Samford University, Birmingham.

equipment raised productivity more than anything men did, steel companies increased the number of hourly workers on their payrolls and narrowed the wage gap between skilled tonnage workers and common laborers by reducing tonnage rates. When companies cut rates, workers either produced more or absorbed the loss of income. The sliding scale had been designed to prevent such employer control of wages.[13]

The rise of the steel industry also altered the structure of the workforce. A government report observed that mechanization in the handling of materials and in the regulation of each stage of steel production "to a large degree displaced [skilled] men either with unskilled laborers or with semiskilled workmen who can be recruited by the thousand whenever it is necessary."[14] As Table 6.1 shows, this happened in Birmingham. Over 40 percent of Birmingham's iron and steel workers in 1880 held skilled jobs. Analyses of samples of production workers in 1900, 1910, and 1917 reveal a steady decline in the size of the skilled segment of the workforce after 1880. During the same period the proportion of workers in semiskilled jobs increased sharply. Most of these semiskilled workers operated the cranes, charging machines, and other equipment used in open hearth steel production.

The expansion of semiskilled work meant increased opportunities for un-

Table 6.1. Occupational Structure, Iron and Steel Industry, Birmingham, 1880–1917 (percentages)

	1880	1900	1910	1917
Skilled	41	22	29	24
Semiskilled[a]		3	6	22
Unskilled	58	74	65	54
Total	99	99	100	100
Sample	207	334	618	1515

Sources: Figures for 1880 represent all iron workers listed in the manuscript census for that year. Data for 1900 is based on a sample of the Jefferson County Manuscript Census. I included all iron or steel workers on every fifteenth page of the census beginning with the randomly selected sixth page. Data for 1917 is based on a sample of World War I draft registration cards for Jefferson County. I selected every fiftieth iron or steel worker registered, beginning with the first such worker encountered in each district. Because men over age thirty-five were not required to register, the figure for the skilled segment is probably slightly low. It is, however, consistent with the 1900 figure, which included all ages.

[a]Men placed in this category operated a variety of machines or were the helpers of craftsmen. Their jobs clearly did not require the level of knowledge of the skilled craftsman but involved more than a strong body. To determine where an individual should be placed, I relied upon detailed descriptions of work that can be found in government documents from the period. Most useful is U.S. Bureau of Labor, *Labor Conditions*.

skilled workers or rural migrants to secure jobs that paid relatively well. Ladle liners, ladlemen, and melters' helpers all earned forty to forty-five cents an hour, a wage not much below that of melters. Charging machine operators, cranemen, stationary engineers, ingot strippers, second helpers, steel pourers, and stopper setters earned twenty to thirty cents an hour. The next level included unclassified laborers, stockers, pitmen, and door operators who earned between nine and eighteen cents per hour.[15]

The impact of advancing technology was not limited to the steel production. Jigs that guided the path of a machine tool, fixtures that held the piece to be machined in position, and specialized high-speed automatic machine tools that could perform multiple operations simultaneously reduced dependence upon the highly skilled, all-around machinist. The master machinist would set up power-driven lathes, milling machines, drilling machines, and planers, which less skilled specialists could then operate.[16]

In Birmingham's rapidly expanding cast iron pipe industry, improvements in production methods and technology in the molding of pipe subdivided the task of skilled molders, creating a number of semiskilled specialists. One of the more innovative companies in this regard was the American Cast Iron Pipe Company, which in 1909 began to use a circular casting method that made possible more efficient, continuous operation. The company also purchased air-jolt rammers, which eliminated the need for a molder's skill to pack the sand around a pattern uniformly. These innovations, combined with the use of steam "dinkeys"—locomotives—to pull trams and iron ladles, enabled the company to raise productivity and lower per unit labor costs.[17]

Skilled workers in the city understood the threat posed by the transformation of work. Because local industries had relied on outdated methods, the city's craftsmen had been able to achieve a degree of status and authority that craftsmen in other industrial centers had lost as mechanization displaced them. Now the forces that had driven many out of Pittsburgh, Wheeling, and Chicago were changing the city that had been their refuge. By adopting modern methods of production, the *Labor Advocate* explained, Birmingham industrialists reduced their dependence on skilled workers and made possible increased use of men who needed short training periods on machines rather than lengthy apprenticeships. The *Advocate* warned that corporations would lower "existing labor . . . standards" by exploiting this new class of specialists. Unions must take steps to regulate the new order, it declared.[18]

Birmingham unions did try to expand their jurisdiction to many of the new jobs being created in the metal industries. Employers, of course, believed that the potential benefits of mechanization could not be fully realized if labor unions imposed all of their rules governing hiring and production. After all, many of them had bought new equipment from salesmen who promised that the machines would allow employers to replace skilled union men with unskilled, unorganized workers.[19] Employers therefore responded to the unions with a well-organized campaign to impose the open shop and to firmly establish their power in the workplace.[20] By taking advantage of the weakened position of craftsmen in the city's industries and the tension that existed between the "aristocracy of labor" and semiskilled and unskilled workers, employers made Birmingham an open shop city.

Ironically, the changes that organized labor feared initially provided favorable conditions for unions' efforts to improve and secure their positions in the iron and steel industry. Birmingham boomed during the first three years of the twentieth century as Sloss-Sheffield Steel and Iron and Woodward Iron Company joined TCI in expanding their operations. Republic Iron and Steel purchased several establishments that had been idle and returned them to production. All of this activity sharply increased demands for labor. The *Birmingham News* reported a 100 percent increase in employment in the iron and steel industry between 1897 and 1900. In 1902 the *News* complained of shortages of skilled men, and the *Labor Advocate* reported that "good men are in demand all the time."[21]

Labor unions recognized a chance to expand their power and took advantage of it. They soon learned that employers were just as determined to prevent union growth. Not surprisingly, the initial confrontation in what would become a lengthy struggle took place at TCI's Ensley steel works. The Amalgamated Association of Iron and Steel Workers had begun to organize workers at the plant shortly after it went into production, and by 1900 the company had signed an AAISW scale agreement.[22] Relations between the union and TCI seemed to be harmonious until September 1900, when company officials denied a union request for a day off to observe Labor Day. After twenty-four members took the day anyway, the company fired them. The company's action was part of President Don Bacon's larger plan to remove from the plant a union that he believed deprived the company of profits. He had complained that "the operations were greatly hampered, almost directed, in fact, by labor organizations, and the cost of production largely increased as a result." So when AAISW officials demanded an explanation for the dismissals, the plant manager replied that the company would no longer tolerate the organization. Soon thereafter the company fired all union men and replaced them with nonunion workers. AAISW officials demanded that TCI rehire union workers and recognize their right to organize the steel plant. They also ordered the local at TCI's Bessemer plant to strike until the company recognized the union at Ensley.[23]

As the conflict spread, some local newspapers joined the union in demanding recognition and urged the public to support the workers as well. The *Ensley Enterprise* vigorously defended workers' right to organize. It criticized companies for treating men like "slaves, to be driven by the absolute will of the master." The paper urged employers to reach an accord with the unions and thereby "gain and hold the support of those who work with us and for us." When the AAISW held a mass meeting at Ensley's Knights of Pythias Hall, Ensley mayor W. G. Powell attended and endorsed the union's demands. The meeting attendees adopted a resolution stating that "we the merchants and citizens of Ensley, Alabama, are in full accord with the victimized employees of the Ensley steel mills, believing their cause to be a just one, and we do hereby pledge them our hearty support, moral and financial, in their struggle for right and justice."[24]

Initially the company revealed little sensitivity to the union's and the community's pressure for concessions. It imported nonunion workers from as far away as Cleveland, Ohio, and enlisted the aid of the county sheriff in protecting the replacements. But in early November the company gave in to the popular pressure for a settlement and conceded the AAISW's right to organize in the Ensley plant.[25] The AAISW also reached an agreement with Republic Iron and Steel covering all of its operations in the district.[26]

Union successes in 1900 and 1901 left employers fuming. N. F. Thompson no doubt expressed the sentiments of many when, in testimony before the U.S. Industrial Commission, he denounced union control of "all classes of labor." He declared that such power posed the "greatest menace to this Government that exists inside or outside the pale of our national domain." Thompson charged that labor organizations denied people the right to work where they wanted and forced employers to pay "arbitrary wages" they could not afford. Union regulations, he continued, shackled individual initiative in the workplace and violated the rights of property owners. These conditions, Thompson concluded, retarded the economic growth essential to continued prosperity.[27]

Thompson advocated an organized open shop movement but generated little support until the summer of 1903. Since the summer of 1902 the International Association of Machinists (IAM), the International Molders' Union, the Patternmakers League, and the Brotherhood of Boilermakers had been locked in a conflict with a number of shops over their demands for the nine-hour day, increased pay, restrictions on output from new machines, and union regulation of the hiring of machine operators and apprentices. The shops affected had recruited nonunion workers and had secured an injunction to stop picketing and alleged harassment of strikebreakers. When Nick Smith of the International Molders' Union continued to meet with replacement workers, the companies had him arrested for violating the injunction. Soon thereafter the companies organized the Birmingham Citizens' Alliance to protect members "against strikes and lockouts" or any other organized attempts to deprive them of their rights to manage their businesses as they wanted within the law, and "to give regular employment to union and non-union workmen." Thompson urged anyone "who wishes to see Birmingham and her people free, independent and prosperous" to enlist in this struggle against "class dictation, class interference, and class rule of any kind."[28]

Advocates of the open shop in Birmingham joined a nationwide campaign. Embracing the philosophy of D. M. Parry and the National Metal Trades Association, they contended that unions violated fundamental American economic principles. Local industrialist T. G. Bush defined the philosophy and goals of Birmingham's "Parryites" in an article in the *Birmingham News*. Unions, he charged, manipulated workers through their propaganda, blinding them to the interest they shared with their employers. Suspicion, distrust, and class tension resulted from this cynical exploitation of people's fears. Harmony between capital and labor, rooted in a spirit of cooperation for the good of all producers, could not survive in such a conflict-ridden society. Workers, Bush wrote, possessed the right to organize, but organized labor had no right "to dictate who shall be employed, who shall be discharged, and further, to decide as to numbers of helpers and apprentices." He warned that if unions continued to have their way, they would "wrest the management of the business from the hands of the owner." Conflict between capital and labor would end only when workers abandoned all claims to the right to determine conditions of employment. The employer should pay "reasonable wages," while the employee conceded to the owner "the right to manage his own business and to employ such labor as is best suited for the work to be done." And what was the basis for employers' power? "They furnish the capital and the knowledge, and know how best to direct the business; therefore, their views must command the respect and consideration of those who are employed," answered Bush.[29]

Union leaders rejected the idea that employers had a right to arbitrarily dictate the terms and conditions of work to the men who created capital. To them the open shop movement was nothing less than another phase of capitalists' plan to reduce men to a state of wage slavery. Corporate officers' rhetoric about the union threat to individual liberty obscured their true intent, labor leaders warned. Employers spoke the language of individualism even as they organized themselves "to corner labor and business, reducing the former to the point of starvation and monopolizing the latter." While paying respect to individual liberty, spokesmen for organized labor argued that unbridled individualism could be a "menace to the community," tending "to the destruction of the freedom of the whole." Dismissing the argument that the open shop movement defended the rights of the nonunion worker, labor leaders charged that advocates of the open shop sought to foster among the working people the kind of destructive competition capital organized to prevent. If workers did not counter organized capital with their own organizations, they would be denied their rights to determine conditions of their employment, especially the fair price for their property—their labor—"which is a fair share of that which [one] produces."

Union leaders also linked poor working conditions and lower real wages to instability in families and the community. Long hours of labor, they contended, deprived men of time with their families and the wholesome recreation essential to the development of their moral lives. In a speech to Fidelity Lodge Number Seven, James O'Connell, president of the IAM, suggested that extended workdays and low pay fueled intemperance and sexual immorality. Tired men, said O'Connell, went to saloons to revive themselves and perhaps to consort with the prostitute who had no other way to earn an adequate income. Wives and children waited at home for the meager amount their husbands and fathers might bring home. A victory for advocates of the open shop would, O'Connell concluded, undermine the values on which the social order rested.[30]

Thus organized workers cast themselves as opponents of men whose sole concern was their individual economic well-being. Labor spokesmen pleaded with nonworkers not to be taken in by capitalists' promotion of themselves as public benefactors. The "Parryites," wrote B. H. Ryder, the business agent for the IAM in Birmingham, sought to "poison the minds of the people" with propaganda about their defense of the rights of labor. Merchants and other members of the community would suffer at the hands of corporations free to impose their will, he warned. If the open shop movement succeeded, a few employers would flood the district with "a stupid and improvident class of labor." They would use their "'pluck-me stores' and rents for shacks" to "collect every surplus dollar that under open, free and fair conditions might find its way into legitimate business channels and go to the building of homes and the general upbuilding of the community." Ryder blamed the open shop movement for bringing Birmingham to the verge of the class warfare the founders of the Magic City had hoped to avoid.[31]

Organized labor's arguments struck a responsive chord among citizens who feared the growing power of corporations. The *Birmingham Age-Herald* believed that organized labor protected the community from the abuses of organized capital. An editorial in the *Bessemer Workman* agreed. It argued that "the trusts and great aggregations of capital . . . continually force down the wage paid labor, while the prices demanded of the consumer for their products is continually rising." Working people had no choice but to organize.

"The labor union is simply a defensive measure which was made necessary by the aggressions of its inferior partner, capital, and the labor question can never be considered as solved until a basis is reached whereby the toiler is guaranteed a just and liberal portion of his product," the paper concluded.[32]

The Parryites responded to their critics by reiterating that the open shop employed all men regardless of union affiliation. They conceded the right of workers to organize but rejected unions' demand for closed shops which discriminated against many workers.[33] The open shoppers hoped to exploit division between the unorganized and the organized. Their arguments did indeed resonate among men, especially blacks, who had worked for years as helpers to machinists, molders, patternmakers, and boilermakers or who had held jobs as common laborers and hoped to advance to better-paying, higher-status jobs. They could become operators of cranes, charging machines, and lathes earning wages substantially higher than they had ever earned in their lives. Many workers feared that if unions controlled these jobs they would limit their access to them. The Parryites certainly encouraged such reasoning when addressing the unorganized, but workers' antiunionism cannot be attributed to the open shop movement alone. Workers' support for open shops reflected rational appraisals of their self-interests. Many migrants from the countryside and men who had lived in Birmingham for years knew that unions would deprive them of opportunity. Black workers in particular had long suffered discrimination at the hands of unions and now saw a chance to strike back at those whom they held responsible for their subordination.[34]

The appeal of the Parryites was more than rhetoric. From 1903 to 1904 employers offered thousands of nonunion workers jobs many of them had never been allowed to hold before. Often the unorganized took the jobs of striking union members.[35] When five hundred to six hundred men struck TCI's Bessemer rolling mill, the company reopened it in just over a month with a nonunion workforce. By 1906 TCI had established itself as an open shop company, and U.S. Steel continued the open shop policy when it took over in 1907. The company hired union members but refused to recognize the union as the representative of any of its workers. Many of TCI's AAISW members chose to move to Republic Iron and Steel, which signed an agreement with the union in the fall of 1904.[36]

Court decisions and legislation supported the open shop movement. Local courts consistently ruled in favor of employers who sought injunctions against workers engaging in picketing or employing other tactics designed to hinder the importation of strikebreakers. Constitutional guarantees of the rights of property, judges reasoned, extended to the means of making use of that property; thus the owner of an industrial establishment must be allowed to employ anyone he chose. A corollary to this defense of employers' property rights was a defense of the right of nonunion workers to work wherever and whenever they pleased without having to face what the courts considered to be unlawful intimidation. Labor leaders objected to the charge that they infringed upon the rights of employers and nonunion workers. They claimed the right to publicize their grievances and to present them to strikebreakers in a public place, such as the street in front of offending establishments. In none of the cases documented did local judges agree with the unions.[37]

Leaders of the open shop movement also secured the passage of antiboycott legislation. After failing to win approval of an antiboycott bill in early 1903, lobbyists for the Birmingham Citizens' Alliance renewed its campaign for its passage that summer. P. J. Collins, secretary of the Citizens' Alliance, demanded that the state legislature defend employers' property rights against infringement by unions. He complained that "the business interests of Birmingham are at the mercy of labor unions." He asked that the legislature protect employers from the "illegal interference" labor organizations relied upon to deprive them of their right to employ anyone they wanted.[38]

When the legislature convened in late August, state representative Felix Blackburn of Jefferson County reintroduced the antiboycott measure and with August Benners, another Jefferson County representative and a partner in a law firm that represented TCI, led the fight for passage. The measure passed in the Alabama House of Representatives with the support of all but one Jefferson County representative. A few weeks later the state senate approved the bill, and the governor signed it into law. Alabama's antiboycott law prohibited striking workers from "loitering" around a place of business for the purpose of persuading others not to trade or work there. It banned picketing, boycott notices, and blacklists.[39]

Leaders of organized labor denounced the antiboycott law as a fundamental violation of workers' rights as free men and a blueprint for their subjugation by self-serving capitalists. The *Labor Advocate* called the measure "anti-liberty, anti–free speech, anti–human rights." Before the measure passed, the *Advocate* had warned its readers that the antiboycott law would "draw close the lines of the class struggle and make more acute the class feeling, the existence of which only the ignorant will dispute." It denounced employers who advocated class legislation designed to reduce producers to abject dependence. The *Advocate* argued that the consequences for the community could be disastrous, for "the regard for the law that is inculcated by true unionism may wane and the secretive methods taught by our enemies will take the place of the open and manly fight; the pleasant relations existing in the district through the excellent understand [*sic*] of organized capital and organized labor may be disturbed and a happy and prosperous people brought to face the terrible probability of industrial suicide." Conceding a victory for "the arch anarchist Parry and his confederates," the *Advocate* affirmed workingmen's continued resistance to efforts to "crush and enslave them."[40]

Unions won a few victories in their struggles against the open shop, but the movement continued to spread throughout the district between 1904 and World War I, making its greatest gains during the economic recessions of 1907–08 and 1912–13, when employers took advantage of increased unemployment to rid themselves of troublesome unions. Strikes against the Louisville and Nashville Railroad (1907–8) and two foundries (1912–13) illustrate the pattern. Machinists at the L&N shops in Birmingham and Decatur walked out in May 1907 after the company refused to recognize the union and to replace a piece rate with a uniform scale of payment. The company quickly replaced the strikers with nonunion workers, including some blacks. Despite reports that the strikebreakers' lack of skills caused a number of accidents, the company maintained its commitment to the open shop. Union molders at the Eureka Stove Foundry and the Avondale Stove Foundry experienced the same fate when they demanded increased wages and reduced hours. Both companies replaced strikers with nonunion blacks and joined a number of other Birmingham foundries that had already established open shops.[41] This policy represented quite a departure for Avondale; in the 1880s the company had recruited white skilled workers by advertising its belief that blacks could not handle such work.

By 1916 writers in the labor press were calling Birmingham an open shop city. In the summer of that year the *Machinist's Journal* warned its readers to stay away from Birmingham, where shops would not hire union members and discharged all those who joined labor organizations. A visiting machinist reported that the open shop campaign had virtually eliminated unions in the city, and employers reported that only 10 percent of workers belonged to unions. While the *Labor Advocate* claimed that employers inflated their figures, it conceded that organized labor no longer enjoyed the honored place in the community it had held twelve years earlier.[42] Much had changed since the heady days of the late 1880s and 1890s when organized labor had paraded proudly down streets crowded with admirers of the producers of the community's prosperity.

World War I provided organized metal workers an opportunity to restore their power. A number of companies in the Birmingham district manufactured goods for the war effort. U.S. Steel produced billets for the manufacture of shells and plate used in the construction of ships. Hardie-Tynes Machine Company produced shell casings. U.S. Cast Iron Pipe manufactured pipe for the government. Other plants did contract work for companies with government orders or manufactured products considered essential to the war effort. Birmingham Machine and Foundry, for example, made condensers used in nitrate plants.

Increased production, of course, meant increased demand for labor. At the same time, opportunities in other parts of the country attracted many workers, while thousands of men entered the military after the United States declared war on the Central Powers. J. W. McQueen, president of Sloss-Sheffield Steel and Iron, estimated that the company lost over seven hundred employees to military service alone.[43] The combination of increased production, emigration, and military service tightened labor markets.

Workers in Birmingham and across the country did not hesitate to use their market power to win improvements in working conditions and wages. They received encouragement and support from a federal government intent upon maintaining production in war industries.[44] To ensure workers' cooperation, the Wilson administration required contractors to improve working conditions and increase wages.[45] AFL leaders responded to this policy with a promise to discourage unions from taking advantage of wartime conditions to close open shops.[46] But where contractors did not comply with government labor policies, organized workers often defied national leaders and struck to force compliance.

This was the case in Birmingham, where few companies with government contracts observed guidelines on hours and wages.[47] In late January 1918 members of the Patternmakers League at TCI's Ensley works demanded that the company reduce their hours from ten to eight as the government had mandated. Ensley's superintendent met with the disgruntled men on January 31 to inform them that the corporation would not agree to their demands. The patternmakers then requested a meeting with TCI president George Gordon Crawford.[48] By this time other metal workers at several companies, united under the auspices of the Birmingham Metal Trades Council, had joined the patternmakers. The secretary of the American Federation of Labor's Metal Trades Department informed the secretary of labor that a major strike at Birmingham was imminent and asked that he send an investigator to the city to look into the situation. The Labor Department assigned to the case W. R. Fairley, a former leader of the United Mine Workers in Alabama. In early February Fairley reported that patternmakers, machinists, and molders intended to carry out their threat to strike if companies could not be "induced" to grant the eight-hour day and double time for work on Sundays and holidays.[49]

After Crawford and other employers rejected workers' demands, the Birmingham Metal Trades Council set a February 20 strike deadline. In justification of its action, the council insisted upon workers' right to share equally in the production increases modern methods made possible, challenging employers' claim "that because they own the improved machinery and new processes they alone should receive the benefits." The workday should be reduced, the council argued, because a man could not physically withstand the pace of work for more than eight hours. Long periods of intense, uninterrupted labor left men exhausted at the end of a day, so that they had little energy left for their families.[50]

Metal trades unions did not demand closed shops, but employers thought that opening negotiations would provide unions with the credibility they needed to expand their power and challenge the reign of the open shop. They suspected that labor leaders would portray any company concessions as an example of the effectiveness of collective action and use their "victory" to appeal to nonunion workers. Therefore, the companies, now organized as the Birmingham Metal Trades Association, refused to bargain with union officials, and Fairley's efforts to mediate failed.

Though union leaders undoubtedly understood the potential long-term benefits to the city's labor movement if the companies met their demands, they insisted that their only aim was to secure obedience to federal regulations. Since the companies would not comply with government standards, metal workers across the city struck on February 20, 1918. The next day, according to Fairley's estimates, as many as 10,000 iron and steel workers were out of work because of the strike. Local newspapers placed the number of union, nonunion, skilled, and unskilled workers affected by the strike at between 3,000 and 3,500. Three weeks after the strike began Fairley estimated that 5,000 skilled men were actually on strike. Exactly how many workers joined the strike remains unclear, but the walkout certainly disrupted production. It forced U.S. Cast Iron Pipe's Bessemer facility, Birmingham Machine and Foundry, and Bessemer Machine and Foundry to shut down temporarily. The Woodward Iron Company requested that all of its employees on jury duty be released so it could continue to operate. Many plants were able to remain in production, but at sharply reduced levels of output.[51]

The local press wasted little time in branding the strike a traitorous plot to undermine the war effort. Workers, asserted the *Ensley Industrial Record*, demanded changes of a "revolutionary" nature during a time of grave national emergency. Their strike, under the circumstances, was nothing less than treason, and only the Kaiser would benefit from workers' selfish desire to take advantage of wartime conditions. To the *Birmingham News*, winning the war was more important than relatively petty differences over wages and hours. An editorial in the paper insisted that all strikers return to work. It suggested that anyone "who positively is averse to working for his present employer or someone with whom or for whom he worked just now, let him find some useful occupation with someone else or for someone else. Productiveness is the main thing."[52]

Patriotic appeals had little discernible impact on the strikers. Mass meetings and marches near the Ensley works of TCI affirmed workers' determination to force the companies to abide by government regulations. Speakers turned the surging patriotism of the day against employers, particularly U.S. Steel. The steel corporation, they charged, undermined the war effort by refusing to comply with government standards. Corporate "autocracy" caused the strike, interrupting the flow of vital war material to the front. In this way, the strikers reasoned, the corporation aided the dictators of Europe. The strike was therefore a battle in the war against worldwide "autocracy."[53]

Federal officials sought a settlement with TCI, the largest of the companies affected by the strike, hoping that an agreement with TCI would set a precedent smaller operators might follow. Early in March Fairley and Rowland B. Mahany represented the Labor Department at a conference with Elbert H. Gary, chairman of the board of U.S. Steel, James A. Farrell, president of U.S. Steel, and George Gordon Crawford. Gary agreed to discuss strikers' demands with the presidents of the subsidiaries. Several weeks later he again met with Fairley to inform him that the corporation would not grant the eight-hour day where it was not already in effect. Gary insisted that any reduction in hours would require corresponding reductions in production levels. Such a policy, he maintained, would violate the government's guiding principle of maintaining full production in critical industries. Gary then pointed out that the corporation had just raised wages 15 percent and ended the meeting.[54]

Gary's position exposed a contradiction in the government's economic policy. From the beginning of the war, a primary goal of government policy had been to assure full production in war industries. The administration implemented regulations governing hours and wages in order to prevent strikes and other disruptions of production. Such policies appeared to mandate the kinds of changes the Birmingham Metal Trades Council demanded, but at the same time the government discouraged actions that caused conflict and reduced output.[55] In the spring of 1918, it was not at all clear which principles the government considered more fundamental. Gary clearly assumed that full production was the top priority and based his decisions on that premise. He forced the administration to reconcile the glaring inconsistencies its policies contained.

Before they could solve this dilemma, federal officials had to determine whether the eight-hour standard even applied to the Birmingham companies. In response to a Labor Department request for a ruling on the issue, an official at the War Department cited several exceptions to the eight-hour law. Whether the law applied to individual companies, he explained, depended on what they produced and the availability of those products on the open market.[56]

The War Labor Board (WLB) would answer this and other questions arising from the Birmingham strike. In mid-April, Secretary of Labor William B. Wilson informed the Metal Trades Council that the WLB had accepted its case for arbitration and urged strikers to return to work while waiting for the board's ruling. The Metal Trades Council agreed to end the strike only if employers allowed strikers to return to work without discrimination and removed all strikebreakers. Since dismissal of strikebreakers under union pressure would have implied recognition of unions' right to control hiring, the companies refused to meet the council's demand, and the strike continued.

The companies could afford to resist the council's demands because they had begun to fill strikers' jobs. A number of them increased wages for employees who ignored the strike. James Bowron, an officer of Gulf States Steel, complained that U.S. Steel implemented wage scales that compelled Gulf States to "advance . . . mechanics 20 to 30 percent and common labor 50 percent." The Hardie-Tynes Machine Company reportedly employed black men as molders and black women as core makers. Companies also trained and promoted unskilled and semiskilled men. Such a policy entailed, of course, the elevation of black laborers to jobs traditionally reserved for whites, a point B. W. King, the secretary of the Metal Trades Council, always emphasized in his reports to government officials.[57]

Birmingham's city commission cooperated fully with employers. Complaining of labor shortages, employers in mid-April demanded a strictly enforced vagrancy ordinance requiring that all men who could not show proof of regular employment be forced to work. Representatives of the metal trades unions protested that the ordinance was a thinly disguised attempt by iron and steel manufacturers and fabricators to enlist city government assistance in undermining the strike. Their objections had little impact on the city commission. The commission approved the ordinance, which provided for the establishment of an "employment service" with agents who would patrol the streets and arrest vagrants. To charges that the ordinance violated citizens' rights, one commissioner responded, "This is not a time to cry for the rights of American citizens; it is the time to win the war." By July 1918 Henry King, the director of the city's employment service, could report few vagrants on city streets, especially in black districts. It is impossible to determine, however, exactly how many "vagrants" were strikers or were forced to replace strikers.[58]

Draft board officials helped suppress the strike by threatening to withdraw exemptions from striking workers. According to affidavits filed with the U.S. secretary of labor, the chairman of the District Exemption Board warned several striking TCI employees to return to work or risk losing their draft exemptions. The chairman did not offer them the option of returning to work with another firm. Unions, he allegedly told the workers, pursued a treasonous plan to create turmoil. Secretary of War Newton Baker had assured labor leaders that strikers would not be considered unemployed, but the government apparently did little or nothing to enforce his guarantees.[59]

The combination of positive incentives and outright repression did undermine the strike. Crawford reported to Secretary Wilson as early as March 12 that TCI had suffered the inconvenience of training new workers but maintained full production in all departments. Some labor leaders repeatedly denied such reports; as late as July 16, B. W. King reported that the strike continued to hamper production. Others told a different story. J. A. Lipscomb, a representative of the Patternmakers League, conceded that most companies had rejected strikers' demands and few workers remained on strike. Fairley informed the secretary of labor that TCI had enough men working to maintain production and therefore "declined, as they have from the commencement of this trouble to grant an eight hours day." Fairley added that though the men still worked ten hours a day, they received wages 56 percent higher than the wages TCI paid in December 1916.[60]

As if to demonstrate the truth of its claim that the strike had failed, TCI held Labor Day festivities in September 1918 for three thousand black and white workers. Oscar W. Adams, the editor of the *Birmingham Reporter*, a prominent leader of the black community, and a featured speaker at this gathering, urged his audience to work hard and to reject the appeals of those who would cause conflict between them and their employers. Speakers denounced unions for trying to deprive men of jobs. They urged the crowd to remain faithful to a company that would not give in when organized labor attempted to force it to fire many of them.[61]

Clearly, TCI wanted its employees to understand that any improvements in their working conditions had more to do with corporate goodwill than union power. This may have been a way to prepare workers for the company's announcement of the eight-hour day a few weeks later. Publicly TCI and other companies denied that union pressure affected their decision to cut hours. They emphasized that their open shop policies remained in place and that they did not intend to negotiate with unions in the future. The companies portrayed their change of heart as a selfless act for the good of the community and the nation.[62] Privately, however, at least one company official acknowledged the key role the unions had played in bringing about wage increases and other improvements in working conditions. In a report on labor for the Executive Committee of Sloss-Sheffield Steel and Iron, J. W. McQueen attributed a large part of wartime wage increases to an "appeal to the National War Labor Board by labor interests."[63]

Labor leaders hoped to rebuild the labor movement by convincing workers that organization was essential if they were to protect the wartime gains union officials claimed their organizations had won for all laborers. Unions launched a renewed assault on the open shop in 1919 under the auspices of the American Federation of Labor's National Committee for the Organization of Iron and Steel Workers. National Committee organizers warned workers that employers would extend hours and reduce wages now that the war was over. Working people, they insisted, must use their collective strength to defend themselves.

Employers unwittingly assisted labor's cause. Just as labor leaders had predicted, the Southern Metal Trades Association announced in January 1919 that its members had agreed to reduce wages and reimpose ten-hour days. In February 1919 some manufacturers in the city began to extend hours and to reduce wages as much as 20 percent. Not surprisingly, many workers reacted angrily. Some nonunion metal tradesmen across the district applied for union membership after the extension of hours and the pay cut.[64] During the summer of 1919 the metal trades unions held well-attended meetings every Friday night to spread the gospel of organization to white nonunion craftsmen. According to reports in the *Labor Advocate*, union membership increased because of the meetings.[65]

But the organizing drive of 1919 failed to close open shops. During the strike of 1918 many men, particularly blacks, had advanced into skilled and semiskilled jobs previously reserved for skilled whites. They doubted that the unions would allow them to continue in those positions. The economic decline of the postwar years weakened the campaign as well. Returning soldiers flooded labor markets at a time of economic contraction, so employers could find plenty of nonunion workers. When some workers joined the national steel strike of 1919, Birmingham employers quickly replaced them, and the strike accomplished nothing.[66]

Organized labor's failed attempts to take advantage of wartime conditions to restore its strength in Birmingham only underscored its profoundly diminished influence. The transformation of the workplace had created conditions the labor movement inadequately understood. Thus union leaders in Birmingham paid little attention to the masses of semiskilled workers of both races who constituted a majority of the workforce. So in 1920 labor relations in the city returned to "normalcy." Birmingham remained an open shop city.

CHAPTER 7

Remaking the Working Class

According to advocates of the open shop, elimi-
nation of unions would enable southern industrialists to realize the benefits of a large and
growing supply of cheap labor. But an employer could not simply walk out
into the street and find men to operate cranes, lathes, or rammers. Much
of the local labor force lacked the necessary knowledge and would have to
be trained before the theoretical benefits of more up-to-date methods could
be realized. Efficient operation of a modern foundry, machine shop, or steel
plant required a large number of semiskilled operatives who could be trained
quickly and would work twelve hours each day.

Some companies continued to rely upon the market to supply them with
the workers they needed and to use threats of dismissal and other forms
of coercion to force workers to behave as they wanted. Others thought that
such a strategy generated discord and hampered production. They believed
that through enlightened management they could create a disciplined, well-
trained workforce. Thus between 1904 and 1920 two of the city's largest
corporations designed extensive welfare and educational programs to recruit and train workers and to reward them for loyal service to the company.
They and other companies also encouraged and financed public school reforms, which they thought would improve the quality of the local laboring
population.

Out of this effort arose serious questions about the racial order within
the city's industries. The racial division of work as established in the nine-

teenth century had conferred upon whites virtually total control of skilled jobs. White craftsmen decided who would learn their trades, and they rarely if ever extended such an opportunity to blacks. With the growth of the semi-skilled sector of the occupational hierarchy, decreased dependence upon skilled workers, and the decline of craft union power, some employers and social reformers, particularly supporters of the industrial education movement, began to question the logic of older arrangements. They thought blacks should be prepared to compete with whites for semiskilled and many skilled jobs within the sphere of manual labor. A number of influential white reformers encouraged employers to modify the racial division of work to provide more opportunities for black advancement. Black leaders cooperated with the reformers, even if they objected to the restrictions whites placed on black social and economic progress. They saw a chance to chip away at the system of segregation that had impeded black progress in Birmingham since the city's founding. Black workers did make gains during the period as employers redefined racial lines in their companies.

These changes in the racial status quo generated considerable anxiety among white workers and the general public. Because employers respected the social practices and values of the community and wanted to reduce the appeal of labor organizations, they maintained a Jim Crow system, albeit, one they controlled. Industrial segregation, however, no longer rested on as firm a foundation as it had in the past when whites had been able to rely upon their monopoly of skills to enforce restrictive union rules. Labor organizations struggled to regain control of the racial division of work. Some labor leaders urged their organizations to adopt a more enlightened approach to the race problem, one that would attach black workers to the labor movement without threatening white control of the best jobs. This more inclusive strategy found little support among rank-and-file whites, who preferred absolute exclusion of blacks. African Americans also rejected a plan designed to perpetuate their subordination. Employers, in the end, retained control of the racial division of work.

During the first decade of the twentieth century Birmingham industrialists complained constantly about shortages of adequately trained workers. While technological change had reduced their reliance on the highly skilled craftsman, it had increased employers' need for workers with more training than common laborers. After U.S. Steel took over TCI, it issued a report citing the existence of a largely unskilled, unstable workforce as one of the major obstacles standing in the way of successful development of its Alabama properties. Company officials reported to a government investigator that native whites would not work year round and that blacks worked just long enough to earn some money to go out on the town. The president of Sloss-Sheffield Steel and Iron informed his Board of Directors of similar problems.[1]

Don Bacon, the president of TCI from 1901 to 1906, implemented a plan designed to reduce labor costs and to attract and retain more skilled and disciplined labor. He believed that his labor problem might be solved by replacing troublesome black common laborers and undisciplined local whites with European immigrants. Bacon had spent his career in the northern iron and steel industry and associated its success, as did many southerners, with its ability to attract Europeans who would work hard long hours. TCI, the Louisville and Nashville Railroad, and the state government joined forces to recruit workers from Germany, England, France, Italy, and the Slavic countries. Soon Italians, Poles, and Slavs began to move to Birmingham. By 1913 approximately 20 percent of Birmingham's iron and steel workers had been born in European countries; almost half of foreign-born workers were natives of Italy.[2]

Migration chains channeled immigrants to companies where relatives or acquaintances from Europe had already obtained employment, usually as common laborers. For example, Frances Oddo's father, a farmer in Bisaquino, Italy, made the journey to Birmingham in the early 1900s and joined his brother-in-law, Charlie Raia, as a blast furnace laborer. Sometimes companies placed immigrants who could speak English in charge of labor gangs consisting of men from the supervisor's country in order to facilitate communication between management and workers. These labor gang bosses naturally hired relatives and people they knew. This was undoubtedly one reason why TCI's workforce in 1917 included a number of Italians with the same last names.[3]

Despite the growth in the number of immigrant laborers, immigration proved to be an unsatisfactory solution to the labor problem. Not enough Europeans moved to Birmingham to replace black labor, and those who did often performed as poorly as or worse than local labor, white or black. Employers found that Europeans with limited experience in industrial work were no more efficient than blacks or whites from the farms of Alabama. Turnover and absenteeism continued to plague Birmingham companies.

Birmingham employers could continue to deal with these problems by hiring more workers than they needed, and many did. But officials at American Cast Iron Pipe Company (ACIPCO) and TCI came to believe that turnover and absenteeism were symptoms of labor unrest that cost them money and might lead to widespread unionization.[4] John Eagan, chairman of the board of ACIPCO, thought that the solution to both problems could be found in the teachings of Christ. He urged Christian businessmen to extend the Golden Rule to those who toiled in their establishments. Eagan compared the employer to a father who had a divinely sanctioned responsibility for his children, the employees. Of course, paternalism carries with it the expectation that the children will defer to the humane and caring father, the source of their well-being.[5] Though Don Bacon and his successor, George Gordon Crawford, did not claim divine sanction or inspiration, they did believe that positive incentives and education must be fundamental parts of any strategy for solving the company's labor problem. Thus ACIPCO and TCI undertook long-term programs designed to alter workers' habits, stabilize workforces, and create more humane work environments. Both companies financed the construction of housing for workers, created health services, built churches, provided social workers, established recreational facilities, and helped finance a system of education for adults and their children.

Through the various institutions that made up their welfare plans, TCI and ACIPCO sought to instill habits of efficiency and thrift and promote loyalty to the company. They believed that improved residential and educational facilities would attract family men less prone than single men to extended weekends following paydays. In addition, if a company owned workers' housing, it added a weapon to its antiunion arsenal. Provisions in leases allowed the company to ban certain visitors and to evict workers who consorted with "undesirables."[6] A former resident of the Sloss quarters identified yet another benefit companies derived from employee housing. When workers lived close to the plant, he explained, companies could more easily find workers "in case of an emergency at the plants. . . . If a breakdown occurred in the middle of the night, all they had to do was send someone down to the company quarters and knock on the doors and tell them we need them."[7]

TCI and ACIPCO established an array of benefit programs to address the problem of worker turnover. In November 1915, ACIPCO inaugurated a "Savings Bank Plan" that encouraged workers to save by paying them interest on income they invested in the plan. Company officials believed this benefit would encourage workers to stay with ACIPCO to accumulate interest. Two years later the company offered employees a pension plan. To be eligible for benefits ACIPCO required that employees complete at least fifteen years of uninterrupted loyal service. Pension eligibility could be terminated if the pension board found an employee guilty of misconduct. ACIPCO also created the Mutual Benefit Association for the relief of employees who could not work because of sickness or injury. For ten cents a week a member of the association received a $6.00 payment for each week of work missed. Again the company hoped that workers would be less likely to leave a company that offered such benefits.

TCI instituted similar programs to encourage worker longevity and good behavior. For example, it offered employees the opportunity to enroll in U.S. Steel's profit-sharing plan. Workers could purchase U.S. Steel stock and pay for it in installments; the corporation charged 5 percent interest on unpaid balances and allowed employees three years to pay for their sub-scriptions. Before employees could collect the full value of their stock, the corporation required them to demonstrate "a proper interest in the welfare and progress" of U.S. Steel by completing five years of service.[8]

Neither TCI nor ACIPCO depended solely upon benefit programs as they tried to remake the working class. They and other companies also relied on formal education to teach workers the skills and habits they desired and to reduce the influence of unionized craftsmen. As Magnus W. Alexander wrote in the *Iron Age*, by developing "effective systems of apprenticeship, factory schools, special training courses," corporations could end their de-pendence "on the grown up men as they float around the country" and "effectively take hold of the youth of the country and train them in the ways of our industry, and in loyalty and intelligence."[9]

Long before Alexander's article appeared in 1914, industrialists and civic leaders around Birmingham recognized that educational institutions could be used to upgrade local labor. John Lapsley, in his 1885 testimony before a U.S. Senate committee, called for the creation of an educational system that would train native whites and blacks for industrial labor. He and later pro-ponents of industrial education emphasized its disciplining effect. Workers' lack of discipline, Hastings N. Hart wrote, would be "gradually overcome by the training of the children in public schools, the community houses and the playgrounds." J. L. M. Curry, Alabama's leading advocate of education reform, wrote in 1899 that instruction in the manual trades would "bring in-creased productive industries, better wages, steady employment." Workers would then be more content and less likely to "nurse imaginary troubles and engage in strikes and conspiracies." Education, Curry suggested, should be a key weapon in employers' battle against organized labor. In his testi-mony before the U.S. Industrial Commission, N. F. Thompson was more explicit about the relationship between education reform and antiunionism. He called for an end of union-controlled education and the development of "counteractive education." Social workers and teachers, Thompson said, would teach academic and practical skills essential in the modern industrial world.[10]

Leading educators in the state encouraged this idea that formal state-supported education would prepare the next generation of industrial workers. Birmingham's superintendent of education called general education a "great economic force, continually and surely tending to develop the productive capacity of our citizenship and to increase the values of the state." Schools would contribute to the creation of a more disciplined and efficient workforce by "elevating the standards of home life, and awakening desires for greater comforts and conveniences." In order to satisfy these desires, the superintendent concluded, men and women would work harder and longer. The president of the normal college at Florence, Alabama, remarked in a speech the same year that "one of the requisites for a good, useful citizen is conscientiousness in the performance of duty, and a most important part of a child's education is to be taught to be regular in his habits, in his attendance at school, and in every part of his life." Educators cast themselves as agents of economic progress and the purveyors of the discipline and consumerism many corporate officials and reformers believed working people lacked. Regularity, discipline, and efficiency, rather than independence in the workplace, defined the ideal worker.[11]

Reformers placed the education of blacks high on their list of priorities. Since the 1880s some industrialists and local civic leaders had been advocating the use of the educational system to train blacks for what the vice president of the Southern Industrial Convention called "the higher grades of mechanical skill."[12] Reformers such as Edgar Gardner Murphy and B. F. Riley, a Birmingham minister, argued that industrial education would make it possible for blacks to compete with whites within the limited sphere of manual labor. Murphy criticized skilled workers' exclusion of blacks from the trades. He argued that white privileges in the workplace distorted the free market for labor by preventing blacks from competing with whites. When blacks had no incentive to work hard, they became a burden to the economy and society. Moreover, failure to fully develop black potential, reformers argued, artificially inflated white workers' wages and raised the prices of southern products higher than the region's competitors. Under such conditions, the South could not compete in world markets. W. H. Baldwin, a northern philanthropist active in southern education reform, warned N. F. Thompson that "the union of white labor, well organized, will raise the wages beyond a reasonable point." Then southern employers would be forced to employ

"Negro labor in the various arts and trades" to remain competitive. Baldwin forcefully argued that "the labor of the now despised Negro" would produce the economic revolution the South's leaders had been awaiting.[13] Thompson revealed the influence of Baldwin when he later told the Industrial Commission that the future prosperity of the South depended upon the instruction of blacks in all manual occupations and in "proper discipline."[14]

Advocates of black education encountered intense opposition in the white community. Many whites feared that educated blacks, no longer satisfied with the racial status quo, would use their learning to challenge white domination. If that happened, the southern social order would probably collapse, warned some concerned citizens. As early as 1890 the *Birmingham Age-Herald* had expressed its fear that "negro education" would "sharpen the conflict between the races" by undermining "that relation between the races which is now the strongest bond of amity—the relation of employer and employed."[15]

In response to such criticism, reformers came up with a justification for black education that maintained the relationship between education and mobility, while emphasizing the importance of schooling in the subordination of blacks. They conceded that blacks and whites would compete at the lower levels of the social order but insisted that most whites would, because of their superior intellectual capacity, rise out of the manual trades into supervisory, managerial, and professional positions. Education, wrote Curry, would actually eliminate the problem of competition between the races by providing the white "laboring classes" open "avenues of wealth and highest respectability." Thompson argued that as blacks learned industrial pursuits, whites would be freed to attend school and prepare for more suitable roles. Increased black competition, Murphy explained, would force whites from the lower classes to strive harder to achieve the stratum of the socioeconomic order reserved for the superior race. And since whites would leave behind menial jobs, blacks must be prepared to fill the demand for labor.

The potential for conflict in a more competitive racial order would be reduced as well by social segregation and white political control, reformers promised. During the first decade of the twentieth century a distinction among social, political, and economic spheres began to appear in discussions of race relations. Editorial writers reaffirmed white social and political superiority, while assuring blacks of at least the opportunity to compete with whites for jobs requiring "manual or mechanical labor." The *Birmingham News* remarked in 1902 that though "social equality with the white race will forever be denied [to blacks]," the rights of blacks to jobs and property would be "determined by [their] own worth, retrogression if unworthy, advancement if deserving." Another *News* editorial declared that "the Negro's mission is to do what he can to elevate his race along that parallel channel, which keeps ever in the same direction as the progress of the white American, but never touches the latter's social side." As for political equality, Thompson advised blacks to "begin to realize that their future lies along industrial lines rather than political lines." When they accepted this fact, "no trouble will exist in any department . . . they will become efficient laborers and be so recognized in every department of production in the South." The *News* declared that "when [the black man] has accumulated something from his own individual efforts he develops a pride and self-respect which will do far more for his material welfare than dabbling in politics for which he is in no way fitted." By depriving black workers of political power, W. E. B. Du Bois explained, white capitalists and their allies hoped to produce a "more docile and tractable" labor force.[16]

Officials at TCI and ACIPCO drew on the ideas of education reformers as they developed their own extensive educational programs. Both companies built schools and provided financial assistance to the public school system. Under Crawford's leadership, TCI began to subsidize schools near company properties. With this financial support, Superintendent John Herbert Phillips upgraded city schools, particularly white schools, and instituted a curriculum that included training in "the use of mechanical tools and . . . the elementary practical arts." In 1909 he reported that the city's high schools taught courses in carpentry, patternmaking, forge, foundry, and machine work. Three years later TCI and Jefferson County reached an agreement under which TCI promised to build and maintain schools around its plant, while the county paid the salaries of teachers. ACIPCO did not build its own school for whites before World War I but did conduct an apprenticeship program for boys beginning in 1915. After World War I ACIPCO lent $40,000 to the public school system to finance the construction of a grammar school for white children near its plant. The company also established a day school for employees without a common school education. Company officials hoped the school would teach students basic reading, writing, and math skills so they could then enter apprenticeships or improve their job skills through courses from the International Correspondence Schools.[17]

Neither corporations nor the county excluded African Americans from their educational programs. Companies included them in private programs, and the county made at least a limited effort to improve black public schools. As Carl Harris has documented, black schools did not progress as rapidly as white schools in Birmingham, but they did improve. Indeed, blacks in Birmingham fared better when it came to education than did blacks in the rest of the state. Under the leadership of Dr. W. R. Pettiford, blacks secured in 1900 a commitment from the school board to build a black high school; the school opened in 1901 under the principalship of Arthur H. Parker. Black organizations sponsored private educational institutions as well. The Knights and Ladies of Honor led the campaign to create the C. A. Tuggle Normal and Industrial Institute, where black children were to be trained for "better usefulness."[18]

TCI and ACIPCO built and supported their own schools for the children of African American employees. Though they endorsed the racist notion that it was, as the *Acipco News* put it, "more or less natural for a negro to be shift-less and lack ambition," they thought they could "help him get away from these natural racial characteristics." Thus TCI provided schooling for black children from kindergarten through the eighth grade. ACIPCO, with the as-sistance of the YMCA, established the Negro ACIPCO School in 1916. The company hired L. B. Bascomb, a graduate of Lincoln University and West Theological Seminary in Pennsylvania, as principal. According to Bascomb the company created the school "with the view of making efficient and in-telligent workmen." A year after the opening of the Negro ACIPCO School the company expanded its black educational system with a new school for blacks in West ACIPCO, the company's black housing project. The city of Birmingham operated the school.[19]

As more and more blacks received the training they needed for skilled and semiskilled jobs, and the open shop movement spread, employers began to hire them. The proportion of blacks in skilled occupations in the iron and steel industry increased sharply after 1900. In 1910, 8 percent of all boiler-makers, machinists, and molders were black. Black gains in molding were particularly impressive; in 1910, 19 percent of Birmingham's molders were black.[20] Firm-level data reveals continued growth after 1910 in the propor-tion of black skilled workers; in 1917, 14 percent of sampled skilled workers were black. The proportion of black molders increased to almost half of all molders, while black representation among machinists and boilermakers re-mained about the same as in 1910. (See Table 7.1.) Judging from a 1920 sample of workers, the growth in the proportion of skilled African American workers in Birmingham continued after World War I. Of the black workers in the sample, 11 percent held skilled jobs; these black skilled workers were 22 percent of all skilled workers.

This growth in the number of black skilled workers might have been a

Table 7.1. Racial Segregation in Selected Skilled Occupations,
Birmingham, 1917–1918 (percentages)

	Black	White
Molders	48	52
Machinists	7	93
Boilermaker	10	90
Roller	0	100
Patternmaker	0	100
Heater	0	100
First helper (open hearth)	0	100
Melter (open hearth)	0	100
Sample	52	311

Source: World War I draft registration cards.

product of the deskilling process. For instance, many skilled blacks worked
as molders, an occupation that certainly did not require the level of skill it
had demanded less than two decades earlier. Perhaps this deskilling lowered
the stature of molding among whites, making it more acceptable to employ black molders. But workers in Birmingham still considered molding a
skilled job, one that whites should therefore control. The other metal trades
in which blacks gained a foothold during this period remained among the
best jobs in the industry as well.

Black representation in the many semiskilled positions created by technological innovation and economic expansion also increased. According to
census figures, 35 percent of semiskilled workers at blast furnaces and rolling mills were black. Of semiskilled workers working at various firms in the
city, 64 percent were black and 36 percent were white.[21] (See Table 7.2.)
Blacks were clearly making slow but steady progress in the iron and steel
industry between 1900 and 1920.

Though, as these figures demonstrate, employers during the first two decades of the twentieth century challenged and altered racial divisions of
work, they had no desire to eliminate racial distinctions among workers.[22]
The technology of modern steel and iron production still supported occupational hierarchies.[23] White workers and their employers believed that the
"superior race" should continue to control most of the best jobs. Employers
therefore maintained a racial division of work that allowed blacks some
gains, while satisfying white desires for privileged status in the labor market, though one less privileged than unions had established. As Will Battle,

Table 7.2. Race and Occupational Level, Iron and Steel Industry, Birmingham, 1917–1918 (percentages)

	Black	White
Skilled	14	86
Semiskilled	64	36
Unskilled	89	11
Sample	992	523

Source: World War I draft registration cards.

a black employee at TCI from 1906 to 1965, said, "the negro had his job, what he was doing, and the white man had his." Whites dominated semiskilled work, especially the better-paying positions, and held most skilled and supervisory positions. Of the men in the draft card sample employed at U.S. Steel's Ensley and Fairfield operations, 97 percent of skilled workers and 60 percent of semiskilled workers were white. With the influx of European immigrants, the size of the white unskilled population increased between 1900 and 1920, but TCI's unskilled labor force remained close to 80 percent black. (See Table 7.3.) Patterns of job distribution at U.S. Steel's subsidiary, American Steel and Wire, differed little from those at Ensley and Fairfield.[24]

Job segregation at ACIPCO, U.S. Cast Iron Pipe, Sloss-Sheffield, and Republic Iron and Steel varied somewhat from those observed at TCI. All the skilled men in the sample who identified ACIPCO, U.S. Cast Iron Pipe, and Sloss-Sheffield as their employers were white, but those companies employed more blacks as semiskilled workers than did TCI. Stockham Pipe and Republic Iron and Steel differed from all the larger companies represented in this data when it came to racial hiring policies in that both companies employed a number of blacks in skilled jobs. Smaller companies not listed in Table 7.3 hired blacks for skilled jobs as well.[25]

Though some form of segregation remained firmly entrenched at the major Birmingham corporations, racial lines in industry had certainly shifted enough to cause considerable concern among white workers.[26] To many whites the mere existence of segregation at a plant was less than reassuring when the boss possessed the authority to change the system as he saw fit.[27] Organized workers had always recognized that a racially divided workforce served their interests only as long as they controlled access to their trades and hiring. As early as the 1890s some labor leaders, realizing that

Table 7.3. Race and Occupational Level for Selected Companies, Birmingham, 1917–1918

	Black		White		Total	
	%	N[a]	%	N	%	N
TCI						
Skilled	3	2	97	76	100	78
Semiskilled	37	40	63	68	100	108
Unskilled	81	270	19	61	100	331
ACIPCO						
Skilled	0	0	100	8	100	8
Semiskilled	90	18	10	2	100	20
Unskilled	100	75	0	0	100	75
USCIPCO						
Skilled	0	0	100	12	100	12
Semiskilled	80	8	20	2	100	10
Unskilled	100	16	0	0	100	16
Stockham						
Skilled	80	20	20	5	100	25
Semiskilled	91	10	9	1	100	11
Unskilled	100	26	0	0	100	26
Sloss						
Skilled	0	0	100	4	100	4
Semiskilled	100	9	0	0	100	9
Unskilled	97	83	3	3	100	86
Republic						
Skilled	76	16	24	5	100	21
Semiskilled	71	15	29	6	100	21
Unskilled	89	48	11	6	100	54

Source: World War I draft registration cards.
[a]Represents raw number of employees in sample.

changes in the process of production could undermine union control of the racial division of work, began to look for new ways to regulate the employment of black workers. Some of them advocated the organization of blacks in separate labor unions. They agreed that since the vast majority of unskilled laborers in the metal-producing and -finishing industries were black, such an approach would avoid violation of local proscriptions against racial mixing and ease some of the tensions between blacks and organized labor.[28]

In 1903 David U. Williams, an officer of the AAISW and the Birmingham Trades Union Council, pleaded with all "wage-workers" to rise above "all malice and prejudice against color, creed, or nationality and . . . work with one end in view."[29]

Williams did not call for an end to the racial division of work in Birmingham's iron and steel industry; nor did he articulate a growing class consciousness that transcended racial divisions among workers. He knew that metal trades unions had no intention of opening their doors to African Americans. But white craft unions could support the idea of black organization without abandoning racial segregation. Advocates of this policy insisted that it would complement and reinforce traditional racial restrictions while offering benefits to black laborers. Because black workers would make gains in their sphere of labor through organization, they would develop an interest in the success of the broader labor movement and be less likely to assist employers in the destruction of the craft unions. Whites would control blacks through segregation rather than exclusion. "It is time," said the *Labor Advocate* in 1895, "that white labor was turning to and using the colored man for its own good."[30]

The AFL unions did attempt to organize blacks in segregated locals. By 1904 approximately two thousand black workers had joined AFL unions. But, while local labor leaders applauded this campaign, rank-and-file members continued to resist interracial cooperation. Members of International Molders' Union (IMU) locals in Bessemer and Birmingham reaffirmed their racial restrictions in 1902. A number of white unions withdrew from the Alabama Federation of Labor after it voted to admit blacks. When the all-black Rolling Mill Helpers and Laborers Union struck Republic Iron and Steel's Gate City plant in 1904, skilled white members of the AAISW continued to work and helped the company break the strike.[31]

Increased black employment in traditionally white jobs between 1905 and 1910 caused some whites to reconsider their position on the race issue. One Birmingham local of the IMU decided in 1911 to allow black membership. Organizer Nick Smith had urged the local to do this to "take away from the [employer] his most effective tool, the Negro strikebreaker." The issue severely divided the local, however, and it actually admitted few, if any, black molders.[32] Then in 1916 the larger labor movement left little doubt about its continued support of racial exclusion. Birmingham's "labor forward movement" sought to convince white workers that only labor organizations could defend white privilege in the workplace. Organizers appealed to men such as Robert Lewis, who migrated to Birmingham in 1916 from rural Elmore

County. Lewis found a job as a helper at TCI and never advanced beyond what whites had long considered primarily "nigger work."[33] One spokesman for the labor forward movement bitterly attacked employers for allowing men like Lewis to languish in such demeaning occupations, while blacks moved up to skilled jobs. He wrote in 1916 that if whites "are a superior race, and I maintain we are, then we should not be expected to perform labor on an equality with an inferior race or class."[34] He pleaded with white workers to unite in the labor movement to defend against employer violations of the ideology of white supremacy.[35]

The labor forward movement failed to generate much interest among Birmingham's white workers. Economic hard times during the campaign accounts in part for its failure. Men did not want to place their jobs at risk by joining labor unions. Moreover, organizers still focused their energies on white craftsmen and a limited segment of the white semiskilled workforce. Thousands of white workers cast their lot with their employers, hoping they would maintain a racial division of work.

Union leaders experienced little more success in their continuing efforts to control black labor. Again they chose a strategy of solidarity that assigned blacks to separate and unequal labor unions. White craftsmen still wanted to defend their dominance of the metal trades by offering blacks the possibility of improvements within the lower levels of the occupational hierarchy. During the metal trades strike of 1918, they encouraged blacks to join a union of unskilled and semiskilled mine and furnace workers called the International Union of Mine, Mill, and Smelter Workers.[36]

At first it appeared that this union might be the solution to organized labor's race problem. But the union had to contend with a hostile community willing to use violence to prevent the organization of blacks. The activities of "several negro agitators" in Ensley elicited a warning from the *Industrial Record* that "interference" with men who wanted to work would not be tolerated. A month later vigilantes dynamited the Oxmoor home of black organizer William Hale. In June a "Vigilance Committee" took Edward Crough, general organizer for the Mine, Mill, and Smelter Workers Union, and Hale from a union meeting. The committee ordered Crough to get out of town on the next train and stripped, whipped, tarred, and feathered Hale. According to a government investigator, representatives of mining and smelting companies convinced the vigilantes that Hale and Crough promoted racial equality.[37]

Vigilante violence undoubtedly intimidated many black workers, but the more difficult problem Mine, Mill, and Smelter Workers Union promoters confronted was black suspicion of organized labor. Many middle- and working-class blacks understood the motivation of the craftsmen and pleaded with black workers to ignore the appeals of union organizers. White unions, black leaders reminded readers of their newspapers and members of their organizations, had always worked to limit black opportunity in the iron and steel industry and had not abandoned that objective. Organization of separate unions for blacks and the unskilled was just another way to secure whites' monopoly of the best jobs. Indeed, some whites were eager now for blacks to join labor organizations under white control because they feared the consequences of open shop conditions.[38] The *Birmingham Reporter* warned its readers that white union members "whose qualifications as craftsmen do not exceed those of the blacks" most vigorously defended the racial division of work. Even if whites welcomed blacks into their unions, blacks would not be treated as equals. The kind of interracial cooperation whites proposed, the *Reporter* warned, would deprive black workers of the bargaining power they gained from divisions among whites. Already, the paper argued, blacks had seen opportunities for advancement increase as employers broke union control of their plants. If African Americans wanted to organize, the *Reporter* advised, they should create their own independent organizations and use their collective strength to achieve their goals. Many black workers embraced this self-help philosophy and defended the editor of the *Reporter* when the *Labor Advocate* attacked his antiunion editorials.[39]

While some blacks joined the few unions that welcomed them, many others experienced little that would cause them to question the argument that unions considered them unequal partners and would do little or nothing for black workers. They no doubt understood the meaning of a 1919 Labor Day parade in which the Mine, Mill, and Smelter Workers marched at the rear of the procession. Their experience taught them that predominantly white unions wanted to lock them into the menial jobs long reserved for African Americans. They had learned that they stood to gain more by exploiting class divisions among whites than by uniting with white unions as separate and unequal allies.

Though most unorganized workers responded to organized labor's appeals with indifference, they had not become the loyal, docile employees welfare capitalists hoped to produce. Employers could not congratulate themselves for creating a loyal and disciplined workforce. Turnover and absenteeism had soared during the war years. Beginning in late 1916 black workers left the city by the trainload, heading for that "promised land" of opportunity in the North labor recruiters so vividly described. Articles appeared in the local press warning those contemplating joining the exodus that agents promising blacks greater opportunity in the North deceived them. Black and white newspapers published stories of the abuses black migrants suffered at the hands of white unionists and foreign immigrants in northern cities. The *Acipco News* published a series of articles describing violence against southern blacks in St. Louis and other northern cities. Though blacks in Birmingham still suffered from racial discrimination, the editor of the *Reporter* wrote, they had made progress and would continue to do so. If they moved north they faced a struggle just to acquire what they had already achieved in Birmingham. Black ministers, such as J. H. Eason of the Jackson Street Baptist Church, advised their congregations to stay in Birmingham, where open shops hired blacks for positions that had always been for whites only.[40] Despite such appeals blacks continued to leave the city throughout the war.

Workers who stayed in Birmingham demonstrated their discontent in other ways. Strikes, though unsuccessful, exposed a level of hostility between workers and employers that troubled corporate executives. ACIPCO officials complained of widespread employee theft and instances of tool breaking. They published articles in the company newspaper chastising workers who were disloyal to their employers and the company. One told workers that they should be grateful to an employer who provided for their well-being and should always "speak well of him, think well of him, stand by him, and stand by the institution that he represents." Another explained that employers deserved respect because they had risen in the world "by reason of some measure of intelligence, thrift and energy." Radicals who attacked such exemplars of the work ethic, the author asserted, only revealed their own flawed character.[41]

Neither ACIPCO nor TCI relied on moral suasion alone as they addressed the problems of the postwar years. Both companies continued to offer employees rewards for faithful, disciplined service. ACIPCO consolidated all of its welfare programs under a single service department in order to more effectively coordinate welfare activities that would "stimulate workmen to better perform their jobs, and the employer to make the jobs more worthwhile." A few months later the company announced a stock purchase plan for employees. Under the plan the company would sell preferred stock to workers at reduced prices. Those who could not pay for the stock up front could borrow the money from the company at nominal interest rates and pay off the loan in installments. The company would pay 6 percent interest per year plus $2.00 per share annur 'ly for as long as an employee remained with the company. Longevity would pay dividends at ACIPCO.[42]

John Eagan also ousted James R. McWane, whom he blamed for the company's labor troubles, from the presidency of ACIPCO. Eagan then ordered wage increases, construction of quality housing for all employees, and improvement of working conditions in the plant. To enhance workers' employment security, Eagan and his managers tried to eliminate the production peaks and valleys common in the industry. By 1922 the company had begun to offer consumers reduced prices for goods ordered during slow periods. If employment levels could not be maintained in this way, the company assigned workers to repair and construction projects. If layoffs still could not be avoided, the company helped those released find other jobs or took care of them in other ways.[43]

Finally, Eagan made all employees owners of the company as part of his "plan" for "industrial democracy." He created a Board of Management and an employee-elected Board of Operatives to cooperatively develop company policy. Black employees could not sit on the Board of Operatives, but Eagan's plan did provide for black access to that body through their own twelve-member board. A month after the creation of the Boards of Management and Operatives, Eagan placed the 1,085 shares of common stock he owned in a trust for the employees of the company. All dividends were to be distributed or invested by the joint trustees—the Board of Management and the Board of Operatives—"to insure to each of said employees an income, which, together with the wage or salary paid to said employees, will enable said employee to maintain a reasonable standard of living." [44]

In his speeches and writings, Eagan argued that his program would restore to workers not just a sense of proprietorship but its reality. Once again the roles of employee and employer would be merged, for everyone who worked at ACIPCO would share ownership. Adversarial relationships between manager and managed would be superseded by an ethic of mutuality among members of a corporate family. As Gerald Zahavi has argued in a study of a program at the Endicott Johnson Corporation that served as one of the models for the ACIPCO program, the family metaphor was reinforced by corporate appropriation of certain family responsibilities, such as the provision of healthcare and recreation. The Board of Operatives and the Board of Management would resolve any conflicts that might occur from time to time.[45]

How much power Eagan's plan gave to workers remains a controversial issue. Some company officials objected to the plan because they thought

it would so fragment authority that they could not run the company effi-
ciently. They worried that day-to-day decisions would require the approval
of a majority of employees or their representatives. When questioned about
this in the latter years of his life, Eagan made it clear that he did not intend
to alter radically the prevailing power relationships at ACIPCO. He assured
the Board of Directors that management would retain operational control of
the company. The Board of Operatives, he explained, possessed the power
only to make recommendations to the Board of Management when issues
affecting the workforce arose. If the two boards failed to reach agreement,
the Board of Directors, which included representatives of management and
labor, would act as mediator. Eagan envisioned a company that operated like
a democratic family, or his ideal of a democratic family. Just because the
head of a family discussed important decisions with other family members
did not mean that he no longer possessed the authority to make the final
decision.

Eagan's plan only appeared to give workers an equal role in the development of company policy. As originally formulated, it provided no alternative
grievance procedures should the Board of Management and Board of Directors reject employee appeals. In other words, the plan deprived workers of an
independent voice. Soon after its implementation, workers complained that
the Board of Management made decisions concerning wages without even
consulting representatives of the workers. When the Board of Operatives
protested, management ignored them.[46]

Even though Eagan's system did not provide workers at ACIPCO the power
an independent worker organization might have, it did create a means
through which workers could influence the decisions that affected their lives
and an alternative to unionization. By providing workers this limited access
to power, a model company welfare program, and relatively secure, well-
paid employment, the company extended to the unorganized benefits unions
could not yet guarantee to the minority of workers they sought to organize.
The program at TCI accomplished the same end. Both companies used their
education programs to teach workers that they had an obligation to work
diligently for their beneficent employers.[47]

This is not to suggest that workers thoroughly absorbed the lessons companies and schools taught, as Henry T. Ware learned in 1928. He went to
work for ACIPCO that year as part of his field experience for the YMCA Graduate School. Ware found that laborers, regardless of race, "had no scruples
[sic] against making 'easy time.'" On one occasion, he reported, he and a
black helper were working for a carpenter and were left to work unsuper-

vised. Ware's associate waited until no supervisors were in sight and told him to "set [sic] down and rest" while he watched for approaching bosses. Another black helper warned him not to do all of the work assigned to him on a given day because they would just be given more to do. Such attitudes, which Ware maintained were widespread, proved a constant source of irritation for white supervisors, who attributed workers' behavior to intellectual inferiority or laziness. One foreman complained of his weariness after years of having "to explain to him [a black helper] every little detail" of a job. "Dese here G— D— niggers," he continued, "won't do a damn thing ef a man don't jest stay on 'em all the time."[48]

Ware saw during his stay at ACIPCO that workers continued to find ways to assert a degree of control over their working lives even in the most closely supervised shops. The comments of the men with whom he talked reveal patterns of behavior that sixteen years of welfare capitalism had failed to change. Yet managers had limited the power of workingmen to determine for themselves the conditions of their work. No longer were the open assertions of autonomy one might have observed in a foundry or rolling mill in early Birmingham acceptable. Now men relied solely upon their ability to dissemble and to deceive. Their reliance upon subterfuge to maintain a degree of self-respect said much about their understanding of the realities of power on the shop floor.

As long as organized labor shunned the vast majority of the unorganized through exclusion of blacks, employers would maintain the upper hand. Their ability to control hiring and the racial division of work, combined in many cases with improved benefits, provided them with an effective defense against worker challenges to their power. Recognizing the critical role racial division played in the relationship between capital and labor, labor leaders struggled mightily to find a way to bring blacks into the labor movement while defending white control of the best jobs. They knew that they must convince black and white workers that only through some form of biracial unionism would all workers regain the power to free themselves of dependence on employers. But the terms of such an alliance and widespread doubts about the benefits of unionism continued to generate severe conflict within the union movement and the working class as the era of World War I came to a close.

CHAPTER 8

Life Away from Work, 1900–1920

T he growth of Birmingham's iron and steel industry during the first two decades of the twentieth
century brought profound and lasting change to
the community. Companies built new plants on the fringes of the old city
that attracted thousands of workers. By 1920 most iron and steel workers
had moved away from the center of the city to neighborhoods closer to their
jobs. Their neighborhoods and their institutions continued to reflect and
reinforce the racial, occupational, and ethnic divisions of the workplace.

In some cases companies financed and controlled "industrial suburbs"
as part of their larger strategy for creating efficient and loyal workers. They
offered workers comfortable housing in relatively pleasant surroundings designed to provide a refuge from the rigors of the workplace. The same patterns of segregation that existed in independent neighborhoods carried over
to company projects as well. Indeed, companies institutionalized such divisions by assigning workers to living quarters arranged according to race and
occupation.

To ensure that workers maintained their domestic haven, companies instructed them, their spouses, and their children in "domestic science" and
inspected their homes to make sure they applied the lessons. Believing that
the way workers used their leisure time should reinforce the habits they tried
to instill at work, companies sponsored "productive" recreational programs
in hopes of getting their employees out of saloons and brothels. Never before

had Birmingham companies intervened in the private lives of their workers to this extent.

Company efforts to control all aspects of their employees' lives was one part of a larger campaign to limit workers' and other citizens' choices when it came to their leisure time. Industrial expansion intensified some citizens' fears that the community might fall into a state of moral anarchy. Though their concerns for the souls of their fellow citizens extended to all classes, moral reformers tended to focus on the behavior of workers, particularly black workers. They linked the growth of the working class to what they perceived to be increasing disorder. The reformers articulated an almost apocalyptic vision of saloons, prostitutes, and violent crime engulfing the city, thrusting it into chaos. They demanded that city, county, and state governments approve and enforce legislation to force men to go home after work to their families rather than to their favorite saloon or house of prostitution. Government must, they believed, stop the moral decay of the community.

Workers responded to all of this in different ways. Many workers resented company intrusions into their private lives and refused to live in company houses or to participate in company programs. Others embraced company welfare programs that improved the quality of their lives. Still others fell between these two extremes. In any case companies failed to render workers as dependent upon their largesse as they had hoped. Working people still looked to family and friends during hard times. Their continued reliance on their own system of social welfare shielded them from total dependence on their employers. When it came to moral reform, the same range of response emerged. Many working people objected to drinking and prostitution but believed that individuals, rather than the state, should be responsible for their behavior. Others supported moral reformers' demands for state intervention, though they did not necessarily endorse the arguments reformers used to justify legislated morality.

During the 1880s real estate speculators had begun to develop suburbs around Birmingham's perimeter in response to increased demand for housing. Typically these early suburbs included an industrial plant, but they were primarily residential developments. Near the end of the nineteenth century, as Birmingham recovered from the depression of the 1890s, investors began to look outside the city for new plant sites. Around these plants they hoped to build thriving communities. This was what Tennessee Coal, Iron, and Railroad planned to do when it created the Ensley Land Company in 1887. TCI sold the company four thousand acres of land west of Birmingham for $5 million in stock, which it distributed among TCI stockholders. At the time of the sale, wrote James Bowron, a TCI official, "there was nothing at Ensley . . . except the blast furnaces and the company's [TCI] office and laboratory." Bowron described the rest of Ensley as "nothing but bare ground or corn patches."[1]

Enoch Ensley, president of the Pratt Coal and Iron Company until TCI bought it in 1886, and H. G. Bond, a land speculator, controlled the TCI subsidiary. They directed the clearing of land, laying of streets, building of a hotel, and division of the property into lots. But nothing came of the Ensley project until TCI decided to locate its steel plant there in the late 1890s. Then the town began to expand rapidly, soon becoming the center of TCI's operations in the district.[2]

TCI's steel plant attracted thousands of men and their families to Ensley during the first two decades of the twentieth century. Race, ethnicity, and occupational status defined the spatial distribution of workers in Ensley and other industrial suburbs, such as the Sloss quarters in North Birmingham. Black workers concentrated in small, one- or two-room structures in the shadows of the Ensley steel plant and about five or six blocks east of there, near an area that would become known as Tuxedo Junction. Will Prather, a resident of the Sloss quarters, described houses there as little more than shacks. He remembered sitting in his house, watching people through the gaps in the boards. "You didn't have no walls," Prather explained, "[and] wind got so bad you had to stop up cracks."[3] Few laborers' houses included plumbing or electricity. Residents retrieved water from common wells, and waste water ran into the unpaved streets to dry in the sun and air. The hogs and chickens tenants raised to supplement their diets roamed freely through the neighborhoods, contributing to unsanitary conditions. In 1912 John Fitch described one company's laborers' quarters as "an abomination of desolation."[4]

A few companies improved the quarters of white unskilled workers so they could be distinguished from black quarters, but inadequate sanitary facilities, wandering livestock, and the ever-present soot from the furnaces that loomed over the villages created a depressing sameness. In Ensley unskilled whites, mostly Italians, lived in long, narrow shotgun houses constructed of clapboards on brick piers, one room wide and two to four rooms deep. Sloss-Sheffield Steel and Iron housed Italian employees in houses identical to those of black residents. Frances Oddo, whose father worked for Sloss, lived in the company's quarters as a child. Italians, she remembered, occupied a row of houses in front of black residences, but "one [house] wasn't no better than the others." Her family's house, she recalled, "didn't have but two rooms, a bedroom and a kitchen" furnished with "one little stove and a bed, maybe a couple of beds." With five members in the Oddo family, the house was crowded. Oddo's parents slept in one room and she, her brother, and her sister slept in the kitchen.

Though the conditions in which blacks and Italians lived at Sloss differed little on the surface, the residents established a clear boundary within the quarters that might not have been apparent to a casual observer. Frances Oddo emphasized that Italians "didn't mix with the colored families in the company houses" and that they moved into the quarters only because they "didn't know any better." Will Battle, who worked at TCI in the early twentieth century, confirmed Oddo's description of relations between Italians and blacks in company towns, adding that blacks had no desire to socialize with Italians. According to him, "they'd be in the company housing and they'd be in one side of the housing and we'd be in one side."[5] Shared experience clearly did not transcend racial differences.

To accommodate the many unskilled single men who worked in their establishments, companies built boardinghouses or allowed a number of workers to rent a house together. Some enterprising individuals, recognizing an opportunity to earn a profit, rented a house for the purpose of renting extra space to boarders. This "boarding boss system" was more prevalent among immigrants than native blacks or whites and was one reason for the overcrowding often noted among immigrants in the district. Men with families also rented space to boarders; a few rented one house for their families and one for boarders.[6]

Skilled and semiskilled white workers lived in houses and neighborhoods that contrasted sharply with those of blacks or unskilled whites. If they lived in company-owned quarters, investigators for the U.S. Immigration Commission observed, they did not occupy "the ordinary type of 'company house.'" Companies provided skilled workers with the best facilities available in their projects. In one town skilled workers occupied spacious, two-story houses on large lots with grass yards and indoor plumbing. The houses were located on wide paved streets, and livestock was not allowed into the neighborhood.[7]

Regardless of race, ethnicity, occupation, or marital status, most workers preferred to live in residential suburbs rather than company towns. They wanted to escape the grime and noise of life near industrial plants and, most important, the supervision of company police and managers. Often the houses in Tuxedo Junction and Moro Park, where many black workers settled, were no better than those in company towns, but they provided their residents a measure of independence from their employers.[8] Skilled whites sought houses in residential suburbs because they wanted to separate themselves from "coloured settlements" and the "low-class white population." They chose, one contemporary study observed, "to live in neighborhoods where their children will mix with the children of the commercial classes in the public schools." The populations of suburbs such as East Lake, Woodlawn, and West End included many skilled and semiskilled whites in addition to people engaged in a variety of nonindustrial pursuits. (See Map 4.2.) Paul Worthman found that approximately one-third of a sample of semiskilled and skilled whites lived in residential suburbs in 1909, while less than 10 percent of unskilled whites and blacks lived in the same areas.[9]

Seeing that men with families avoided filthy, overcrowded neighborhoods, a few companies took steps to improve the housing they offered workers. As part of their efforts to attract and retain reliable workingmen, they constructed higher-quality housing for all workers and upgraded the physical surroundings in company quarters. In 1909 TCI built housing projects at some of its operations that had winding streets rather than the monotonous grid pattern, a variety of house styles painted different colors, and houses with electricity and running water. Likewise, ACIPCO remodeled houses in its quarters and improved the landscape. The company equipped houses for blacks and whites with indoor plumbing and included hot water, electric lights, and pens for livestock. A visitor to all-black West ACIPCO in the early 1920s observed that "the attractively laid-out streets, individual design for all houses, varied color of paint, water and sewer connections, and the attractive detached bungalow type of architecture . . . make West ACIPCO indeed a model village."[10]

Having upgraded its housing, ACIPCO incorporated maintenance of the projects into its larger strategy for improving workers' habits. Managers thought the education of workers should not be limited to the shop floor or the schoolroom. Workers and their families, they believed, should use their leisure time engaged in productive activities that complemented and reinforced other educational programs. Thus company publications sought to convince employees that the state of one's yard reflected the state of his or her soul. The company newspaper reminded workers regularly of their responsibility for their animals and the appearance of their yards. To encourage employees to keep their neighborhoods as the company thought they should, ACIPCO offered prizes for the most attractive yard. It urged workers to plant vegetable gardens that might provide a hedge against hard times; employees with the most productive gardens received awards.[11]

The most ambitious project for workers was the development of Fairfield.[12] After Robert Jemison's Corey Land Company purchased land from U.S. Steel for a "nominal sum," it began to build a model community for company employees. Fairfield was not to be a typical company town, however. Corporation executives opted for private development of the community because they had learned that overt company paternalism tended to breed resentment. They wanted to create opportunities for their employees to purchase reasonably priced homes in pleasant neighborhoods free of obvious corporation control.

Though U.S. Steel wanted to be less directly involved in the development of Fairfield, it clearly considered the project an integral part of its strategy for improving its workforce. Workers who owned their homes, planners believed, would be less likely to roam than those who did not. One observer wrote that U.S. Steel invested in the Fairfield venture because it wanted "ideal living conditions for its employees, appreciating the fact that better home conditions mean better labor, more contented labor—an actual return in dollars and cents in dividends and interest." The *Jemison Magazine*, a Corey Land Company publication, thought it essential that workers "be induced to purchase and own homes" so that "labor can be held in the South, which has been a difficult thing in the past." Workers would be "contented and satisfied" living in a " 'show town' that will be the talk of the industrial world." [13]

The builders of Fairfield constructed houses of varying sizes and quality so that all workers could find one they could afford. Under the watchful eyes of corporation officials, the Corey Land Company laid out a "model community" divided into several zones; within each zone it built similarly priced houses. It built more expensive houses for higher-paid skilled workers and foremen on primary residential streets and less expensive houses for those of less means on secondary residential streets. To create an attractive environment, the builders painted houses different colors, planted yards with grass and flowers, and constructed parks and playgrounds throughout the development. Common areas would not become chicken yards or pastures for grazing livestock, for each house had a pen for pigs, cows, and chickens. The developers hoped that the product of their endeavors would be an environment that would "promote health, peace, permanency, pleasure, and recreation for the workmen who live in the influence of such an environment and be conducive to the increase of efficiency, in citizenship, and in work." [14]

For thousands of Birmingham's workers, Fairfield provided an opportunity to escape the squalor of dingy, filth-ridden company towns. Workers did not, however, escape regulation of their behavior. A variety of restrictions on property use forced residents to maintain their neighborhoods in a manner developers and U.S. Steel officials deemed appropriate. Although most of the men and women who moved to Fairfield presumably wanted to keep their community attractive, the builders of the town assumed otherwise. A contributor to the *Jemison Magazine* wrote that regulation of property use was "the part of the work of home building which the citizen, the wage-earner, must have done for him, and when it is done along intelligent, far-sighted lines he accepts the effort." The wage earner, he continued, was to be given "the foundation for standard esthetic, sanitary, utilitarian and economic home conditions that are the equal to the best in the world. These are the kinds of things which make for a better and greater future for Birmingham, the laying down of that foundation upon which can be based ideal homes for the highest or the humblest of the community." The objective of the town planners was worthy of praise, but it was rooted in an elitist sense of obligation to teach the masses how to take care of themselves.[15]

What corporation officials offered workers was much different from what the early promoters of Birmingham had promised and reflected a transformation of Americans' ideas about upward mobility. When the men who built Birmingham had been recruiting skilled workers, they spoke of the opportunity to rise to a position in life where one possessed the power of self-determination at work and in the community. Contentment and satisfaction would derive from equitable productive relations and the critical role of the worker therein. But the increasingly impersonal and authoritarian nature of relations in the workplace, and the systematization of work itself, alienated workers. Corporate officials recognized the alienation and discontent social relations in their plants produced, so they offered workingmen more comfortable lives away from work rather than control of their working lives. One of the rewards for disciplined labor would be a nice house in a nice neighborhood.[16]

Company intervention into the lives of their workers did not end at the threshold of their houses. ACIPCO and TCI employed social workers to go into homes and ensure that residents maintained an acceptable level of cleanliness and order. Again the companies assumed that their employees lacked either the will or the ability to take care of themselves. The companies hired social workers, Hastings N. Hart wrote, "because the people are without experience or training and their social sense has to be developed."[17]

TCI's social workers provided wives instruction in child care, housekeeping, and nutrition. Visiting nurses offered workers' families medical care and advised mothers and daughters on hygiene and the "fundamentals of eugenics." U.S. Steel's health and sanitation department inspected houses regularly; if a resident failed the inspection, the company could evict the family. ACIPCO instituted a similar system of visitation, inspection, and education in "domestic science." It was particularly concerned with the living conditions of black employees. Believing that blacks had a natural tendency toward slovenly living, ACIPCO officials in June 1918 hired Hattie Davenport, a former president of the "colored women's branch" of Birmingham's Red Cross, to teach cooking and sewing to the wives and daughters of black employees. Davenport held her classes in the Domestic Science House, which the company built in West ACIPCO.[18]

Companies across the district also devoted increased attention to workers' recreational activities. Even companies that did not embrace welfare capitalism believed that productive use of leisure time could teach workers habits that would enhance their job performance. Company officials placed an emphasis on team sports rather than the individual contests more typical of rural life. They thought that participation in competitive athletics as a member of a team would teach employees the importance of cooperative individual effort to achieve collective goals. At the same time, they believed, sports contests would foster pride in the company and dedication to making the company a winner in athletics and in the marketplace. Companies created internal baseball, football, and basketball leagues consisting of departmental teams. In addition, they sponsored white and black teams that played in the city's industrial league. The industrial league games attracted large crowds of employees eager to see their respective teams succeed. Such participation, the *Acipco News* remarked, proved that the company's sports program did "more toward the development of the 'Acipco Spirit' than any one phase of the [welfare] work."[19]

Companies did not limit their recreational programs to competitive, exclusively male team sports. They sought to reach the entire family with a range of activities. They built churches, community centers, and playgrounds in their housing projects. Employees could attend company-sponsored Labor Day and Fourth of July festivities each year, in addition to other picnics, banquets, and barbecues. ACIPCO held a fair each year where women demonstrated their gardening, cooking, and sewing skills. J. D. Ross, secretary of the black YMCA at ACIPCO, praised such activities for producing "better working men." "Men," he wrote, "are social beings, and this side of man should be developed to its highest in all classes of men." A company that did this, he argued, "makes [employees] love the company more. It makes them care more for the interest of the company and make better pipes, better everything."[20]

With benefit plans, health services, housing projects, and recreational programs, companies expanded their influence over workers' leisure hours far beyond what it had been during the nineteenth century. But not even the all-encompassing programs at TCI and ACIPCO could replace workers' own systems of support. Nor did workers rely solely on companies for the spiritual sustenance of a church or the camaraderie of a picnic or sporting event. Most attended their own churches and engaged in recreational activities free of company influence. Workers struggled to maintain independent lives away from work.

Despite some companies' increased attention to the social welfare of their employees, workers continued to depend primarily upon their own family-based welfare system. For example, the wife of a Polish worker who worked only six months during 1909 added $20 a month to the household income by taking care of a boarder. The household of Squire Jordan, a black furnace laborer, adopted a different strategy; his wife and two daughters took in wash so the family could get by. An unskilled Italian laborer with two young children could not pay his house rent and other expenses on the $1.25 he made per day in 1909. Since his house was not large enough to accommodate a lodger, and his children were too young to work, his wife found work as a seamstress, sometimes earning more in a day than he did.[21]

These cases reveal the critical role all family members played in the household economy. They also suggest that economic strategies may have changed since 1900. Few white women in 1900 listed an occupation regardless of ethnicity. Was the case of the Italian laborer in 1909 an exception, or did economic circumstances force many unskilled Italians and other white laborers to alter their attitudes toward wives working outside the home? Among blacks only about 10 percent of spouses in 1900 listed an occupation and their children were no more likely to work than were the children of other groups. Did black households after 1900 rely more heavily on the contributions of wives and children than did other groups? Analyses of samples from the 1910 and 1920 census records yield some answers to these and other questions.

In 1910 and 1920 the proportion of nuclear households among both whites and blacks was higher than in 1900. If someone other than members of the core nuclear family lived in a household, he or she was more likely to be a

Table 8.1. Household Structure, 1910 and 1920 (percentages)

	1910		1920	
	White	Black	White	Black
Nuclear	62	65	74	62
Extended	20	17	15	20
Augmented	16	9	7	9
Augmented-extended	1	5	1	3
Single	1	5	3	6
Total	100	101	100	100
Sample	152	196	163	271

Source: Jefferson County Manuscript Census, 1910, 1920.

relative than a boarder. (See Table 8.1.) Examination of changes in household structure across the life cycle reinforces the impression that boarding was becoming less important to the household economy. Households took in boarders at all stages, but more first-stage households included boarders than second- or third-stage households. During the second and third stages, when more children were likely to be present, many households shed unrelated members. (See Tables 8.2 and 8.3.) Judging from these samples, workers, particularly black workers, in 1910 and 1920 still provided support for transient or needy relatives but were abandoning boarding as a household survival strategy.

Exactly why boarding declined among workers at a time when they should have needed extra income the most cannot be determined with certainty. Increased availability of housing for single men and workers' desire for privacy may explain part of the change. The change did not reflect some dramatic improvement in the economic circumstances of households that had always relied on the income derived from boarding. Poorer households still required more income than the household head could generate, but they seemed to be adopting other survival strategies. Among the poorest of Birmingham's workers—blacks—the decline of boarding coincided with a sharp increase in the proportion of wives and children listing occupations. As the city grew, demand for domestics increased, and black women filled most of that demand. Approximately one-quarter of all black households included wives who worked as cooks, laundresses, and housekeepers; most of these wage-earning wives still worked at home, though the proportion had declined sharply between 1900 (over 95 percent) and 1910 (about 70 per-

Table 8.2. Household Structure by Age of Household Head, 1910
(percentages)

	Age Group				
	18–27	28–37	38–47	48–57	(N)
Nuclear					
White	58	61	77	53	(94)
Black	67	66	63	61	(127)
Extended					
White	21	22	7	28	(31)
Black	23	16	11	17	(33)
Augmented					
White	21	13	11	18	(24)
Black	6	9	11	7	(17)
Augmented-extended					
White	0	2	0	0	(1)
Black	2	4	4	7	(9)
Single					
White	0	2	4	0	(2)
Black	0	4	9	7	(10)
Total					
White	101	100	99	99	
Black	98	99	98	99	
Sample					
White	43	54	27	28	(152)
Black	43	68	44	41	(196)

Source: Jefferson County Manuscript Census, 1910.

cent). The proportion of 1920 households with wives employed was slightly below that for 1910. At least some of this change can be explained by the growth in the percentage of skilled black workers during the decade. With higher incomes from the household head, the households of many skilled black workers did not require the help a wife could provide by entering into wage employment. Only 13 percent of the spouses of skilled black household heads listed an occupation, while 21 percent of the wives of semiskilled and unskilled black household heads did so.

Black households also looked increasingly to children to augment the household head's income. About one-quarter sent children to work in 1910,

Table 8.3. Household Structure by Age of Household Head, 1920
(percentages)

	Age Group				
	18–27	28–37	38–47	48–57	(N)
Nuclear					
White	63	82	74	68	(121)
Black	56	69	60	64	(168)
Extended					
White	20	12	14	20	(25)
Black	27	13	21	20	(55)
Augmented					
White	17	1	7	8	(11)
Black	11	9	13	0	(25)
Augmented-extended					
White	0	1	0	0	(1)
Black	1	4	0	6	(7)
Single					
White	0	3	5	4	(5)
Black	5	4	6	10	(16)
Total					
White	100	99	100	100	
Black	100	99	100	100	
Sample					
White	30	65	43	25	(163)
Black	79	75	67	50	(271)

Source: Jefferson County Manuscript Census, 1920.

a proportion more than twice that of 1900. Of the households in the 1920 sample, 31 percent included an employed child. For some households the employment of children was an alternative to a wife working outside the home, but that does not appear to have been the case for most. Indeed, wives with no employed children were *less* likely to identify an occupation than those with at least one employed child living at home. Households with employed children included fewer boarders, suggesting that as black families grew during the life cycle, they shifted from reliance on income from outsiders to exclusive reliance on family members. Boarders occupied needed space in the home, so households looked for ways to generate income. If the combined income of parents could not support larger families, they relied on older children for assistance.

This trend toward dependence upon the earnings of children and wives to supplement the income of a household head set blacks apart from all whites. Regardless of ethnic group or income level and despite a larger average number of children than blacks, the vast majority of the wives of white workers in 1910 and 1920 identified no employment outside the home. White households sent far more children to work than wives and mothers, though still fewer white households included working children than did black households. This is not to say that wives in white households never supplemented their husbands' incomes. Many white households took in boarders, and wives bore the burden that practice incurred.

Some historians have suggested that distinctions between white and black household economies reflect a more favorable attitude toward female spouse employment within African American culture. It is more likely, however, that these employment patterns were dictated by economic hardship. Given the large proportion of black households with no spouse employed and the lower proportion of employed spouses among skilled blacks, it would appear that African American attitudes toward the division of household labor differed little from that of their white counterparts. Discrimination in the workplace, however, held most blacks in lower-paying jobs, forcing upon them survival strategies at odds with prevailing attitudes toward wives' employment outside of the household. Economic reality rendered cultural commitments, whatever they may have been, largely irrelevant.

Reinforcing household-based systems of support were institutions that linked households together in distinct subcommunities largely free of employer interference. Racially and ethnically defined fraternal and other voluntary organizations continued to be a popular source of financial assistance during hard times as well as centers of recreational activity. Voluntary associations scheduled a number of recreational events during each year. Labor unions held picnics and dances to, as the Ladies Auxiliary of the Brotherhood of Boilermakers put it, "promote more social and cordial relations between the members of the union." Italian and Irish associations sponsored communitywide festivities celebrating important dates or events in the history of their native countries and their adopted country. Each year the Irish Democratic Club sponsored a Saint Patrick's Day parade, which was one of the major events on Birmingham's social calendar. An Italian organization, the Societa Italiana Umberto Di Savora Di Piemonte, sponsored Columbus Day activities in the city and successfully lobbied Alabama's legislature for a state holiday honoring Columbus's voyage.[22]

For many workers churches became the focus of community life. African American churches, such as the Mt. Ararat Baptist Church in Ensley and Bethel Baptist in North Birmingham, not only met the spiritual needs of congregants, but they also helped members survive hard times. They provided shelter and food to newly arrived migrants until they could find their own places, to the unemployed, and to others in need. In addition, they brought congregants together for a variety of social functions. Deprived of equal access to theaters, parks, and most public recreational facilities, black workers spent much of their leisure time engaged in church-sponsored recreational activities.[23]

Recognizing the critical role religion played in the African American community, some companies built churches for their black employees. Many then hired ministers and urged them to teach their congregants the virtues of discipline, thrift, and loyalty. Some workers participated fully in company-sponsored religious activities, while many others rejected them completely. For example, most of ACIPCO's black employees, feeling the presence of the company every time they entered the company church, built their own church away from company property and company influence. The company complained often about poor attendance at its church and chastised workers for rejecting its benevolence.[24]

Italian community life revolved around churches as well. Father John Canepa, originally from Genoa, organized the first predominantly Italian Catholic congregation in Thomas, Alabama, in 1904. Because Ensley had no Catholic church, he held services for Italians there in a house in "Little Italy" until 1913, when the construction of Saint Joseph's Catholic Church was completed. Mass and church-sponsored picnics on secular and religious holidays were well attended and helped maintain old country traditions essential to the ethnic and communal identities of parishioners. On such occasions Italians gathered for early mass before indulging in games, dancing, and eating.[25]

For many workers saloons remained popular places to socialize during the first decade of the twentieth century. As the laboring class grew, so did the number of saloons serving workingmen. C. M. Stanley, a resident of Birmingham in 1901, described a section of the city containing a number of saloons that catered to workers. He remembered that "no lady ever walked along the block on 20th Street between Third and Fourth Avenues because of the drunks and saloons and beer kegs."[26]

Many in the city were still eager to do something about saloons. During the early years of the twentieth century, moral reformers intensified their crusade against drinking, especially working-class drinking in saloons. They thought that workers must be forced out of saloons and into more productive leisure activities. Thus some reformers proposed the banning of games and music in saloons, with the intention of eliminating the "social feature" that they believed attracted workingmen to drinking establishments. Others proposed sharp increases in taxes that would, they hoped, drive many of the smaller grogshops out of business. The city government tried both solutions, but neither had much impact on the problem.

Failure to regulate saloons effectively fueled agitation for an election to decide whether alcohol sales would continue in Jefferson County.[27] A referendum was scheduled for the fall of 1907. During the weeks before the voters went to the polls, prohibitionists, led by the Anti-Saloon League and the Birmingham Pastors Union, and antiprohibitionists ("antis") engaged in a bitter struggle for citizens' votes. Both groups devoted much of their time to convincing white workers to support their respective positions. Though disfranchisement had reduced the size of the working-class electorate, the antagonists clearly believed that white workers could make a difference in the campaign. The prohibitionists aggressively exploited white workers' fears of black competition in an effort to win their support. They sought to connect destruction of the liquor traffic to the "Negro problem," imploring white men of all classes to unite in what they defined as a movement to eliminate the main source of black criminality in the community. Race loyalty, prohibitionists insisted, should be placed before relatively petty class differences. While this was not a new strategy, earlier agitation against the liquor traffic had not been cast in such stark racial terms.[28]

Prohibitionists also exploited the presence of "corporationists" among antis in their effort to attract working-class votes. Officers of leading iron and steel corporations opposed the ban on alcohol because, they thought, it would eliminate one of the city's attractions for black laborers. Speakers at Prohibition gatherings responded to this argument in three ways. First, they charged that many antis who took this position lowered white men to a level with drunken blacks and urged white workers to prove them wrong by voting against alcohol. Second, prohibitionists pointed out that many of the same men who had led the open shop movement opposed Prohibition because they wanted to maintain a large force of black laborers in order to minimize the influence of labor organizations. Third, they attacked employers for running their plants on the Sabbath. Men who violated the Sabbath, prohibitionists explained, naturally cooperated with their fellow Sabbath breakers, the saloon owners and their customers.[29]

Not all corporate leaders opposed Prohibition, however. Some thought that the destruction of the saloon was essential to maintaining workplace discipline. James Bowron complained that so many men, white and black, failed to report to work on Mondays that it was often difficult for the pipe works he managed to function. Blacks, he and others alleged, were especially fond of "Saint Mondays" and would never become disciplined workers as long as saloons that pandered to their dissolute ways existed.[30]

Workingmen among the antis argued that Bowron and his friends represented the mainstream of the Prohibition movement. The crusade against liquor, they contended, had always been directed against the working class and should be seen in the context of a design against workers' rights in all areas of life. Free men, anti-Prohibition workers declared, should have the right to choose for themselves how to conduct their private lives. They warned that the populistic appeals of the prohibitionists only obscured their desire to take this freedom away from all workers regardless of race, ethnicity, and occupation.[31] Workers, then, could find a number of reasons to vote for or against Prohibition, none of which had anything to do with rural origins, fundamentalist backgrounds, or embourgeoisement. This is not to suggest that such factors had no impact on individuals' votes. But exploitation of class and racial tensions was at least as important to the strategies of both campaigns as religious appeals.

On election day white workers who voted were as divided as the rest of the community.[32] Support for Prohibition tended to be weaker in heavily working-class industrial satellite towns, such as Ensley and Bessemer, than in more heterogeneous residential suburbs, such as East Lake, Woodlawn, and Avondale. In the latter communities, prohibitionists won more than 70 percent of the vote compared to 53 percent and 60 percent in Ensley and Bessemer respectively. Of course, disfranchisement and the ineligibility of recent European immigrants reduced the size of the working-class electorate, magnifying the voting strength of the middle and upper classes of the county and perhaps insuring the prohibitionist victory.[33]

The prohibitionists had always insisted that a victory for them would bring peace and order to the community. After the county went dry violent crime in the community did decline rather sharply. By the end of 1908 arrests for drunkenness, disorderly conduct, and assault and battery had fallen to 70 percent, 60 percent, and 46 percent of the 1907 totals for each of those crimes. These figures did not continue to improve, however; Prohibition failed to rid the county of the "liquor problem" and the violence associated with saloons. Local law enforcement agencies found it impossible to control the spread of the illegal saloons—"blind tigers"—that met continued citizen demand for alcohol.[34]

Disappointed with the failure to end the liquor traffic in Alabama, local prohibitionists looked to the state government for help. They argued that blind tigers could continue to operate because liquor companies continued to do business in the state. Antiliquor legislators therefore proposed an amendment to the state constitution that would ban the "manufacture, sale, offering for sale, and keeping for sale" of liquor. Shops selling legal beverages would be closely supervised to make sure that they did not spike their coffee or lemonade. Finally, the "Carmichael" amendment would permit alcohol use in the home only.[35]

Opponents of the amendment, including some prohibitionists, immediately launched an attack on the measure, claiming it would allow the state to violate civil liberties. The state, they warned, could enforce the law only if they invaded private homes to determine whether the residents possessed liquor for personal use or for sale. Few of these critics called for a return of the saloon, but they could not endorse a law they believed to be an unnecessary expansion of state power, one that would lead eventually to violations of the "sanctity of the home." [36]

Spokesmen for organized labor in the city, even some of those who had voted for Prohibition in 1907, endorsed the position of the amendment's opponents. In addition, they questioned the sincerity of local advocates of the law who claimed to be friends of the working people. James B. Drake of the International Association of Machinists ridiculed Governor B. B. Comer's attempt to sell the measure as a benefit to working people. He reminded readers of the *Labor Advocate* that Comer had always been willing to exploit employees at his cotton mill. Another supporter of the bill, he charged, had represented Birmingham Machine and Foundry when it sought and won an injunction against striking machinists. Drake concluded that neither man had much interest in helping workers.[37]

While many workers might have agreed with Drake's criticism of Comer and other prohibitionists, they did not necessarily come to the conclusion that they should therefore vote against the Carmichael amendment. After all, some workers had benefited from the Birmingham Machine and Foundry injunction. Others found among the opponents of the amendment men who had been as hostile toward organized labor as any of the amendment's supporters. In a response to Drake, Edward Flynn pointed out that Frank Evans, the editor of the *Birmingham Age-Herald*, opposed the Carmichael amendment and had been one of the most vocal opponents of striking coal miners in 1908. A local judge who opposed the amendment, Flynn continued, once sent a union member to jail for violating an injunction he had issued. Given these facts, Flynn asked, why should a union member vote against the law? [38]

The voters of Jefferson County rejected the Carmichael amendment. Citizens of the county continued to openly disregard the 1907 ban on alcohol. By the summer of 1911 the number of violations of drinking ordinances had increased sharply, while the number of convictions had declined. [39] Of 1,066 people arrested for liquor law violations between April 10 and August 10, 1911, only 109 paid fines. Complaining of the difficulty and expense of enforcement, city officials called for the establishment of high-license saloons to eliminate the problem of blind tigers. In late August 1911 voters endorsed that proposal, and legal saloons returned to the city. [40]

But the era of the saloon as a center of working-class social life had passed by this time. With workers' migration to the suburbs, the neighborhood ties that had been so central to the culture of the saloon dissolved. [41] At the same time workers discovered other amusements, particularly motion pictures. While the struggle over alcohol raged, working people and their families began to spend much of their leisure time viewing movies. On their day off, they headed for the nearest movie theater, where, as one man put it, the workingman relaxed and recovered from the previous week's work.

To many moral reformers this new form of entertainment offered little improvement over saloons. They did not object to movies per se, especially those that reinforced their ideas about good and evil. They did, however, object to moviegoing on Sunday, the only day many workers were free to attend. In February 1915 the Reverend A. J. Dickenson, of the Birmingham Pastors Union, and the Woman's Christian Temperance Union demanded that the city commission extend Sunday closing ordinances to include movie houses. If the commission failed to act, they warned, Birmingham might fall into the same morass of sin and general decadence that had swallowed New Orleans and Memphis. [42]

Many workingmen opposed what they considered to be another attempt to limit their control of their leisure time. A worker named J. R. Smith wrote a letter to the editor of the *Birmingham News* asking why the ministers wanted to deprive working people of the one day they had for "good and clean recreation" but said nothing about the Sunday activities of more well-to-do citizens. He ridiculed the notion that movies took people away from church, arguing that most working people went to the movies after church services. Smith then reminded the ministers that " 'Remember to keep holy the Sabbath' does not mean to crawl into your shell and stay there for fear of doing wrong on the Sabbath." [43] J. B. Wood of the Birmingham Trades Union Council placed the Sunday movie controversy in the context of a larger struggle between workingmen and those who sought to deprive them of control over their own lives. Already, he said, employers forced the workers to spend their "daylight in toil," which left them exhausted and able only to go home at night and sleep. "On Sunday," Wood continued, "he is ready for recreation, it is the only day, yet there is none for him in Birmingham." He urged the commission to respect the right of the working people of the city to use their one day away from work as they chose.[44]

Others in the community, including several ministers, opposed a complete ban on Sunday movies. They thought movies with a moral message would be appropriate, especially if they were shown for a good cause. The commissioners found this compromise appealing and decided to permit the screening of approved Sunday movies to raise money for charity. Although the Trades Council began a series of Sunday movies for workers to raise money for the unemployed, the commission's decision sharply reduced workers' opportunities to see a film on Sunday.[45]

Discontent over these restrictions contributed to the election of Arlie Barber to the city commission in late 1915. Barber promised voters, among other things, that he would work to end all limits on Sunday movies. Shortly after Barber took his seat, the commission did remove the restrictions it had imposed a year earlier.[46] Dickenson and the Pastors Union reacted to the return of Sunday movies with a demand for a referendum on the issue, and in February 1918 the commission finally succumbed to their pressure.[47]

The campaign that ensued was as divisive as the struggle over Prohibition. Dickenson and his allies exploited rising anti-Catholicism in the city, warning that the pope used movies to recruit followers. Supporters of Sunday movies responded to such tactics with ridicule and the usual defense of individual liberty. The *Labor Advocate* tried to convince workers that a ban on Sunday movies would deprive them of Sunday recreation while allowing largely middle-class amusements, such as East Lake Park, to remain open.

Many workers found the *Advocate*'s argument persuasive, but Dickenson won the support of many others, a number of whom had joined his chapter of the True American Society of Guardians of Liberty. When a representative of the Trades Council told the city commission that workers opposed restrictions on Sunday movies, a man who said he represented a union contradicted him. The Trades Council, he countered, did not speak for the majority of workers, who had no desire to violate the Sabbath. On election day the vote was evenly divided across the city, but a majority approved a ban on Sunday movies. Again majorities in working-class suburbs such as Ensley and Fairfield voted with the moral reformers.[48]

Between 1900 and 1920 Birmingham's workers confronted a number of challenges to their autonomy outside of the workplace. Employers sponsored a variety of programs designed to extend lessons of discipline and loyalty beyond the workplace in order to expand and reinforce their power on the shop floor. Their efforts did not reach all workers, and even those they did reach maintained varying degrees of independence from the company when they left work. Still, by 1920 the influence of some employers extended well beyond the shop floor, encompassing almost all facets of their employees' lives.

Company welfare programs always deepened existing divisions within the workplace. Some scholars have argued that this policy was part of companies' effort to divide workers in order to secure an unchallenged ascendancy. The evidence here suggests, however, that occupational, racial, and ethnic division in company towns reflected the workers' own preferences. After all, the vast majority of workers who lived in independent neighborhoods segregated themselves along occupational, racial, and ethnic lines and created institutions that reinforced those distinctions.

Working-class divisions also appeared during controversies over reforms designed to impose certain ideas about morality. Many workers saw the campaigns of moral reformers as extensions of the strategies of control they confronted at work; to them the goal of reformers was identical to that of the builders of company towns—to limit individual freedom. Other workers joined the reformers in hopes of defeating forces they believed threatened the economic and social ascendancy of white Americans. Although workers shared a desire to maintain control of their lives away from work, the sharply different means they employed reflected distinct and conflicting views of their world.

CHAPTER 9

Workers and Politics, 1894–1920

When organized workers confronted challenges to their authority at work and in the community, they used their political power to defend their interests.[1] The Birmingham Trades Union Council, through the *Labor Advocate*, repeatedly warned members against political passivity in an era of rapid change in the relationship between capital and labor. In 1898 the *Advocate* defined politics as "a craft by which one class oppresses another class. The burdens of laws enacted in the interest of certain classes, cliques, or corporations is the fruit of the present political machine." It concluded its comments by reminding readers that politicians made possible "the placing of capital over labor; the control of labor by the control of wages constituted the subtle craft which took the place of powder and ball."[2]

The "political machine" the *Advocate* vilified here consisted of men who had risen to office promising a restoration of social harmony through a purge of political bosses David Fox and Sylvester Daly, both of whom many workers embraced as their own. Now the *Advocate* pleaded with workingmen to unite once again behind political leaders who would place the interest of labor (the "people") first. It understood that organized labor's power to shape public discourse and policy declined after 1894. Labor's loss of influence can be attributed in large part to increased division and tension within the white working class. White workers who held semiskilled and unskilled jobs in steel plants and iron foundries did not always share the concerns of organized skilled workers. For example, proponents of antiboycott legislation found supporters among unorganized workers, who resented union intimidation of nonunion workers during strikes. Many workers whose families relied on the income of children opposed restrictions on child labor supported by organized labor. Institutional changes undermined organized labor's political influence as well. A resurgent movement for reform of city government swept away the aldermanic system of government that had been the traditional source of working-class political strength within the city.

Having failed to block the establishment of the commission form of government, the Birmingham Trades Union Council became the leading critic of city government. It helped foster a populistic movement to return power to the "masses." Politicians emerged who exploited working-class resentment of the elitism of the first city commissioners, racial tension, and surging nativism, linking all to corporate disregard for the interests of working people. Though this new force sometimes generated hostility toward unions, it did eventually provide the building blocks for a political coalition that began to bridge divisions among white workers.

Although the Citizens' Reform Union did not survive the 1894 election, men active in the Commercial Club, who had been instrumental in the formation of the Citizens and the Municipal Democratic Club, continued to advocate a political agenda that often set them at odds with organized labor. The most prominent leader of the Commercial Club faction was future "progressive" governor B. B. Comer, whose relationship with organized labor in the district was somewhat less than amicable. During the coal miners' strike of 1894, he joined a vocal group of businessmen in support of Tennessee Coal and Iron, continued to do business with the company, and praised Governor Thomas Goode Jones for using troops against strikers. Although Comer's opposition to the strike was initially unpopular, he subsequently benefited politically from the mistrust of labor organizations that was a legacy of the violent end of the strike.[3]

Comer's role in the economic revival of Birmingham after the depression, particularly the opening of his textile mill in the suburb of Avondale, also contributed to his rise to local political prominence. Comer promoted the mill to the Commercial Club as a way to attract more white labor to the city. The mill, he argued, would utilize the labor of women and children, while husbands worked in the city's growing steel industry. A number of the members of the Commercial Club invested in the project, and the organization became Comer's political base.[4]

Labor organizations bitterly denounced the employment of women and children at Avondale Mills. Such a practice, labor leaders argued, was barbaric and a threat to the integrity of the family. The *Labor Advocate* suggested that industrialists like Comer wanted to provide work to women and children rather than pay men enough money to provide their families with the necessities of life. Pay men a fair wage, the *Advocate* argued, and their wives and children would not be forced to work. Abolition of child and female labor became one of organized labor's primary legislative goals.[5]

As early as 1898, a year before Comer's mill was scheduled to be completed, the Trades Council and its constituent organizations began lobbying for legislation that would prohibit the employment of children under thirteen years of age and would require children to attend school. If not educated, warned the *Labor Advocate*, children would become "social slaves, the tools of unscrupulous capitalists, helpless as babes in the hard conflict for existence, dependent upon the whims and caprices of those in possession of the things they lack—money and learning." The Trades Council endorsed a child labor bill the state legislature considered in 1899.[6]

The Birmingham Commercial Club opposed this measure. Club members viewed agitation for restriction of child labor as an attempt to enlist the power of the state in organized labor's campaign to limit the rights of employers to hire anyone they pleased. Such an expansion of the power of the state would, they warned, hinder economic development. Opponents of child labor legislation also raised the specter of state interference with the right of heads of families to decide what was best for their children. A majority of state representatives found these arguments persuasive and voted against the bill.[7]

The Trades Council blamed the defeat of the child labor bill on legislators controlled by corporations and the workingmen who voted for them. It offered two solutions to these problems. First, it endorsed the disfranchisement provisions of the 1901 constitution as a way to cleanse the electorate of "foreigners" and blacks who, in the judgment of the *Labor Advocate*, lacked the independence to resist their bosses' coercion at election time. Depriving such men of the right to vote not only would advance organized labor's political agenda, argued the *Advocate*, but it also might encourage men who took jobs away from "respectable" whites to leave the state.[8] Second, in May 1902 the Trades Council's Committee on Political Action urged union men to form ward and precinct Majority Clubs that would work for the election of Democratic candidates friendly to the labor movement. The clubs spread across the district during the next two months. In July they nominated Ed

Veitch, an iron molder from Bessemer; J. H. Leath, a printer and vice president of the Typographers Union; W. C. Cunningham, a barber; and James Liddell, a miner from Wylam, to represent the county in the legislature.[9] Labor's candidates hoped to defeat a group of candidates the Birmingham Citizens' Alliance nominated. The *Labor Advocate* reminded its readers that the Citizen's Alliance wanted to use the legislature to defend corporate practices, such as exploitation of child and female labor, convict leasing, and the commissary and scrip systems.[10]

All of labor's candidates did well in the election, though only Cunningham won a place in Jefferson County's delegation. Nonetheless, labor leaders hoped that their strong showing might demonstrate to those who advocated antiunion legislation that workers still wielded considerable political clout and therefore force them to reconsider their positions. But the antiunion Birmingham Citizens' Alliance had won a clear victory and quickly moved to secure legislative approval of an antiboycott measure. All of the representatives chosen in 1902, with the exception of Cunningham, voted for the antiboycott bill.[11]

The victory of the Citizens' Alliance reflected increased middle-class power in a restricted electorate. It also exposed deep divisions between organized and unorganized workers. The *Labor Advocate* explicitly blamed the Citizens' electoral success on workers who found the right-to-work philosophy of the open shop movement appealing. After the legislature approved the antiboycott bill in 1904, the *Advocate* denounced the "stupid and improvident" class of worker who voted for Citizens' Alliance candidates. The Trades Council organized the United Labor League to defeat the men responsible for a law it claimed was designed to replace union workers with "non-union labor" and reduce all workers to "a level with the peon labor of Mexico and the pauper labor of other countries."[12] It pleaded with union labor to unite and defeat this plot to "destroy the ancient constitutional guarantees—freedom of the press, free speech, and the right to seek happiness and prosperity." The United Labor League, the *Labor Advocate* argued, would "enable the toiling masses to act in concert against the vicious onslaught of their enemies, whether in the courts, before the law making power at the ballot box or through whatever concerted action may become necessary for the protection of their lawful rights and best interests."[13] Of course, the "toiling masses" did not include "stupid and improvident" nonunion workers.

In 1906 the United Labor League led a campaign to replace Felix Blackburn, one of the legislators who had voted for the antiboycott bill, with one of its own candidates. The league also endorsed C. P. Beddow in his race against Nathan L. Miller for the state senate. Beddow did not oppose the antiboycott bill, but he had been a miner and after becoming a lawyer had consistently taken the side of workers in legal conflicts with corporations. This record contrasted sharply with that of his opponent, who, according to the *Birmingham News*, worked for "convict-hiring corporations." [14]

Blackburn lost his bid for reelection, but so did labor's candidate. And the winner, L. J. Haley, was as supportive of the antiboycott bill as Blackburn had been. Beddow also lost but immediately contested the election, charging that Miller's corporate backers had used their power to ensure that their candidate won. After recounting the votes, county officials ruled for Miller. The election of 1906, then, seemed to confirm organized labor's political impotence.

This evidence of political weakness undoubtedly encouraged labor's political opponents in city politics. For years, as we have seen, corporate-backed reformers had campaigned for a change in city government that would weaken or destroy the political machine David Fox and Sylvester Daly had built among workers who lived in Ward One. While the reformers had managed to reduce the level of working-class influence Fox and Daly had brought to city government, they had not eliminated it. Ward One continued to elect aldermen associated with the "machine," and as late as 1901 David U. Williams, president of the Trades Council and a member of the Amalgamated Association of Iron and Steel Workers, served on the City Democratic Party Executive Committee. But discontent with "machine" politicians, and the ward system of government that reformers believed supported them, remained.

George Ward, a reform-minded mayor, renewed the attack on "machine rule" in 1907. His campaign grew out of a conflict with his opposition on the Board of Aldermen. John L. Parker, the president of the city council and the leader of the anti-Ward faction, had taken advantage of Ward's absence from the city to place his own men on important committees. When the mayor returned, he asked the Alabama Supreme Court to reverse Parker's action. After the court rejected his appeal, Ward attempted to remove two of Parker's supporters, who, the mayor alleged, had accepted kickbacks and bribes; one of the men, R. D. Burnett from Ward One, controlled the Fox-Daly machine.[15] An investigation exonerated both men, but Ward filed similar charges against three more aldermen the next year.

Such factional fighting might have been dismissed as business as usual in another time, but proponents of government reform seized upon the episode to build a powerful challenge to the aldermanic system of government. They joined Ward in calling for the creation of a city commission. In December 1908 Walker Percy, an attorney for TCI, organized a mass meeting to discuss the "crisis" in city government. Percy and other speakers argued that the aldermanic system encouraged political division and graft that paralyzed the government. They demanded the replacement of the Board of Aldermen with a commission and payment of salaries to elected city officials, who would serve full time.[16] With a commission, its advocates insisted, "business" government would become a reality in Birmingham. Percy and the *Birmingham News* believed that commission government would reduce the power of "undesirable elements" with voting strength and place municipal affairs in the hands of a "few men of intelligence, business, experience, industry and character."[17]

The Trades Council opposed the movement for commission government from the beginning. All the talk about corruption and efficiency, warned the *Labor Advocate*, concealed an attempt to deprive the people of representative government. Those who proposed the commission, continued the *Advocate*, rejected the fundamental principle of American democracy that the people rule. They looked down upon the average workingman and claimed to be more capable of governing the city than representatives of the average citizen. The *Advocate* compared the commission movement to the creation of the police commission during the Fox regime (see Chapter 4). Leaders of both movements, the paper concluded, wanted to impose "aristocratic" government upon the city.[18]

The voters paid little attention to such warnings. Residents of the suburbs, angry about the Board of Aldermen's decision to appoint their representatives after their incorporation in 1910, joined citizens disgusted with government corruption in giving the commission plan a huge majority. In the same election, Percy won a seat in the state legislature.[19]

Soon after the legislative session of 1911 began, Percy secured the chairmanship of the House Committee on Municipal Organizations, an assignment that allowed him to closely supervise the progress of his commission bill. A difference soon arose among proponents of the bill over the method of selecting the first commissioners. A majority of the Jefferson County delegation wanted Governor Emmet O'Neal to appoint the first commission. The men they suggested as candidates were Culpepper Exum, the sitting mayor; Harry Jones, the incumbent city council president; and Alexander O. Lane, a former mayor. Commission forces protested that this plan would return the city to "aldermanic rule" since both Exum and Jones were sitting on the Board of Aldermen. Percy argued for election of the first commissioners but eventually accepted a compromise that allowed the governor to appoint the first group of commissioners, if he replaced Jones with James M. Weatherly, a Birmingham corporation attorney and a man with no ties to the old government. The governor signed this version of the bill.[20]

While the change to a city commission had won the blessing of the voting public, the first two years of the commission's life tended to reinforce opponents' warnings that the corporations and the privileged would use it to achieve their own selfish ends. Three decisions in the spring and summer of 1913 were particularly antagonistic to organized labor. First, commissioners provided police protection to contractors in their campaign to destroy building trades unions; policemen who refused to cooperate were fired. Then they sided with the Birmingham Railway, Light and Power Company during a strike by white men who claimed the company forced them to work for lower wages than the company paid nonunion blacks. Finally, the commission dismissed all union members in the fire department. Union men all over the city, most of whom had been fighting the open shop for years, were outraged.[21]

Opposition to the commission began to spread beyond organized workers after it approved the sale of the People's Telephone Company to Southern Bell. The sale, contended the *Labor Advocate*, reduced competition and increased telephone rates. Walker Percy, the man who engineered the deal, according to the *Advocate*, had created the commission to serve the corporate interests who employed him, and it appeared to be fulfilling its purpose effectively.

Revelations of commission favoritism toward prominent individuals in the dispensation of justice expanded popular opposition even more. Commissioners routinely arranged for some well-known men in the city to receive private hearings when charged with morals violations, while the average citizen stood trial publicly. The practice became public knowledge after the arrest of Henry Gray, a former lieutenant governor, on charges of consorting with a prostitute. A young recorder's court judge named Clement Wood insisted that Gray be tried in open court like everyone else. The city commission did not agree with the judge and dismissed him. The firing immediately became a cause célèbre for anticommission forces. The people needed no further evidence that the new aristocratic rulers of their city had abandoned the democratic principle of "equal rights to all, special privileges to none." [22] At a mass meeting labor attorney White Gibson demanded the destruction of a system of government that ensured the dominance of "concentrated wealth." Under the commission form of government, he continued, "the working man has very little chance to either rule or be rightly ruled." [23]

The beneficiary of what had become a popular movement against "aristocracy" was the politically ambitious Clement Wood. Wood consciously exploited class tensions in building a following among workers and others struggling to regain influence in the governing of their community. While on the bench, he had defended striking workers who appeared in his court and had encouraged organized workers' struggle for the right to determine the conditions of their employment. In a speech before the Trades Council, Wood declared that "as long as exploitation continues, as long as the product of labor does not belong to labor, but he [the laborer] receives only a small fraction of it, so long will the class struggle continue. The exploitation goes on whether you strike or not; it is to seek to lessen or end this class struggle that you strike." [24]

In July 1913 Wood, riding a wave of popular protest, announced his candidacy for the city commission. In the announcement and throughout his campaign, Wood sought to breathe life into the old populist struggle between the producing classes and the corporations. He insisted that "local conditions require that a man be elected to this office who stands for a complete break from the old corporation control of the city, both in financial and moral matters, and a return of the powers and benefits of city government to the people. . . . Citizens of Birmingham have a right to demand, and by their votes enforce the demand, that the city government shall no longer be used as a weapon against them; that it must represent them and be used in their favor." [25] Workingmen, petty proprietors, and all others who suffered from the tyranny of concentrated economic power constituted the people in Wood's view. Wood and his supporters identified B. B. Comer as the representative of the forces that wanted to deprive the people of their government. Comer became the campaign's symbol of the corporate arrogance and narrow self-interest that threatened the rights of workers and representative government. The *Labor Advocate* urged its readers to reject "Bombastic Buncombe" Comer and his henchmen and "to rise in . . . righteous indignation and demand a square deal for every man, every citizen of our city, regardless of craft, need or standing in the community" and vote for Clement Wood.

Wood's platform reflected the breadth of the constituency he wanted to reach. It called for, among other things, equal enforcement of morality laws, expanded educational facilities, municipal ownership of public utilities, creation of city markets where consumers could buy directly from producers, equality in taxation, and lower license fees for small businesses. His opponent, former mayor George Ward, branded the platform socialistic and warned that Wood sought to disrupt the social order with his revolutionary, anarchistic ideas.[26]

Ward's strategy proved to be effective; he defeated Wood by three thousand votes. Ward's strength was concentrated in "Old Birmingham," while Wood won much of his support in the suburbs where many white workers lived. Wood won just 22 percent of the vote in the whole city, but won a third of the suburban vote. In the heavily working-class suburb of Ensley, he finished a close third in an evenly divided vote. He was strong in North Birmingham, lost by only two votes in Pratt City, a coal mining community, and finished first in East Birmingham.[27]

Wood's showing in the suburbs exposed the continued hostility of working-class and middle-class voters in those areas toward the residents of Old Birmingham who continued to dominate city politics. During the next four years suburban politicians sought to harness the potential political power of the suburbs in a challenge to the "downtown crowd." In a 1915 race for city commissioner, Arlie Barber, the candidate of the suburbs, resorted to a familiar tactic: he attempted to incite fears that the city was controlled by giant enterprises and their puppets. He and his supporters charged that his opponent, Alexander Lane, allowed the industrial interests to dominate city politics. Barber defeated Lane on the strength of the suburban vote. The suburbs also controlled one of two seats the legislature added to the city commission.[28]

City elections in 1917 again featured conflict between the suburbs and Old Birmingham. The Birmingham Civic Association (BCA) had become the center of a continued suburban challenge to the political power of the downtown interests identified with the Commercial Club and the chamber of commerce. The BCA emphasized issues that concerned workingmen and many businessmen. For instance, its demand for a ban on company stores attracted workers, who felt that the stores exploited them, and merchants, who considered the stores unfair competition.[29]

Suburban politicians also exploited widespread anxieties about the continued growth of the black and immigrant population.[30] The institutional expression of this anti-immigrant, antiblack sentiment in 1917 was the True American Society of Guardians of Liberty. A secret society under the leadership of the Reverend A. J. Dickenson of Birmingham's First Baptist Church, the True Americans advocated the restriction of immigration, the imposition of more stringent Sunday closing laws, and the defense of white Protestantism against alien and black threats. Little is known about the organization's membership, but comments in the local press indicate that it attracted mainly middle-class suburbanites and white, mostly nonunion, workers.[31]

In 1917 the True Americans entered the political arena when they endorsed Dr. Nathaniel A. Barrett, a former mayor of East Lake and an officer of the BCA, for president of the city commission. Barrett, like Barber and Wood before him, claimed to be a crusader against an alleged alliance between the "downtown crowd" and the industrial interests. He combined the now standard denunciations of the corporations with strong doses of racist, nativist, and anti-Catholic invective. Concentrating on the suburban electorate, Barrett charged that his opponent, George Ward, was the servant of corporations such as Birmingham Railway, Light and Power and the Alabama Power Company. In a speech in the working-class suburb of Ensley he charged that Ward hired blacks rather than whites to build his house in an exclusive section of Birmingham. Barrett's credibility as a defender of white privilege received a boost when the *Birmingham Reporter*, a black middle-class newspaper, warned its readers that Barrett represented the worst element of white society.[32]

The *Labor Advocate* disapproved of Barrett's association with the True Americans, his exploitation of anti-Catholicism, and his opposition to unions. It urged workingmen to vote for George Ward, the man the paper had vilified as a puppet of the corporations just four years earlier. The thousands of white nonunion workers, and probably many union members, who lived in the industrial suburbs paid little attention to the opinions of the *Advocate*, however. Defense of unions made little sense to men whom labor organizations often treated as inferior, men whom a writer in the *Advocate* once called "parasites." Furthermore, the *Advocate*'s criticism of the True Americans was often condescending, suggesting that workers who joined the organization lacked enough intelligence to identify their real enemies. Perhaps most important, Barrett and the organizations that supported him addressed issues that had a direct bearing on many workers' lives at work and in the community. Immigrants and blacks posed a more immediate threat to the unskilled and semiskilled worker, socially and economically, than they did to the skilled worker. Barrett and the True Americans rode such fears to a massive victory in the suburbs, one that overcame Ward's 59 percent of the Old Birmingham vote.[33] The *Labor Advocate* complained about the support Barrett received in industrial suburbs such as Ensley, East Lake, Wylam, and Pratt City.[34]

Barrett's administration proved to be as antiunion as the *Labor Advocate* had warned. He employed nonunion labor on city projects and cooperated with U.S. Steel management and other industrialists in their efforts to break the metal workers' strike of 1918. Unfortunately for Barrett his cooperation with the corporations eventually alienated nonunion white workers, who saw a dangerous precedent in the use of vagrancy statutes to force blacks into white men's jobs. Barrett's failure to maintain order and morality in the city disappointed his fundamentalist following as well. In 1921 he and his entire administration faced a challenge from suburban candidates who promised to do a better job of cleaning up vice in the city and who did not take the strongly antiunion position Barrett had assumed. They won four of five seats and established suburban dominance of the commission until 1950.[35]

The city election of 1921 gave organized labor reason to celebrate, for one of the victorious candidates was William L. Harrison, a former United Mine Workers and Alabama State Federation of Labor official from West End. Harrison had entered local politics in 1919 as organized labor's candidate for the state legislature. The 1919 campaign had exposed once again the hostility toward industrial interests that had appeared in campaigns since 1913. Harrison left no doubt in the voters' minds that he was the candidate of labor, believed in the need for further union expansion, and would vote for an anti-injunction bill then before the legislature. His opponent, Judge L. J. Haley, ran as the candidate of the Alabama Manufacturers' and Operators' Association, an organization then engaged in a campaign to prevent unionization in the district and to roll back some of the gains workers had made during the war. The association pronounced Harrison a dangerous man who would deprive employers of the courts' protection in conflicts with labor organizations. Harrison won the election with a large majority; the *Birmingham Age-Herald* called the result a victory for organized labor.[36]

The *Age-Herald* failed to mention that Harrison also found much support among unorganized whites and social conservatives. Barrett's campaign had suggested the potential of a coalition of union and nonunion workers and moral reformers. His electoral success, and the popularity among workingmen and the middle class of organizations like the True Americans and later the Ku Klux Klan, taught local politicians that they needed the support of social conservatives if they hoped to win in Jefferson County. Judging from Harrison's campaigns, organized labor had learned this lesson well. He and the *Labor Advocate* publicized his active membership in the Presbyterian Church, one of the Protestant denominations active in the campaign to suppress immorality in the Birmingham district.[37]

The U.S. Senate campaign of 1920 in Jefferson County left little doubt that organized labor had adopted a new political strategy. In his attempt to unseat O. W. Underwood, L. B. Musgrove indulged in Catholic-baiting in Jefferson County and elsewhere. At the same time he devoted much energy to cultivating the opposition to Underwood among organized and unorganized workers after the senator's support for the inclusion of a no-strike clause in the Esch-Cummins bill. Musgrove's campaign skillfully linked Underwood to the chamber of commerce, the Manufacturers' and Operators' Association, and the Manufacturers' Union, all of which advocated the open shop, increased hours, and reduced pay. Underwood tried to win over nonunion workers by portraying himself as a victim of union aggression, but met with limited success. Although Musgrove lost the election, he won in Jefferson, Underwood's home and a county that had always been loyal to him.[38] In explaining the loss of Jefferson County, Underwood's campaign manager, R. H. Mangum, provided a keen analysis of political and social conflict in the Birmingham district as the decade of the twenties began. He reported to Underwood a "phenomenal cleavage between the working classes and the business interests." Musgrove's supporters, he continued, "interpreted [the campaign] as a contest of the well-to-do against the working man." "Musgrove men" traveled about the county dressed in overalls encouraging this "false impression." Mangum assured his boss that his campaign workers had attempted to convince voters that Musgrove was the candidate of organized labor, but were unable to "satisfactorily overcome" the Musgrove campaign's more populistic "point of view." Thus, according to Mangum, Underwood lost in heavily working-class Avondale, North Birmingham, Woodlawn, and East Lake.[39]

The phenomenon Underwood's manager observed was a revival of working-class political power in Jefferson County. For many years thereafter candidates for the city commission and other local offices eagerly sought support among all white workers. They linked corporate arrogance, black competition for white jobs, and threats to white dominance in the community. These candidates appealed to groups such as the Ku Klux Klan, while advocating reforms workingmen in Birmingham had sought for years. When they won office, they supported legislation their constituency demanded.

In politics organized labor joined a coalition that transcended divisions among white workers. Thousands of workers believed that their class interests depended upon the subordination of blacks and other minorities at work and in the community. They held their bosses responsible for the deterioration of white dominance that had taken place during the first two decades of

the twentieth century. Thus white workers voted for politicians who promised to defend them from the aggressions of large corporations and to protect
the supremacy of the white race in all areas of life. This combination of class
resentment and racism would shape Birmingham politics for almost half a
century more.

CONCLUSION

━━━━━━━━━━━━━━━━━━━━━━━━━━━━━━━━

When Birmingham's promoters articulated their vision of the city they hoped to create, they confronted problems of race and class relations directly. They assured Alabamians that African American workers would fill the most menial jobs in the iron and steel industry, freeing whites to achieve as much as their talents would allow. Whites of all classes would join together, united by their interest in the subordination of blacks and their pursuit of prosperity. Racial oppression, then, would shield Birmingham from the class conflict that had long plagued older industrial centers in the United States and Europe.

This New South variant of the "mudsill" theory of social order has been the source of a long-standing historiographical tradition. Historians for many years have cited such booster rhetoric to support the argument that southern elites manipulated the racism of the white masses to dominate them as well as African Americans. They maintain that though the long-term interest of working-class whites and blacks lay in unified resistance to those who exploited them, workers rarely transcended the racial tension their bosses and political leaders actively fostered.

What this interpretation fails to understand, and what this study has demonstrated, is that the ideas about race and class expressed by early boosters reflected the attitudes of the white workingmen they were trying to attract to Birmingham. As David Roediger has shown, white workers experiencing working conditions uncomfortably similar to those they believed suitable only for blacks continually struggled to defend their status by defining for themselves a privileged sphere of labor. They distinguished between their jobs and what they called "nigger work."[1] When civic leaders and employers began trying to find much-needed skilled labor to build and operate the furnaces and rolling mills that were essential to the success of the "workshop town," they soon learned that white workers, especially skilled workers, were reluctant to move to a place where they thought they might someday be forced to compete with black men for jobs and thereby lose the economic, social, and political privileges of their race. So recruiters adjusted their sales pitch. They addressed white workers' fears, promising them that they would never compete with African Americans in a region so deeply committed to white supremacy. Their status at work and in the community would, therefore, be guaranteed.

White workers, however, remained skeptical. They knew that southern employers before the Civil War had employed free blacks and slaves to counteract the influence of white workers. They never believed that the color of their skin alone would protect them from competition with blacks and descent into what they called wage slavery, especially should employers decide that workplace segregation no longer served their interest. Thus the first generation of skilled workers demanded control of the racial division of work. Through union rules which deprived blacks of access to the metal trades, white workers played a primary role in defining "nigger work" and in the institutionalization of Birmingham's industrial color bar. White labor constructed an ideology of white supremacy to secure and to justify their power and status in their places of work and in the community.

This is not to suggest that labor unions were solely responsible for racial discrimination in Birmingham's nineteenth-century iron industry. Clearly the decline of craft unions in the 1880s did not mean an end to white dominance of skilled jobs. The racial division of work that evolved in the 1880s was rooted in a productive system dependent upon craftsmen, the vast majority of whom were white. Employers who managed to free themselves of union rules, and who were willing to violate racial etiquette, could not find enough replacements among African Americans, since few blacks possessed requisite skills thanks to white control of access to the skilled metal trades during much of the 1880s.

Even though employers did not alter the system of segregation in the mid-1880s, whites feared that they might. Thus they desperately searched for organizational strategies that would restore their control over the shop floor and a racial division of work that would relegate blacks to menial labor.

Some embraced the Knights of Labor's racially inclusive philosophy. They believed that until blacks joined the labor movement they would always pose a threat to whites engaged in struggles with their employers. Most white workers, however, preferred absolute exclusion of blacks and defied the Knights' attempts to transcend racial barriers. Conflicts over the race issue tore the Knights apart. In the late 1880s and early 1890s white skilled iron workers eagerly joined the revived American Federation of Labor and restored work rules in union shops barring blacks from the trades.

As long as Birmingham relied upon industries with relatively backward production processes, white metal tradesmen enjoyed a degree of economic, political, and social status that craftsmen in older industrial cities were rapidly losing. But forces that undermined and altered this system of production, and the social relations it supported, began to take hold in the late 1890s and early 1900s. The rise of the steel industry and modernization in machine shops and foundries eased demand for skilled workers, while sharply increasing demand for semiskilled workers. Now the racial division of work had to be redefined. Would whites control the new jobs? Similar changes in Pittsburgh and other industrial centers had created opportunities for the European immigrants who dominated unskilled work. Would Birmingham's blacks realize the same gains?

The answers to these questions depended on the outcome of an employer attempt to destroy organized labor during the first two decades of the twentieth century. Recognizing that the transformation of work posed a threat to its power, organized labor attempted to extend its jurisdiction to many of the new jobs being created. Employers had upgraded their plants in large part because they saw an opportunity to destroy the source of skilled workers' power. Determined to define the division of labor on their property as they wished and to reap the lion's share of benefits to be derived from economic growth, employers launched a movement in 1902–3 designed to end union control of hiring. They exploited racial, ethnic, and occupational differences within the working class, offering semiskilled and unskilled workers opportunities to improve their lives as operators of modern machines in open shops. Some companies promised those who would accept their offer a range of benefits that unions could not possibly provide.

Such appeals resonated among blacks and native and immigrant whites who had moved to Birmingham to escape the poverty of rural life. The jobs open shop employers promised seemed to offer a way to achieve the personal freedom and economic security migrants sought in the city. This was especially true of black workers, most of whom saw in the open shop movement a chance to challenge a system of segregation unions enforced. Historians often attribute antiunionism among black workers to black middle-class accommodationists who sought benefits from the white establishment. But black workers responded favorably to middle-class leaders because they had experienced on a daily basis the consequences of union power. For years they had labored in menial jobs with no hope of advancement. They thought that the open shop movement, by ending white unions' domination of shop floors, might bring some improvement, and it did. While whites continued to dominate the best jobs in industry, African American workers during the first two decades of the twentieth century began to move into semiskilled and skilled jobs whites had long claimed for themselves as a birthright.

Though African American upward mobility was limited, it was enough to foster a sense of crisis among white workers, despite employers' maintenance of a modified system of segregation in their plants. Many labor leaders warned that in the absence of white workers' control of racial divisions in the workplace employers would eventually deprive whites of all their privileges. They ridiculed the notion held by some employers and civic elites that a loss of status at work would be offset by continued political and social superiority. They pleaded with white workers to organize for protection against employer practices that threatened to place them on the same level as blacks at work and in the community. Despite disagreements among white workers about subordinate membership for blacks or absolute exclusion of blacks, all agreed that white workers, rather than white capital, must control black labor.

Iron and steel workers' unions, then, attempted to exploit racial fears among white workers to build their strength and restore their power in Birmingham's industries. They achieved little before 1920. Like craft unions across the country, Birmingham's unions struggled within a radically changed context to define a principle of organization that might incorporate the thousands of workers who remained outside of their traditional boundaries. With the exception of a brief period during World War I when union membership increased, organized labor in Birmingham remained only a shell of what it had been at the height of its strength in the nineteenth century.

Labor leaders in Birmingham continued to search for a way to transcend divisions within the working class. In the late 1930s, the Congress of Industrial Organizations' (CIO) philosophy of industrial unionism seemed to offer an answer, but the problem of race complicated organizers' efforts immensely.[2] Judith Stein argues that the CIO overcame the race problem by convincing Birmingham workers that they all shared an interest in interracial unionism. Her major example of the application of this strategy is a coke workers' local made up of blacks and whites. Herein lies the flaw in Stein's argument: coke work had traditionally been defined as black work, and she indicates that this was still the case during the period she studied. Where whites were in a minority in an occupation and did not really care about establishing a monopoly, interracial alliances could be consummated, as Stein demonstrates. But, as Robert J. Norrell has convincingly argued, many white workers relied upon their unions to defend the racial status quo if they had established their control over certain jobs. Thus white workers demanded that the United Steelworkers impose and enforce a racial division of work that allowed them to control the best jobs in the city's industrial plants. The CIO's experience in Birmingham, he concludes, demonstrated that white workers remained as dedicated to a defense of their privileges in the workplace as the men who built the city's first foundries and rolling mills.[3]

The CIO may have provided black workers with organizational experience that they carried into the civil rights movement, as some historians have suggested. In Birmingham at least, the CIO certainly provided them with lessons in the depth of white commitment to a defense of white supremacy. After close to three decades of industrial unionism in Birmingham, Martin Luther King could still tell African Americans "fortunate enough to get a job" that they "could expect that promotions to a better status or more pay would come, not to you, but to a white employee regardless of your comparative talents."[4] Black workers therefore looked to the civil rights movement and the federal government for relief from such discrimination. They knew that white workers would never voluntarily abandon a system that shielded them from competition with blacks in the labor market.

The people who built Birmingham dreamed of a city that would lead the South back into the Union and ultimately to a position of leadership in the nation. Historians have repeatedly written about the failure of Birmingham and the South to enter the national mainstream. They typically cite the city's chronic racial troubles as a primary reason for the city's and the region's distinctiveness. But in a perverse way Birmingham has always epitomized the national experience. Its citizens have had to come to terms with problems of race and class that transcend space and time. It has taken years of struggle in the streets, in the halls of Congress, and in the courts to undermine the barriers to black advancement that have been erected across the nation. A national debate continues to rage over affirmative action programs and other efforts to alleviate the consequences of past and present discrimination. Given the deep historic roots of white claims to a privileged status in the labor market and ongoing economic contraction, such conflict is not likely to end soon.

NOTES

INTRODUCTION

1. The most prominent exceptions are Carlton, *Mill and Town*, pp. 116–21; Newby, *Plain Folk*, p. 462; Arnesen, *Waterfront Workers*.

2. One of the earliest proponents of this argument was W. E. B. Du Bois. See Du Bois, "The Economic Revolution," p. 109. Just a few examples of the argument are Gordon, Edwards, and Reich, *Segmented Work, Divided Workers*, p. 142; Montgomery, *The Fall of the House of Labor*, pp. 84–85; Kulik, "Black Workers and Technological Change," p. 30.

For suggestive discussions of the problem of race and class in the South and elsewhere, see Marvin Harris, *Race in the Americas*, chaps. 2 and 7; Fields, "Ideology and Race," pp. 155–56; Fredrickson, *The Arrogance of Race*, chap. 11; Flynn, *White Land, Black Labor*, pp. 1–5; Wilson, *The Declining Significance of Race*, chap. 3.

3. Worthman, "Black Workers and Labor Unions," pp. 53, 57, 85.

4. Ibid., p. 84. For a thorough critique of the idea that class unity would transcend racial division, see Hill, "Myth-Making as Labor History" (quote is from p. 133); Hill, "Race, Ethnicity and Organized Labor."

5. Wright, *Old South, New South*, pp. 178–87.

6. Bond, *Negro Education in Alabama*, pp. 144–45; Kulik, "Black Workers and Technological Change," p. 30. There are those among historians who consider Kulik the last word on race and class in Birmingham. His conclusions are, however, based on a study of a single furnace company and ignore the activities of white workers during the period.

7. For a theoretical discussion of how a racially divided labor market serves the interest of white workers, see Bonacich, "Position of Free Blacks," and Bonacich, "Advanced Capitalism." See also George Fredrickson's comments on Bonacich and his discussion of labor market segmentation in *White Supremacy*, pp. 212–34.

8. After the completion of the dissertation from which this study has evolved, David Roediger published his important study of the role of "white ethnicity" in working class formation: see Roediger, *The Wages of Whiteness*. Robin D. G. Kelley in a recent article (" 'We Are Not What We Seem,' ") termed this phenomenon "racialized class consciousness."

CHAPTER I

1. Armes, *Story of Coal and Iron*, p. 339.

2. On economic change in the 1850s, see Thornton, *Politics and Power*, pp. 267–91; Flynt, *Mine, Mill, and Microchip*, pp. 40–41.

3. Thornton, *Politics and Power*, p. 271; Armes, *Story of Coal and Iron*, p. 105.

4. Armes, *Story of Coal and Iron*, pp. 108–9.

5. Flynt, *Mine, Mill, and Microchip*, p. 45; Armes, *Story of Coal and Iron*, p. 124.

6. Flynt, *Mine, Mill, and Microchip*, pp. 50–51; Armes, *Story of Coal and Iron*, pp. 161–65; Joseph H. Woodward II, "Alabama Iron Manufacturing," pp. 201–7.

7. McKenzie, "Horace Ware," pp. 57–60; Armes, *Story of Coal and Iron*, pp. 76–81; Vandiver, "Shelby Iron Company," pp. 12–15.

8. Vandiver, "Shelby Iron Company," pp. 15–16, 23–24; Vandiver, "Shelby Iron Company, Part II," pp. 112–27; Vandiver, "Shelby Iron Company, Part III"; Armes, *Story of Coal and Iron*, pp. 173–77.

9. Armes, *Story of Coal and Iron*, pp. 196–99; Somers, *Southern States*, p. 178; McKenzie, "Alabama Iron Industry," pp. 179–83; C. Vann Woodward, *Origins of the New South*, p. 128.

10. Armes, *Story of Coal and Iron*, pp. 246–49; Chapman, *Iron and Steel Industries*, pp. 102–3.

11. Armes, *Story of Coal and Iron*, pp. 216–22; James Harold Clark, "Alabama Railroad to 1872"; Wiener, *Social Origins*, pp. 163–64.

12. *De Bow's Review*, February 1867, pp. 173–77.

13. Armes, *Story of Coal and Iron*, pp. 196–97, 200; Norrell, *James Bowron*, pp. xvii–xviii; Wright, *Old South, New South*, pp. 166–72.

14. Armes, *Story of Coal and Iron*, pp. 255–73.

15. Fuller, "Boom Towns and Blast Furnaces," pp. 39–40; Norrell, *James Bowron*, p. xxv.

16. Agreement between H. M. Caldwell and Levin Goodrich, witnessed by W. J. Milner, Milner Family Papers, Alabama Department of Archives and History; Armes, *Story of Coal and Iron*, pp. 284–88.

17. Armes, *Story of Coal and Iron*, pp. 285, 298–301.

18. Ibid., pp. 298–301; Tait, *Report of the Commissioner*, p. 20; *Birmingham Iron Age*, February 26, 1874.

19. Thornton, *Politics and Power*, pp. vii, 443; Randall M. Miller, "Daniel Pratt's Industrial Urbanism," pp. 29–30. The comments on Jefferson County are based on my analysis of wealth distribution there in 1850. The data for this analysis was taken from the manuscript census for the county. See also Rutledge, "Antebellum Jefferson County, Alabama," pp. 38–52.

20. Thornton, *Politics and Power*, pp. 221–29; Carlton, *Mill and Town*, p. 84; Ford, "Republican Ideology," pp. 421–22.

21. Armes, *Story of Coal and Iron*, p. 117.

22. Knapp, "William Phineas Brown," pp. 119–22; Armes, *Story of Coal and Iron*, pp. 77–78; Bennett, *Old Tannehill*, pp. 13, 42; McKenzie, "Horace Ware," p. 163.

23. Vandiver, "Shelby Iron Company, Part II," pp. 113–25.

24. Bombhart, *History of Walker County*, p. 50; Bell, "Reconstruction in Tuscaloosa, Alabama," pp. 1–2; Greene, "Reminiscences of Julius C. Greene," p. 11, Birmingham Public Library; Armes, *Story of Coal and Iron*, p. 270.

25. *De Bow's Review*, February 1867, pp. 173–77; *Birmingham Iron Age*, June 14, 1876; Dubose, *Jefferson County*, pp. 279–85; U.S. Senate, *Labor and Capital*, pp. 42–46, 189–90. The *Manufacturers' Record* included much comment on the saving grace of industrializa-

tion in the South in the nineteenth and twentieth centuries. For example, see Speakes, "Southern Industry."

26. Tait, *Report of the Commissioner*, pp. 20–23; Aldrich testimony, U.S. Senate, *Labor and Capital*, pp. 481–82; Somers, *Southern States*, pp. 177–78.

27. Armes, *Story of Coal and Iron*, p. 270; Milner, "Building of Birmingham," Milner Family Papers, Alabama Department of Archives and History. On the political manifestation of anticorporation sentiment in the 1870s, see Perman, *The Road to Redemption*, pp. 201–3.

28. *Birmingham Iron Age*, September 28, 1875; Shore, *Southern Capitalists*, p. 170.

29. Danner testimony, U.S. Senate, *Labor and Capital*, p. 108; Milner, *Alabama*, pp. 158–59; *Birmingham Iron Age*, September 28, 1875; Shore, *Southern Capitalists*, p. 170.

30. *Birmingham Iron Age*, February 19, 1874, April 13, 1882; Barefield, *Bessemer, Yesterday and Today*, pp. 34–35; Armes, *Story of Coal and Iron*, pp. 177, 298–99. My understanding of free labor ideology is based on my reading of the following: Eric Foner, *Free Soil*, pp. 9–23; Rodgers, *Work Ethic*, pp. xi–63; Ross, *Workers on the Edge*, pp. 56–61; Montgomery, *Beyond Equality*, p. 31; Conkin, *Prophets of Prosperity*, pp. 192–93; Brian Greenberg, *Worker and Community*, pp. 22–27.

31. *Birmingham Iron Age*, July 25, 1877; *Birmingham Daily News*, July 25, 30, 1890; *Bessemer Journal*, April 19, 26, May 31, 1894; Lewis to McKee, June 13, 1871, McKee Papers, Alabama Department of Archives and History. On antimonopoly sentiment in antebellum Alabama, see Thornton, *Politics and Power*, pp. 108–9. Compare Thornton to Ford, "Republican Ideology," pp. 416–19. For a discussion of the antimonopoly cast of free labor ideology, see Eric Foner, *Free Soil*, pp. 17–36.

32. *Birmingham Iron Age*, February 8, 1883; *Birmingham Age*, November 4, 25, 1887; *Birmingham Daily News*, July 25, 1890, March 11, 1892, February 3, 1893; Cruikshank, *History of Birmingham*.

33. The recruitment of unskilled labor is discussed at length in Chapter 3.

34. *National Labor Tribune*, September 28, 1889; *Birmingham Age-Herald*, March 7, 12, 1890.

35. Testimony of Edwards, Ernest, Patton, and Lapsley, U.S. Senate, *Labor and Capital*, pp. 47–49, 166, 234, 383–85; Dubose, *Jefferson County*, pp. 279–85; Fuller, "Tennessee Coal, Iron, and Railroad," p. 286; Gutman, "United Mine Workers," p. 146; McKiven, "A Community in Crisis," p. 17. Workers' doubts about the commitment to a racial division of work remained, however. Their efforts to ensure the maintenance of their privileges in the workplace is discussed in Chapter 2.

36. Bond, *Negro Education in Alabama*, p. 145; Fredrickson, *Black Image*, pp. 68, 93–94, 213, 226–27, 266–67; Fields, "Ideology and Race," pp. 156–57; Carlton, *Mill and Town*, pp. 116–21.

37. Armes, *Story of Coal and Iron*, p. 284; *National Labor Tribune*, February 26, 1881.

38. Lloyd testimony, U.S. Senate, *Labor and Capital*, p. 356; *Birmingham News*, April 19, 1902; *Birmingham Labor Advocate*, March 17, 1894.

39. Davis, *The Iron Puddler*, pp. 114–15; *Birmingham News*, April 19, 1902; *Birmingham Labor Advocate*, March 17, 1894.

40. Analysis of World War I draft records indicates that many white skilled workers of southern birth migrated from predominantly white counties near Birmingham. As

numerous studies have demonstrated, these counties were experiencing during this period severe economic difficulties resulting from, among other things, declining commodity prices and overcrowding. One of the best of these studies is Wright, *Old South, New South*, chap. 4. For a discussion of late-nineteenth-century conditions in some of the Alabama counties from which migration appeared to be heaviest, see Hyman, *The Anti-Redeemers*.

One of my assumptions here and in subsequent chapters is that draft card data reveals a process that had begun in the late 1880s or early 1890s. Because registrants in the first draft were twenty-one to thirty-one years of age, they probably migrated to Birmingham after 1900. There is no reason to believe, however, that they were the first to leave their home counties.

I decided to use the first draft because registrants provided more personal information than they did for later drafts. The cards identified place of birth, occupation, employer, current residence, and race. Although any analysis based on this source will be biased toward young men, the draft cards do provide more information on Birmingham's workers than any source currently available. They are located at the East Point Federal Records Center, East Point, Georgia.

41. Armes, *Story of Coal and Iron*, p. 177. Manuscript Census Schedules, 1880; Birmingham City Directory, 1883–84. See also Fuller, "Tennessee Coal, Iron, and Railroad," pp. 275–76. For more on the practice of skilled iron workers passing their skills on to their sons, see Davis, *The Iron Puddler*, p. 114.

CHAPTER 2

1. Historians of the South have only recently begun to move capital-labor relations to the forefront in their studies of the industrial towns and cities of the postwar South. See Carlton, *Mill and Town*; Hall et al., *Like a Family*; Flamming, *Creating the Modern South*.

2. Gordon, Edwards, and Reich, *Segmented Work, Divided Workers*, pp. 79–86; Gregory Clark, "Authority and Efficiency," p. 1069; Stone, "Origins of Job Structures," p. 30.

3. See the story of David U. Williams above and in the *Birmingham News*, April 19, 1902; Davis, *The Iron Puddler*, pp. 114–15; Montgomery, *The Fall of the House of Labor*, p. 16.

4. Davis, *The Iron Puddler*, pp. 97–112; J. Russell Smith, *The Story of Iron and Steel*, pp. 74–75.

5. U.S. Bureau of Labor, *Iron and Steel Industry*, pp. 110–17; *National Labor Tribune*, October 27, November 17, 1883, November 30, 1889, December 27, 1890; Pettyjohn testimony, U.S. Senate, *Labor and Capital*, pp. 307–11, 367; Nuwer, "From Batch to Flow," pp. 813–15; Couvares, *The Remaking of Pittsburgh*, pp. 11–13; Montgomery, *The Fall of the House of Labor*, pp. 16–20; Stone, "Origins of Job Structures," pp. 30–31; Buttrick, "The Inside Contract System," pp. 205–7; Englander, "Inside Contract System," pp. 435–42.

6. U.S. Bureau of Labor, *Iron and Steel Industry*, pp. 143–63; *National Labor Tribune*, October 27, November 17, 1883, November 30, 1889, December 27, 1890; Daniel testimony, U.S. Senate, *Labor and Capital*, pp. 307–11, 367; Montgomery, *The Fall of the House of Labor*, pp. 16–20; Stone, "Origins of Job Structures," pp. 30–31; Buttrick, "The

Inside Contract System," pp. 205–7; Englander, "Inside Contract System," pp. 435–42.

7. Richey, *Patternmaking*, pp. 55–63; Rusinoff, *Foundry Practice*, pp. 9–10.

8. Richey, *Patternmaking*, pp. 55–63; Rusinoff, *Foundry Practice*, pp. 45–80; Stecker, "The Founders, the Molders," pp. 279–80.

9. Walkowitz, *Worker City, Company Town*, p. 35.

10. *Striking Machinist* (Birmingham), July 18, 1901; Montgomery, *The Fall of the House of Labor*, 180–87; Peterson, *American Automobile Workers*, p. 35.

11. Ideas about relations between capital and labor in Birmingham during the nineteenth and early twentieth centuries were little different from those one might see expressed in the labor press in most parts of the United States during the same period. See *Birmingham Weekly Review*, June 12, 19, 1883; *National Labor Tribune*, February 28, 1882, October 27, 1883, August 9, November 15, 1884, November 16, 1889, February 8, 1890; *Labor Union* (Birmingham), July 24, November 13, 1886, February 12, 1887; *Tariff and Labor Advocate* (Calera, Ala.), February 18, 1887; *Alabama Sentinel*, April 23, 30, May 7, 28, June 4, 11, 25, December 3, 1887, February 11, March 10, April 28, May 5, June 2, July 21, August 25, September 29, 1888, April 29, 1889, May 3, July 19, 1890, October 10, November 14, 1891, May 7, 1892; *Journal of United Labor*, November 5, December 24, 1887, September 5, 1889; *Birmingham Labor Advocate*, February 24, April 21, 1894, November 27, 1897, September 3, October 29, 1898, July 7, September 8, 1900, January 19, 1901, January 18, February 1902; *Striking Machinist*, July 18, 1901; *Birmingham Daily News*, May 1, 1890, July 6, 1894; *Bessemer Journal*, May 10, 1894. For an excellent overview of the national debate over the place of labor in society, see Fink, "New Labor History," pp. 116–19.

12. A number of fine studies of American workers have influenced my thinking on this subject, including Berlin and Gutman, "Natives and Immigrants"; Montgomery, "Labor and the Republic"; Wilentz, *Chants Democratic*; Montgomery, *The Fall of the House of Labor*; Dawley, *Class and Community*.

13. The availability of sources dictated my emphasis on the AAISW here. Letters that Birmingham members wrote to the *National Labor Tribune* combined with other documents made it possible to reconstruct the activities of Birmingham's AAISW more completely than other organizations.

14. Robinson, *Iron, Steel, and Tin Workers*, pp. 10–23; Pettyjohn testimony, U.S. Senate, *Labor and Capital*, p. 309.

15. *National Labor Tribune*, February 26, April 2, September 24, 1881; Morgan testimony, U.S. Senate, *Labor and Capital*, p. 361.

16. Pettyjohn testimony, U.S. Senate, *Labor and Capital*, p. 361; Stone, "Origins of Job Structures," p. 41.

17. Robinson, *Iron, Steel, and Tin Workers*, pp. 87–117; Pettyjohn testimony, U.S. Senate, *Labor and Capital*, p. 310.

18. The *National Labor Tribune* reprinted the comments of the *Iron Age* on August 13, 1881; testimony of Chamberlain, Hazard, and Aldrich, U.S. Senate, *Labor and Capital*, pp. 133–34, 470, 483.

19. *National Labor Tribune*, August 13, 1881.

20. For this argument in the case of the Birmingham iron industry, see Bond, *Negro*

Education in Alabama, p. 145; Kulik, "Black Workers and Technological Change," p. 30; Worthman, "Black Workers and Labor Unions," pp. 82–84. Michael Reich repeats Worthman's argument in *Racial Inequality*, pp. 244–50.

21. Morgan testimony, U.S. Senate, *Labor and Capital*, p. 309; *Alabama Sentinel*, May 25, 1889; Philip S. Foner, *Organized Labor*, chaps. 5 and 6; Hill, *Black Labor and the American Legal System*, pp. 15–17; Spero and Harris, *The Black Worker*, pp. 56, 250; Perlman, *The Machinists*, p. 17; Worthman, "Black Workers and Labor Unions," pp. 53, 57, 85.

22. For suggestive discussions of the relationship between racial discrimination of this sort and class conflict, see Marvin Harris, *Race in the Americas*, chaps. 2 and 7; Fields, "Ideology and Race"; Fredrickson, *The Arrogance of Race*, chap. 11; Fredrickson, *White Supremacy*, pp. 212–15; Bonacich, "Position of Free Blacks"; Bonacich, "Advanced Capitalism"; Williams, "Capital, Competition, and Discrimination."

Gavin Wright discusses racial segregation in Birmingham during this period but dismisses the role of labor unions in creating the system. Paul Worthman generally takes a position on this issue much more favorable toward unions than I think is warranted. See Wright, *Old South, New South*, pp. 178–87; Worthman, "Black Workers and Labor Unions," pp. 53–57, 85–87.

23. Testimony of Welsh, Claxton, and Fielding, U.S. Senate, *Labor and Capital*, pp. 374–76, 399–400, 404.

24. *National Labor Tribune*, February 26, 1881; testimony of D. H. Lloyd and Fox, U.S. Senate, *Labor and Capital*, pp. 356–57, 362. Generally, scholars have dismissed the unions of skilled iron workers as largely "peripheral" to the history of the city. The AAISW, however, played a key role in bringing to life one of the projects so critical to the realization of promoters' dreams. Clearly, even though a minority of workers in the city were union members, they were certainly not peripheral to its story. See Wright, *Old South, New South*, p. 181.

25. Pettyjohn testimony, U.S. Senate, *Labor and Capital*, p. 309.

26. *National Labor Tribune*, May 13, 1882. This discussion of labor relations at Birmingham Rolling Mills is based largely on letters to the *National Labor Tribune* from men involved in the events.

27. *National Labor Tribune*, May 13, July 29, August 25, September 30, October 2, 1882, April 7, 1883.

28. *National Labor Tribune*, October 13, 27, November 3, 1883.

29. *National Labor Tribune*, October 13, 27, November 3, 1883; Diary of Julia Ward London, Birmingham Public Library.

30. Pettyjohn testimony, U.S. Senate, *Labor and Capital*; *National Labor Tribune*, July 28, August 11, 1883.

31. *National Labor Tribune*, August 11, September 1, 1883; *Birmingham Advance*, August 13, 1883.

32. *National Labor Tribune*, September 1, 8, October 27, November 24, 1883.

33. *National Labor Tribune*, December 23, 29, 1883, January 12, 26, February 2, July 19, 1884.

34. *National Labor Tribune*, February 9, March 1, 1884.

35. *Birmingham Weekly Iron Age*, June 5, 1884.

36. *National Labor Tribune*, February 9, 1884. Employers in Birmingham successfully tapped the labor surplus created by a national depression in iron and steel in the mid-1880s. See Montgomery, *The Fall of the House of Labor*, p. 31, on the national context.

37. *Birmingham Iron Age*, April 3, 1884; *Birmingham Weekly Iron Age*, May 15, 1884.

38. *National Labor Tribune*, July 26, 1884; *Birmingham Weekly Iron Age*, June 5, 1884.

39. *National Labor Tribune*, September 6, 20, 1884.

40. Montgomery, *The Fall of the House of Labor*, pp. 31–34.

41. Abernathy, "The Knights of Labor in Alabama," pp. 28–37; *Labor Union* (Birmingham), November 13, 1886; *Alabama Sentinel*, April 23, June 11, 1887, April 28, June 2, 1888.

42. Abernathy, "The Knights of Labor in Alabama," pp. 37–61; *Journal of United Labor*, September 24, 1887.

43. *Alabama Sentinel*, June 4, 1887, April 28, 1888.

44. *Alabama Sentinel*, June 11, 1887.

45. The Knights hoped to secure their goals in large part through political action and were active in Birmingham politics in the late 1880s. This will be discussed in Chapter 5.

46. The leader of Birmingham's cooperative movement was a Russian immigrant named Emil Lesser. Lesser, a local merchant, joined with a group of other Knights to organize two cooperative communities named Powderly and Trevellick. As will be seen in Chapter 4, neither community realized the vision of the founders. *Birmingham Age*, August 29, 1887; Abernathy, "The Knights of Labor in Alabama," pp. 65–93.

47. *Alabama Sentinel*, July 2, 1887; *Birmingham Age*, July 25, August 9, 10, 18, 28, 1887.

48. *Alabama Sentinel*, July 2, 1887; *Birmingham Age*, July 25, August 9, 10, 18, 28, 1887.

49. U.S. Senate, *Conditions of Employment in the Iron and Steel Industry*, 3:112; *National Labor Tribune*, April 3, 17, June 26, 1886, October 25, 1887, July 14, October 27, 1888, January 26, February 2, March 16, November 30, December 18, 1889, January 10, 18, 1890; *Birmingham Daily News*, January 10, 14, 1890.

50. *Birmingham Daily News*, January 29, 1890; *National Labor Tribune*, February 1, 8, 15, 22, 1890; *Alabama Sentinel*, February 8, 1890; *Birmingham Age-Herald*, February 16, 1890; *National Labor Tribune*, May 21, 24, June 7, July 14, 1890; Amalgamated Association of Iron and Steel Workers, *Proceedings* (1890), pp. 3007–8; Painter, *Standing at Armageddon*, pp. 110–11; Montgomery, *The Fall of the House of Labor*, p. 35.

51. Goldstein, "Labor Unrest," pp. 59–61. The first mention of a May Day or Labor Day parade in the local press was in 1890. The description herein is a composite based on the following: *Alabama Sentinel*, May 3, 1890; *Birmingham Daily News*, September 4, 1894; *Labor Advocate*, September 10, 1898, September 8, 1900, August 31, 1901. See also Kazin and Ross, "America's Labor Day," pp. 1303–4.

CHAPTER 3

1. Determination of the exact proportion of iron and steel workers who were unskilled is difficult because of the lack of specificity in city directories and census records. In both, furnace laborers were identified, but laborers in other metal-working establishments, such as foundries, were not distinguished from other laborers. I limited the sample to only those identified as working in the production or fabrication of iron or steel. If I

included all laborers, the proportion of laborers to craftsmen would be tremendously inflated. Figures cited herein are consistent with national figures cited in Montgomery, *The Fall of the House of Labor*, p. 64.

2. Milner, *Alabama*, pp. 158–59.

3. Testimony of Wadsworth and Edwards, U.S. Senate, *Labor and Capital*, pp. 461, 463; Bond, *Negro Education in Alabama*, p. 149. Robert Gilmour demonstrates that there was significant white migration within the state after the Civil War as farmers moved from poorer areas to districts with richer soils. Many whites migrated west as well. See Gilmour, "The Other Emancipation," pp. 57–60, 63–73.

4. *Birmingham Weekly Iron Age*, September 4, 1884; Caldwell testimony, U.S. Senate, *Labor and Capital*, p. 352; *Birmingham Daily News*, March 24, 1893; Alabama State Senate, *Senate Journal, 1872–73*, pp. 549–50; Gilmour, "The Other Emancipation," pp. 31–35; Flynt, *Mine, Mill, and Microchip*, p. 94; Flynt, *Poor but Proud*, pp. 92–93.

5. Lapsley testimony, U.S. Senate, *Labor and Capital*, pp. 158, 162.

6. Armes, *Story of Coal and Iron*, pp. 77–78, 158; Wright, *Old South, New South*, p. 187; Bennett, *Old Tannehill*, pp. 13, 42; McKenzie, "Horace Ware," p. 163.

7. Aldrich testimony, U.S. Senate, *Labor and Capital*, p. 483.

8. *Birmingham Iron Age*, November 2, December 21, 1882; *Birmingham Weekly Iron Age*, September 4, 1884; Caldwell testimony, U.S. Senate, *Labor and Capital*, p. 352; *Birmingham Daily News*, March 24, 1893; Flynt, *Mine, Mill, and Microchip*, p. 94; Flynt, *Poor but Proud*, pp. 92–93.

9. Rikard, "An Experiment in Welfare Capitalism," p. 60.

10. *Christian Hope*, March 7, 1902.

11. Wiener, *Social Origins*, pp. 63–65; Sisk, "Alabama Black Belt," pp. 75–85; *Acts of Alabama, 1900–1901*, pp. 1208–10; William Cohen, "Negro Involuntary Servitude," pp. 39, 42; William Cohen, *At Freedom's Edge*, pp. 229–30, 248.

12. Morgan as quoted in Wiener, *Social Origins*, pp. 158–59; U.S. Senate, *Labor and Capital*, p. 458; Welsh testimony, U.S. Senate, *Labor and Capital*, pp. 374–75; Fuller, "Tennessee Coal, Iron, and Railroad," pp. 281–82; Murphy, *Problems of the Present South*, pp. 104–5; Fitch, "The Human Side"; William Cohen, "Negro Involuntary Servitude," pp. 39, 42; William Cohen, *At Freedom's Edge*, pp. 229–30, 248.

13. U.S. Department of the Interior, Bureau of the Census, *Twelfth Census of the United States*, p. 529.

14. Thompson testimony, U.S. Industrial Commission, *Hearings before the Industrial Commission*, p. 758; Worthman, "Working Class Mobility," pp. 195–96.

15. Sloss testimony, U.S. Senate, *Labor and Capital*, p. 289; quote is from Wright, *Old South, New South*, p. 96; Du Bois, "The Negro in the Black Belt," pp. 411–13; Laura Clark interview by Ruby Pickens Tartt, Josh Horn interview by Ruby Pickens Tartt, both in Tartt Collection, Livingston University.

16. Brown, *Up before Daylight*, p. 56; U.S. Industrial Commission, *Agriculture and Agricultural Labor*, pp. 449–51.

17. U.S. Immigration Commission, *Immigrants in Industries*, p. 151; Fitch, "The Human Side," p. 1528; Rikard, "An Experiment in Welfare Capitalism," p. 18; Brown, *Up before Daylight*, p. 56; Rawick, *The American Slave*, p. 231; U.S. Industrial Commission, *Agriculture and Agricultural Labor*, pp. 449–51, 919; Wiener, *Social Origins*, p. 83.

18. Thompson testimony, U.S. Industrial Commission, *Hearings before the Industrial Commission*, p. 758; Worthman, "Working Class Mobility," pp. 195–96.

19. U.S. Senate, *Conditions of Employment in the Iron and Steel Industry*, 3:44–47.

20. Ibid.

21. Ibid., pp. 19–27; Kulik, "Black Workers and Technological Change," p. 26.

22. Kulik, "Black Workers and Technological Change," pp. 26–27.

23. Armes, *Story of Coal and Iron*, p. 96.

24. *Bessemer Weekly*, June 17, 1899; *Labor Advocate*, June 24, July 1, 5, 8, 15, 1899; *Arbitrator*, July 26, 1899; Phillips, *Iron Making in Alabama*, pp. 16–17; Voskuil, *Minerals in Modern Industry*, pp. 184–85; Barger and Schurr, *The Mining Industries*, pp. 105–6.

25. Stampp, *The Peculiar Institution*, pp. 73–85; Blassingame, *The Slave Community*, p. 280; Genovese, *Roll, Jordan, Roll*, pp. 315–17; Dodd and Dodd, *Winston*, pp. 54–61; Kulik, "Black Workers and Technological Change," pp. 29–30; Eric Foner, *Reconstruction*, chap. 4.

26. Phillips, *Iron Making in Alabama*, pp. 16–17; Barger and Schurr, *The Mining Industries*, pp. 99, 105–6.

27. Testimony of Patton, Danner, Sloss, and Caldwell, *Labor and Capital*, pp. 50, 103, 288, 352; Fuller, "Tennessee Coal, Iron, and Railroad," pp. 284–86; Kulik, "Black Workers and Technological Change," p. 30.

28. Testimony of Lapsley, Sloss, and Edwards, U.S. Senate, *Labor and Capital*, pp. 159, 282–83, 386.

29. *Birmingham News*, September 27, December 31, 1902.

30. Testimony of Sloss, Hillman, and Wadsworth, U.S. Senate, *Labor and Capital*, pp. 283, 407, 461; Armes, *Story of Coal and Iron*, p. 287; Rikard, "George Gordon Crawford," p. 165.

31. Studies of Birmingham during this period assume that black common laborers had no leverage in the market. Paul Worthman wrote of the "ease" with which employers could obtain black labor ("Black Workers and Labor Unions," p. 58). He and others rely exclusively upon cultural explanations for the problem of turnover and absenteeism and ignore or dismiss employers' complaints about labor shortages. On the connection between turnover and demand for labor, see Stott, *Workers in the Metropolis*, p. 141. In a recent article, Merritt Roe Smith makes the important point that demand for labor, whether skilled or unskilled, must be taken into account when analyzing workers' bargaining power ("Industry, Technology, and the 'Labor Question,'" p. 558).

32. Wadsworth testimony, U.S. Senate, *Labor and Capital*, p. 462; Tennessee Coal, Iron, and Railroad Company, *Annual Report*, 1888.

33. The data on the wages of unskilled workers does not allow for accurate, systematic analysis. The government report on which my comments are based only provided a yearly income. It did not give the number of months worked during the year or the number of days or hours worked each week. Therefore I could not accurately calculate hourly wages and compare them to the hourly wages of farm laborers in 1890, which is available. Given the data that is available, it is very likely that many black workers could earn significantly higher wages in Birmingham than they could as farm laborers. See U.S. Department of Commerce and Labor, *Sixth Annual Report*, pp. 693, 717. Gavin Wright compares furnace keepers' wages in 1890 to farm laborers' wages in *Old South, New South*, p. 176.

The difficulty of securing and retaining unskilled labor during booms was undoubtedly one reason for an 1891 report that Birmingham employers paid more for labor than other iron-producing districts. This report was quoted in Jeans, *American Industrial Conditions and Competition*, pp. 118–19.

34. *Labor Union*, July 17, 24, 1886.

35. Worthman cites American Federation of Labor figures from the early 1900s, which show that approximately two thousand black iron and steel workers joined exclusively black locals ("Black Workers and Labor Unions," p. 73). Given the size of the black laboring population, this is not a very impressive figure and certainly does not justify Worthman's optimistic appraisal of the labor movement's efforts among black workers.

36. *Bessemer Weekly*, June 17, 1899; *Labor Advocate*, June 24, July 1, 5, 8, 15, 1899; *Arbitrator*, July 26, 1899.

37. *Bessemer Weekly*, June 16, 23, 30, 1900; *Bessemer Workman*, June 20, 27, 1900; Worthman, "Black Workers and Labor Unions," p. 78.

38. *Bessemer Weekly*, October 28, November 18, 1899.

CHAPTER 4

1. On institution building and its importance in defining social identities, see Doyle, *Social Order*, pp. 1–17, and Blumin, *The Emergence of the Middle Class*, chap. 6. For a suggestive discussion of the meaning of working-class culture, see Rosenzweig, *Eight Hours*.

2. For a good discussion of working-class neighborhoods as "a precondition for the development of . . . working-class institutions," see Stott, *Workers in the Metropolis*, chap. 7.

3. Conclusions about the spatial arrangement of the city are based on a combination of my own analysis and that of Paul Worthman. I plotted on city maps the residences of workers from samples drawn from the 1883–84 and 1888 city directories. Worthman's city directory samples were for the years 1890 and 1899. See Worthman, "Working Class Mobility," pp. 203–5.

4. Diary of Julia Ward London, Birmingham Public Library; Sloss testimony, U.S. Senate, *Labor and Capital*, pp. 282–86; *Birmingham Weekly Iron Age*, June 5, 1884; Tennessee Coal, Iron, and Railroad Company, *Annual Report*, 1888, p. 210.

5. *Birmingham Age*, August 20, 1887.

6. Birmingham City Directory, 1888.

7. Caldwell, *Elyton Land Company and Birmingham*, pp. 22–23; *Birmingham Weekly Iron Age*, June 5, 1884; Sloss testimony, U.S. Senate, *Labor and Capital*, p. 286; *Birmingham Age*, August 20, 1887.

8. There is a brief description of the rolling mill district in the diary of Julia Ward London, Birmingham Public Library; London was the daughter of Thomas Ward, the first manager at Birmingham Rolling Mills. Also see *Birmingham Weekly Iron Age*, June 5, 1884; *Birmingham Age*, August 20, 1887.

9. Taeuber and Taeuber, *Negroes in Cities*, pp. 45–49. For some suggestive remarks on class-based segregation within neighborhoods and minor civil divisions, see Blumin, *The Emergence of the Middle Class*, pp. 163–79.

10. Analysis of the demographic characteristics of boarders is based on the samples of households taken from the 1880 and 1900 Jefferson County manuscript census records.

11. I have used the 1883–84 sample here, because Birmingham Rolling Mills had opened by then, and I wanted to see if the helpers in rolling mills lived in the households of the skilled workers for whom they worked.

12. *Birmingham Age*, August 17, 20, 24, 28, September 2, 1887; *Alabama Sentinel*, August 20, 1887; Caldwell, *Elyton Land Company and Birmingham*, pp. 22–23.

13. *Birmingham Age*, August 29, 1887; Abernathy, "The Knights of Labor in Alabama," pp. 65–69.

14. Abernathy, "The Knights of Labor in Alabama," p. 67.

15. *National Labor Tribune*, February 21, 1891.

16. Armes, *Story of Coal and Iron*, p. 236.

17. White, *Village Creek*, p. 62.

18. Ibid., pp. 56–59. For a description of an upper-class residential suburb, see White, "Glen Iris Park," pp. 5–7.

19. Birmingham City Directories, 1883–84, 1888, 1903. Increased rent in 1886–87 was one result of population growth. On this period, see Caldwell, *Elyton Land Company and Birmingham*, pp. 22–23; Armes, *Story of Coal and Iron*, chap. 21.

20. Zunz, *The Changing Face of Inequality*, p. 68; Hareven, *Family Time and Industrial Time*, p. 154.

21. The discussion that follows focuses on differences between blacks and whites. When I controlled for occupation and ethnicity among whites, few differences emerged.

22. On the importance of studying the developmental cycle of households, see Chudacoff, "New Branches on the Tree," pp. 68–72; Berkner, "Stem Family," p. 405; Shifflett, *Patronage and Poverty*, chap. 6.

23. When the sample is divided the number of cases in some categories becomes very small and renders statistical analysis somewhat suspect. Therefore I have used the results in many cases as suggestive of trends only. Due to the exceptionally few cases in much of the analysis of the 1880 households, the discussion, unless otherwise stated, is based on the 1900 sample.

On household extension in other contexts, see Sennett, *Families against the City*, pp. 75–82; Hareven, *Family Time and Industrial Time*, pp. 160–61; Gutman, *Slavery and Freedom*, pp. 443–44.

24. As Tamara Hareven and John Modell have explained, boarding became associated with the "dangerous classes" during the late nineteenth and early twentieth centuries. Skilled workers were concerned with the trappings of respectability and no doubt came to see the need to augment their income as degrading. See Hareven and Modell, "Urbanization and the Malleable Household," pp. 164–66.

25. The budget data used for these calculations is in U.S. Department of Commerce and Labor, *Sixth Annual Report*. My analysis of the budgets follows closely that of John Modell in "Consumption, Acculturation, and Family Income Strategies." On the inconvenience of boarding, see Shergold, *Working-Class Life*, pp. 86–87.

26. On the relationship between economic structure and labor force participation by women and children, see Kleinberg, "The Systematic Study of Urban Women," pp. 21–

26; McLaughlin, "Work and Family Organization," pp. 113–19; Stott, *Workers in the Metropolis*, pp. 102–8; Mintz and Kellogg, *Domestic Revolutions*, p. 93.

Claudia Goldin's work on the labor force participation of "secondary workers" contains useful insights into possible determinants of household economic strategies. See Goldin, "Female Labor Force Participation," and Goldin, "Family Strategies," pp. 277–310.

27. Goldin suggests that after the experience of slavery work for pay was not as socially "stigmatizing" for blacks as it was for white women. What we know of the practices of black families after the Civil War indicates that black women did, after their initial withdrawal from the fields in the immediate aftermath of emancipation, return to work on the farms. Their return was not, however, under the direct supervision of a white master. Part of the compromise that produced sharecropping and tenancy was removal of the black family from the direct control of a white landowner. Whether black control of family labor was an illusion or was real could be argued endlessly; that blacks had a desire to control their family lives is unquestionable. See Goldin, "Female Labor Force Participation," p. 101.

28. Figures on spouse employment are based on the 1880 and 1900 data for households taken from the manuscript census records for those years.

29. Figures on the employment of children are based on the household data taken from the 1880 and 1900 manuscript census records. For a suggestive recent analysis of child labor within the context of household economies, see Koditschek, *Class Formation and Urban-Industrial Society*, pp. 365–79.

30. *Birmingham Weekly Iron Age*, June 5, 1884; *Birmingham News*, April 3, 4, 1902; U.S. Department of Commerce, Bureau of the Census, *Religious Bodies*, pp. 380–407; Brown, *Up before Daylight*, pp. 84–85.

31. Carnes, *Secret Ritual and Manhood*, pp. 78–79, 81–89; Clawson, *Constructing Brotherhood*, p. 173.

32. Stephanie McCurry's remarks on the link between male status and power over dependents in the antebellum South is particularly enlightening on this point ("The Two Faces of Republicanism," p. 1246).

33. The following discussion of voluntary associations is based largely on the records of Knights of Pythias Lodge 85, 1896–98, in the Birmingham Public Library and every list of officers and initiates published in Birmingham newspapers between 1890 and 1893, when the activities of the lodges were covered most fully. I used city directories to identify occupations. See also Donaldson, *The Odd-Fellow's Text-Book*, pp. 141–42; Brooks, *Odd Fellows in America*, p. 222.

Because of the secrecy of these organizations, historians have been unable to define with certainty their social functions. Some of the more perceptive interpretations can be found in Doyle, "Social Functions of Voluntary Associations"; Carsten, "Brotherhood and Conflict," pp. 118–37; Judith E. Smith, "Transformation of Family," pp. 167–69; Wilentz, *Chants Democratic*, pp. 58–59; Ross, *Workers on the Edge*, pp. 165–66; Thernstrom, *Poverty and Progress*, pp. 167–71; Fink, "New Labor History," pp. 134–35.

34. Brooks, *Odd Fellows in America*, p. 223; Donaldson, *The Odd-Fellow's Text-Book*, p. 185.

35. Donaldson, *The Odd-Fellow's Text-Book*, pp. 182–83; Clawson, *Constructing Brotherhood*, pp. 146–76.

36. See Brooks, *Odd Fellows in America*, p. 218. Also see Brooks for dates when the order chartered black lodges in the 1880s and 1890s.

37. Donaldson, *The Odd-Fellow's Text-Book*, p. 182; Brooks, *Odd Fellows in America*, p. 223. Records of Knights of Pythias Lodge 85, 1897, Birmingham Public Library.

38. *National Labor Tribune*, May 26, 1883, December 23, 1892; *Birmingham Advance*, August 13, 1883; *Alabama Sentinel*, October 18, 1890; *Birmingham Daily News*, January 27, 1891, October 9, 1892; *Labor Advocate*, March 5, 1898, February 4, 1899.

39. The description of Fourth of July and Labor Day festivities is a composite based on accounts in local newspapers during the period. See *Birmingham Daily News*, September 6, 1891, September 4, 1894; *Birmingham Age-Herald*, September 3, 1895; *Labor Advocate*, September 10, 1898, September 8, 1900, August 31, September 7, 1901; *Birmingham News*, September 1, 1902. Blacks held separate celebrations or sometimes marched in the rear of white parades. Their activities were not well covered by the white or black press.

40. *Birmingham Daily News*, June 14, 1890; Bigelow, "Birmingham's Carnival of Crime," p. 124.

41. This discussion of the saloon is based in part on reports Pinkerton agents sent the governor of Alabama during an 1894 coal miners' strike. The agents gathered information in drinking establishments, and their reports reveal much about the social function of saloons. See Foley to Jones, May 26, 1894; Vallins to Jones, May 26, 28, 31, 1894, all in Jones Papers, Alabama Department of Archives and History. Local newspapers sometimes included comment on activities, usually violent, around saloons. See *Birmingham Iron Age*, April 3, 1884; *Birmingham Weekly Iron Age*, May 15, 1884. For a suggestive essay on the working-class saloon, see Kingsdale, "The 'Poor Man's Club,'" pp. 472–89. Also see Stott, *Workers in the Metropolis*, pp. 217–22.

42. See Chapter 5 on the role of working-class saloons in local politics.

43. Sterne, "Prostitution in Birmingham."

44. On similar campaigns in other cities, see Couvares, "The Triumph of Commerce," pp. 124–27; Ross, *Workers on the Edge*, pp. 164–65.

45. *Birmingham Age*, July 27, August 1, 2, 1887; *Alabama Sentinel*, August 6, 13, September 10, October 1, 1887.

46. Minutes of the Birmingham Presbytery of the Cumberland Presbyterian Church, 1893, Alabama Department of Archives and History. The Presbyterian Church, U.S.A., the Birmingham Baptist Association, and the Southern Methodists differed little from the Cumberland Presbyterians in their comments on drinking. Generally, more liturgical denominations were less outspoken on the issue, preferring a "drink in moderation" approach. See Bigelow, "Birmingham's Carnival of Crime," pp. 124–25, and Sellers, *The Prohibition Movement in Alabama*, p. 128.

47. Sellers, *The Prohibition Movement in Alabama*, pp. 56–57.

48. *Birmingham Daily News*, March 12, April 16, July 5, 6, 1894. The temperance and Prohibition movements in Birmingham were closely linked to campaigns to clean up local government. See Chapter 5 for more on this relationship.

49. *Birmingham Labor Advocate*, October 15, 1898; Carl Harris, *Political Power in Bir-*

mingham, pp. 189–91. Harris attributes the failure of moral reform in the 1890s to the influence of liquor dealers in city government. Clearly saloon owners used their positions in government or their influence to protect their interests. Their position on government regulation of morality was not, however, a reflection of self-interest alone. It reflected as well their supporters' commitment to the right of individuals to decide for themselves how they would conduct their personal lives.

CHAPTER 5

1. On working-class politics, see Dubofsky, *Industrialism and the American Worker*, pp. 92–95; Katznelson, "Working-Class Formation," pp. 3–41; Katznelson, *City Trenches*, chaps. 1 and 2; Shefter, "Trade Unions and Political Machines," pp. 197–276; Oestreicher, "Urban Working-Class Political Behavior"; Carl Harris, *Political Power in Birmingham*, pp. 68–69.

2. On anticorporatism, or antimonopolism, during this era in American history, see Wiebe, *The Search for Order*, pp. 46–53, and Cassity, "Modernization and Social Crisis," p. 47. The attacks on corporate power and the state's role in facilitating it were a legacy of the politics of the Jacksonian era in Alabama and the nation. See Thornton, *Politics and Power*, pp. 53–55, and Welter, *The Mind of America*, pp. 78–81.

3. *Birmingham Iron Age*, December 7, 1882; *Labor Union*, June 26, 1886; *Alabama Sentinel*, July 30, 1887, July 21, 1888. On challenges to the Democrats in the South as a whole during this period, see Grantham, *Life and Death*, pp. 13–14, and C. Vann Woodward, *Origins of the New South*, pp. 82–85.

4. *Labor Union*, August 14, September 11, October 16, November 13, 27, December 4, 1886; Carl Harris, *Political Power in Birmingham*, p. 66.

5. *Alabama Sentinel*, June 11, August 27, September 3, 1887; Head, "Labor Movement in Alabama," p. 70; C. Vann Woodward, *Origins of the New South*, pp. 228–31.

6. *Alabama Sentinel*, March 3, 31, 1888; Abernathy, "The Knights of Labor in Alabama," p. 73.

7. *Alabama Sentinel*, July 30, 1887; *Birmingham Daily News*, August 8, November 29, 1891, December 1, 6, 1892, January 20, 1893; *Bessemer Journal*, April 26, May 10, 1894; *Labor Advocate*, May 5, 1894; *Birmingham Age-Herald*, June 16, 1894; *Birmingham News*, February 1, 1895; *Birmingham State Herald*, November 10, 12, December 8, 1895, April 5, 8, 10, 1896; Carl Harris, *Political Power in Birmingham*, pp. 227–28.

8. After his election, Milner did hold hearings on the convict leasing that made public the corruption of the system under state warden John H. Bankhead. See Norrell, *James Bowron*, p. 103.

9. *Birmingham Daily News*, November 29, 1891, November 17, 1892, February 8, 9, 10, 1893; *Labor Advocate*, February 3, 1894; Vallins to Jones, April 21, 1894, Jones Papers, Alabama Department of Archives and History; Ward and Rogers, *Labor Revolt in Alabama*, pp. 44–46. In 1893 Jefferson County representatives nearly secured passage of a measure that would have removed the convicts by January 1895. The bill was rendered ineffective when the deadline was replaced by a provision that allowed the state to continue the practice until it was financially able to provide other means of dealing with prisoners. Convict leasing continued until the late 1920s.

10. *Birmingham Daily News*, September 21, December 13, 1891, January 3, 9, June 25, October 2, 1892; *Birmingham Age-Herald*, July 6, 1896. State politics during this period is covered fully in Rogers, *The One-Gallused Rebellion*, especially chaps. 10 and 13.

11. *Alabama Sentinel*, April 7, May 19, June 16, 30, July 7, 14, 21, 27, August 4, 11, 1888.

12. *Birmingham Daily News*, July 8, 22, August 12, 1890, September 23, October 7, November 5, 9 1891.

13. *Labor Advocate*, September 21, 23, 1891, March 17, 1894; *Birmingham Daily News*, October 6, 1891.

14. *Birmingham Daily News*, July 28, August 2, 6, 8, 13, 15, 16, 23, 26, 27, September 6, 8, 10, 20, 30, October 18, 1890; Carl Harris, *Political Power in Birmingham*, pp. 66–67.

15. *Birmingham Daily News*, March 26, 27, 31, 1892.

16. *Birmingham Daily News*, March 27, 1892.

17. *Birmingham Daily News*, March 31, 1892; *National Labor Tribune*, December 22, 1892.

18. *Birmingham Daily News*, November 16, December 10, 1892.

19. *Birmingham Daily News*, November 18, 20, December 13, 1892, January 5, 1893.

20. *Birmingham Daily News*, January 5, 1893.

21. *Birmingham Daily News*, January 7, February 14, March 6, 7, 16, 1893.

22. *Birmingham Daily News*, April 1, 11, 13, 18, 1893, March 12, 1894.

23. *Birmingham Daily News*, April 19, 1893.

24. *Birmingham Daily News*, April 19, 20, 1893.

25. *Birmingham Daily News*, April 20, 21, 26, 27, May 3, 11, 1893, January 6, 13, 18, 1894.

26. *Birmingham Daily News*, March 10, 20, 23, April 1, 1894.

27. *Birmingham Daily News*, April 6, 10, 11, 13, 14, 15, 17, 18, 1894; Carl Harris, *Political Power in Birmingham*, pp. 67–68.

28. *Birmingham Daily News*, July 5, 6, 13, 17, 18, 19, 1894; *People's Daily Tribune*, November 20, December 5, 1894; Hackney, *Populism to Progressivism in Alabama*, pp. 123–25; Carl Harris, *Political Power in Birmingham*, pp. 68–69. Harris contends that the campaign did not polarize city politics "sharply" along class lines. True, no evidence demonstrates that all workers voted one way and all of the middle class voted another. It is not likely, however, that any election will produce this kind of clear division. His evidence and the evidence from the period indicate that white workers, especially skilled workers from Ward One, remained in the Democratic Party and saw the reform ticket as not only somewhat antagonistic toward them but also a threat to white supremacy. As Harris points out, the Democrats nominated nine wage earners for office during its conflict with the Citizens' movement, while the Citizens' nominated only two.

CHAPTER 6

1. *Birmingham Labor Advocate*, August 12, 1910.

2. U.S. Department of the Interior, Census Office, *Iron and Steel Production*, p. 26; U.S. Department of the Interior, Bureau of the Census, *Twelfth Census of the United States*, p. 30; U.S. Department of Commerce, Bureau of the Census, *Fourteenth Census of the United States*, p. 42.

3. Armes, *Story of Coal and Iron*, pp. 395, 432.

4. Ensley testimony, U.S. Senate, *Labor and Capital*, pp. 424–25; *Birmingham Age*, October 29, December 5, 1887; Fuller, "Tennessee Coal, Iron, and Railroad," pp. 252–53; Temin, *Iron and Steel*, pp. 137–45.

5. Armes, *Story of Coal and Iron*, pp. 407–8; Warren, *The American Steel Industry*, p. 183.

6. Fuller, "Tennessee Coal, Iron, and Railroad," pp. 265–70.

7. Norrell, *James Bowron*, pp. 152–53; U.S. Steel, *Steel Making at Birmingham*, pp. 56–59. Gary Kulik argues that Birmingham industrialists were slow to adopt modern production methods because they could rely upon a plentiful supply of unskilled, black labor. Basing his argument on a single company, he contends that black migration after World War I created a labor shortage in Birmingham, forcing companies to install labor-saving machinery such as skip hoists to carry fuel to the top of blast furnaces. As has already been seen, Birmingham industries frequently suffered from shortages of labor well before World War I. Moreover many employers found black workers difficult to handle and therefore had an incentive to find ways to reduce their dependence on them. In any case TCI first installed skip hoists at its Ensley works in 1905 and by 1914 had equipped most of its furnaces with them. See *Iron Age* 94 (October 29, 1914): 995. Kulik's argument appears in "Black Workers and Technological Change," p. 24.

8. Fuller, "Tennessee Coal, Iron, and Railroad," pp. 255–58; Warren, *The American Steel Industry*, p. 183.

9. U.S. Steel, *Steel Making at Birmingham*, p. 64; Hogan, *Economic History*, pp. 404–20; Fuller, "Tennessee Coal, Iron, and Railroad," p. 268.

10. U.S. Steel, *Steel Making at Birmingham*, pp. 60–61; J. Russell Smith, *The Story of Iron and Steel*, pp. 103–4.

11. Nuwer, "From Batch to Flow," p. 830; U.S. Steel, *Steel Making at Birmingham*, pp. 60–61; J. Russell Smith, *The Story of Iron and Steel*, pp. 119–21.

12. J. Russell Smith, *The Story of Iron and Steel*, pp. 119–21.

13. U.S. Bureau of Labor, *Labor Conditions*, pp. 96–101; Fitch, *The Steel Workers*, p. 157; Brody, *Steelworkers in America*, pp. 43–47; Stone, "Origins of Job Structures," p. 37; Hogan, *Economic History*, p. 444; Montgomery, *The Fall of the House of Labor*, pp. 40–41.

14. Fitch, *The Steel Workers*, chaps. 4–6; U.S. Bureau of Labor, *Labor Conditions*, chap. 2; Jeans, *American Industrial Conditions and Competition*, pp. 198–203; Brody, *Steelworkers in America*; Stone, "Origins of Job Structures," pp. 34–37; Edwards, *Contested Terrain*, pp. 30–31.

This discussion of the nature of work in steel plants combines general sources on the steel industry with sources specific to Birmingham. The Birmingham sources available have made it possible to establish that work in the city's steel plants differed little from work in any other steel plant—melters, first helpers, etc., did the same jobs they did in Pittsburgh, Youngstown, or Johnstown.

15. U.S. Bureau of Labor, *Labor Conditions*, p. 95.

16. *Iron Age* 92 (December 26, 1912): 1514; *Iron Age* 94 (November 19, 1914): 1171; Gartman, *Auto Slavery*, pp. 66–70; Montgomery, *The Fall of the House of Labor*, pp. 206–7; Stromquist, "Enginemen and Shopmen," pp. 490–91. For a brief but informative discussion of technological change in the machine-tool industry, see Galloway, "Machine-

Tools," pp. 638–57. I would also like to thank my father-in-law, James A. Tucker, a former machinist, for patiently answering many questions I asked about the operation of the various machines found in a machine shop.

17. American Cast Iron Pipe Company, *History*, pp. 4–8; American Cast Iron Pipe Company, *People and Pipe*, pp. 9–10, 18–19. The degree to which other pipe producers in Birmingham used these innovations is difficult to ascertain with the evidence currently available. The evidence suggests that the U.S. Cast Iron Pipe Company employed similar methods. The circular casting method was common among U.S. pipe makers. See Noble, *Cast Iron Pressure Pipe Industry*, pp. 62–63.

For clear and concise discussions of molding and how it changed in these years, see Stecker, "The Founders, the Molders"; Gartman, *Auto Slavery*, pp. 62–63. For a more technical discussion of molding and patternmaking, see Richey, *Patternmaking*, pp. 54–63.

18. *Labor Advocate*, January 19, March 23, 1901, February 21, 1902, November 29, 1907. On the national context, see Haydu, "Employers, Unions, and American Exceptionalism," pp. 27–30, 34–41; Haydu, *Between Craft and Class*, pp. 26–49.

19. *International Molders' Journal* 45 (February 1909): 108, and 45 (August 1909): 568–69.

20. *Birmingham Age-Herald*, May 10, 1904; *Bessemer Workman*, May 13, 1904; Stecker, "The Founders, the Molders," pp. 287–91; Fuller, "Tennessee Coal, Iron, and Railroad," pp. 335–60; Fitch, *The Steel Workers*, chap. 16; Rikard, "George Gordon Crawford," pp. 165–71; Brandes, *American Welfare Capitalism*, p. 33; Montgomery, *The Fall of the House of Labor*, pp. 259–75.

21. *Birmingham News*, April 23, 28, 1900, April 16, June 6, 1902; *Labor Advocate*, August 2, 1902; U.S. Immigration Commission, *Immigrants in Industries*, p. 151.

22. The AAISW's constitution allowed the organization of all men employed in steel mills except for laborers. Individual lodges could define laborer as they wished. See Fitch, *The Steel Workers*, pp. 258–59.

23. *Birmingham News*, October 13, 1900; *Labor Advocate*, October 20, 1900; Armes, *Story of Coal and Iron*, p. 469.

24. *Birmingham News*, October 13, 15, 16, 20, 22, 1900; *Ensley Enterprise*, October 20, 27, 1900; *Bessemer Workman*, October 24, 1900.

25. *Birmingham News*, October 30, 31, November 3, 1900; *Arbitrator*, November 9, 1900; *Labor Advocate*, November 10, 1900, March 2, 1901.

26. *Birmingham News*, August 31, September 24, 1900, May 26, 1902.

27. Thompson testimony, U.S. Industrial Commission, *Hearings before the Industrial Commission*, pp. 766–68.

28. *Labor Advocate*, June 21, July 19, 26, August 2, 9, October 25, 1902, February 7, April 4, May 23, June 6, 1903; *Birmingham Age-Herald*, July 23, 1903, August 6, 9, 11, 1904; *Labor Advocate*, May 23, July 25, October 31, 1903. On the policies of the International Association of Machinists toward apprentices and specialists, see Perlman, *The Machinists*, pp. 22–23. For the molders, see Stockton, "Membership in the Molders' Union," pp. 685–86.

29. *Birmingham News*, July 2, 1903. On the national campaign, see Montgomery, *The Fall of the House of Labor*, pp. 269–75.

30. *Labor Advocate*, February 20, 27, October 29, November 5, 1904, November 4, December 5, 1905, March 31, December 22, 1906, January 18, 1907, June 4, 1915.

31. *Labor Advocate*, April 23, August 7, November 5, 1904, February 4, 1905, January 18, 1907; *Birmingham Age-Herald*, August 9, 1904.

32. *Birmingham Age-Herald*, April 16, 1903; *Bessemer Workman*, July 29, 1904.

33. *Bessemer Weekly*, October 24, 1908.

34. Stockton, "The Molders' Union and the Negro," p. 588; *Labor Advocate*, May 7, 1904; Spero and Harris, *The Black Worker*, p. 252.

35. The effect of these hiring policies is discussed at length in Chapter 7.

36. *Labor Advocate*, February 13, May 7, July 2, October 8, November 12, 1904, February 11, 1905, March 31, 1906, December 18, 1908; *Birmingham Age-Herald*, May 10, 1904; *Bessemer Workman*, May 13, 1904; *Birmingham News*, April 5, 1906. According to a government study published in 1913, only one open hearth steel plant in the entire United States recognized unions as representatives of its workers. See U.S. Bureau of Labor, *Labor Conditions*, p. 111.

37. *Labor Advocate*, February 7, May 9, 1903, August 2, 1912, January 8, 1916.

38. *Labor Advocate*, February 7, 14, 28, May 9, 30, August 22, 1903.

39. *Labor Advocate*, August 22, September 6, 19, 26, October 3, 1903, May 7, 1904; *Birmingham News*, September 21, 24, 26, 1903; Alabama Legislature, *General Laws of the Legislature*, pp. 281–82.

40. *Labor Advocate*, February 7, September 6, 26, October 10, 1903, January 16, 1904.

41. *Labor Advocate*, July 4, 1903, February 13, June 25, October 8, November 12, 1904, March 8, May 28, 31, August 9, September 13, 27, October 18, November 1, 29, December 6, 13, 1907, January 3, 1908, February 26, March 26, August 2, 1909, January 24, February 28, April 4, July 25, 1913.

42. *Labor Advocate*, June 12, 1914, June 18, 1915, January 6, 8, June 3, 24, July 8, October 28, 1916, February 24, March 3, 1917; *Birmingham News*, February 21, 1916.

43. Minutes: Executive Committee, Sloss-Sheffield Steel and Iron Company, March 1919, Birmingham Public Library.

44. For a broad perspective on labor-management conflict during World War I, see Montgomery, "Whose Standards?" pp. 113–38; Dubofsky, *Industrialism and the American Worker*, chap. 4; Nelson, *Managers and Workers*, chap. 8; Jacoby, *Employing Bureaucracy*, pp. 133–37; Kennedy, *Over Here*, pp. 258–70.

45. Jacoby, *Employing Bureaucracy*, pp. 140–42; Kennedy, *Over Here*, pp. 259–67; Dubofsky, *Industrialism and the American Worker*, pp. 110–21; Haydu, *Between Craft and Class*, pp. 140–42.

46. Haydu, *Between Craft and Class*, p. 138; Kennedy, *Over Here*, pp. 265–69.

47. Fairley to Kerwin, February 4, 1918; Pierce to the Acting Chief of Ordinance, War Department, April 4, 1918, both in RG 280, National Archives; Norrell, *James Bowron*, p. 228; *Labor Advocate*, March 10, 1917.

48. Berres to Wilson, January 31, 1918; Kerwin to Berres, February 2, 1918, both in RG 280, National Archives.

49. Kerwin to Fairley, January 31, 1918; Fairley to Kerwin, February 4, 1918, both in RG 280, National Archives.

50. Fairley to Kerwin, February 8, 18, 1918; King and Lipscomb to Employers of

Metal Trades Mechanics, February 18, 1918, all in RG 280, National Archives; *Labor Advocate*, February 16, March 3, 1918.

51. *Labor Advocate*, February 16, 23, 1918; Fairley to Kerwin, February 21, 22, 1918, RG 280, National Archives; *Birmingham News*, February 21, 22, 26, 1918; Preliminary Report of the Commissioner of Conciliation, February 27, 1918, RG 280, National Archives; Birdwell to Kerwin, March 3, 1918; King to Fairley, March 4, 12, 1918; King to Gompers, March 12, 1918, all in RG 280, National Archives; *Birmingham News*, March 12, 1918; *Labor Advocate*, March 16, 1918; *Ensley Industrial Record*, March 22, 1918. According to Fairley's reports, the companies involved in the strike were TCI, U.S. Cast Iron Pipe (Bessemer), Hardie-Tynes Machine Company, Kenn Foundry Company, American Casting Company, Sloss-Sheffield Steel and Iron Company, Central Foundry Company, Bessemer Machine and Foundry Company, North Birmingham Furnace Company, Southern Wheel Works, Stockham Pipe and Fittings, and Birmingham Machine and Foundry.

52. *Ensley Industrial Record*, February 22, 1918; *Birmingham News*, February 22, 27, 1918.

53. *Labor Advocate*, March 2, 1918.

54. Fairley to King, April 12, 13, 1918; Wilson to Crawford, April 17, 1918; Crawford to Wilson, April 19, 1918; King to Wilson, April 31, 1918, all in RG 280, National Archives; *Birmingham News*, March 28, April 2, 1918.

55. Kennedy, *Over Here*, pp. 266–67.

56. Rosensohn to Kerwin, April 5, 1918, RG 280, National Archives.

57. Fairley to King, March 12, 1918; Crawford to Wilson, April 19, 1918; King to Fairley, July 16, 1918; Fairley to Wilson, July 25, 1918, all in RG 280, National Archives; Norrell, *James Bowron*, p. 232.

58. King to Morrison, April 11, 1918, RG 280, National Archives; *Birmingham News*, April 9, 10, 12, 1918; *Labor Advocate*, April 13, 1918; Carl Harris, *Political Power in Birmingham*, pp. 200–201.

59. Statements of Leslie, Schweikert, Jefferson, and Scott, March 7, 1918, RG 280, National Archives; Kennedy, *Over Here*, p. 269.

60. Fairley to King, March 12, 1918; Crawford to Wilson, April 19, 1918; King to Fairley, July 16, 1918; Lipscomb to Wilson, July 21, 1918; Fairley to Wilson, July 25, 1918, all in RG 280, National Archives.

61. *Birmingham Reporter*, September 7, 1918.

62. Fairley to Wilson, July 25, 1918; King to Fairley, July 16, 1918, both in RG 280, National Archives; *Labor Advocate*, September 28, 1918; Brody, *Labor in Crisis*, pp. 58–60.

63. Minutes: Executive Committee, Sloss-Sheffield Steel and Iron Company, March 1919, Birmingham Public Library.

64. *Labor Advocate*, January 11, 14, 25, February 1, 1919; Brody, *Labor in Crisis*, pp. 63–68.

65. *Labor Advocate*, July 5, 12, 19, August 16, September 6, 1919.

66. *Labor Advocate*, September 27, October 4, 11, 1919; Brody, *Labor in Crisis*, p. 70.

CHAPTER 7

1. *Birmingham News*, April 16, June 6, 1902, July 31, 1905, April 11, August 10, 1906; Minutes: Board of Directors Meeting, Sloss-Sheffield Steel and Iron Company, February 18, 1908, Birmingham Public Library; Rikard, "An Experiment in Welfare Capitalism," p. 34.

2. U.S. Immigration Commission, *Immigrants in Industries*, p. 255.

3. Ibid., pp. 151–63; Minutes: Board of Directors Meetings, Sloss-Sheffield Steel and Iron Company, 1905–9, Birmingham Public Library; Perkins, *Industrial History of Ensley, Alabama*, pp. 36–39; *Labor Advocate*, April 29, 1899; *Birmingham News*, April 23, 1900, April 16, June 6, 1902, July 31, 1905, April 11, August 10, 29, 1906; oral testimony of Frances Oddo, March 26, 1981, Paul Lorino, April 2, 1981, and Rose Maenza, March 25, 1981, all in the Birmingfind Collection, Birmingham Public Library; Norrell, "Steelworkers and Storekeepers," pp. 2–3; Rikard, "An Experiment in Welfare Capitalism," pp. 15–16, 24–34; Mitchell, "Birmingham," pp. 24–25, 57–58.

My comments on kinship networks are based on oral testimony and limited data collected from World War I draft cards. The cards do not provide information on relatives and where they worked, so I cannot say with certainty that every Lorino or Plaia at TCI was related. Information on origin and residence in Ensley, however, strongly suggests that some, if not all, were relatives.

4. U.S. Immigration Commission, *Immigrants in Industries*, pp. 203–5; Spero and Harris, *The Black Worker*, pp. 246–47; Rikard, "An Experiment in Welfare Capitalism," pp. 116–17; Jacoby, *Employing Bureaucracy*, pp. 49–52, 119–26. Jacoby points out that reformers concerned with turnover probably exaggerated the real costs of retraining. Exactly how much turnover actually cost a company can be debated, but managers at these two companies clearly preferred to retain trained and experienced workers.

5. Speer, *John J. Eagan*, pp. 125–33.

6. Corporate influence on workers' lives outside the workplace is discussed at greater length in Chapter 8.

7. American Cast Iron Pipe Company, *History*, p. 20; Rebecca L. Thomas, "John J. Eagan and Industrial Democracy," pp. 275–76; Rikard, "An Experiment in Welfare Capitalism," pp. 33–34, 53–57, 108–9, 111–16, 139–49, 161–64, 246–47; Rikard, "George Gordon Crawford," pp. 165–73; U.S. Bureau of Labor, *Labor Conditions*, p. 433; Sloss Furnaces National Historic Landmark, "Like It Ain't Never Passed"; Fitch, "The Human Side," pp. 1532–38; Taylor, "Birmingham's Civic Front," p. 1465; Stone, "Origins of Job Structures," pp. 50–53; Lizabeth Cohen, *Making a New Deal*, p. 171. On welfare capitalism as a national movement, see Brandes, *American Welfare Capitalism*.

For material on specific welfare programs at U.S. Steel's Birmingham operations, I have relied heavily upon Marlene Rikard's detailed account of the corporation's health and social work programs. She is one of the few people granted access to corporate records that document the evolution of its employee policies. Despite repeated written and verbal requests, I was unable to obtain permission to review these and other documents that might shed more light on welfarism in Birmingham than the published government documents and contemporary accounts on which my treatment is largely based. ACIPCO, on the other hand, provided me with all the relevant material its public relations office could find.

My interpretation of welfare capitalism in Birmingham differs substantially from that of Thomas and Rikard, both of whom emphasize the humanitarian motives of TCI and ACIPCO officials. The men and women who built these programs undoubtedly wanted to improve the conditions in which workers lived and labored, but welfare capitalism was primarily a critical component of a larger strategy designed to discipline and control employees.

8. *Acipco News*, August 1916; American Cast Iron Pipe Company, *Mutual Benefit Association*; American Cast Iron Pipe Company, *History*, pp. 21–24. Employees at all subsidiary companies were eligible for participation in pension, bonus, and profit-sharing plans. See Fitch, *The Steel Workers*, pp. 207–14, 306–24; Rikard, "George Gordon Crawford," pp. 165–67; Rodgers, *Work Ethic*, pp. 45–50; Lizabeth Cohen, *Making a New Deal*, pp. 175–79.

9. Alexander, "Waste in Hiring and Discharging Men," pp. 1032–33.

10. Hart, *Social Problems of Alabama*, pp. 10–20; Washington, "Negro Race since the Emancipation," pp. 55–56; Thompson testimony, U.S. Industrial Commission, *Hearings before the Industrial Commission*, pp. 766–67.

11. Testimony of Gardner, Lapsley, and Armstrong, U.S. Senate, *Labor and Capital*, pp. 71–72, 167, 211; *Birmingham Daily News*, August 19, 1894; *Labor Advocate*, December 23, 1899; *Birmingham News*, February 22, March 8, 1902; Murphy, *Problems of the Present South*, p. 139; Carlton, *Mill and Town*, pp. 264–65; Grantham, *Southern Progressivism*, pp. 246–59; Jacoby, *Employing Bureaucracy*, pp. 66–69.

12. Hazard testimony, U.S. Senate, *Labor and Capital*, p. 473; *Birmingham Iron Age*, August 9, 1883; *Birmingham Age-Herald*, February 25, March 18, 1890; Anderson, *Education of Blacks*, pp. 95–96.

13. Du Bois, "The Economic Revolution," p. 109; Baldwin as quoted in Anderson, *Education of Blacks*, p. 91; testimony of Thompson and Coffin, U.S. Industrial Commission, *Hearings before the Industrial Commission*, pp. 766–67, 781.

14. Thompson testimony, U.S. Industrial Commission, *Hearings before the Industrial Commission*, p. 766.

15. *Birmingham Age-Herald*, March 31, 1890.

16. *Birmingham News*, January 2, February 3, 10, 15, September 20, 1902; Thompson testimony, U.S. Industrial Commission, *Hearings before the Industrial Commission*, p. 766; Murphy, *Basis of Ascendancy*, pp. xv–9, 164–65; Riley, *The White Man's Burden*, pp. 193–205; *Labor Advocate*, December 23, 1899; Washington, "The Atlanta Exposition Address," pp. 67–75; *Birmingham News*, January 2, 1902; Du Bois, "The Economic Revolution," p. 109; Bond, *Negro Education in Alabama*, p. 145; Anderson, "Education as a Vehicle," pp. 15–40. For a thorough analysis of Washington's philosophy and of the movement for creation of training schools for blacks, see Anderson, *Education of Blacks*, chaps. 2 and 4; on education and the race problem, see chap. 3. Anderson's understanding of Murphy's philosophy differs somewhat from my own. I agree with his argument that Murphy saw no place for blacks in the southern power structure, but, given Murphy's remarks in *Basis of Ascendancy*, I do not understand Anderson's conclusion that he

saw education as a way of "arresting the upward and downward momentum of blacks." Education was essential to the subordination of blacks, as earlier chapters of this work have, I think, shown. Anderson is correct in his assertion that Murphy did not promote the complete destruction of the racial caste system; whites of his own class would continue their economic and political ascendancy. But there can be little doubt that Murphy advocated an end of special economic privileges for much of the white working class. The best analysis of the ideas of progressives like Murphy remains Fredrickson, *Black Image*, pp. 294–97.

17. *Acipco News*, January, February 1916, September 1918, July 1919; *Birmingham News*, July 31, 1909, October 12, 1912; Bond, *Negro Education in Alabama*, pp. 144–46, 241; Carl V. Harris, "Stability and Change," pp. 387–88.

18. Carl V. Harris, "Stability and Change," pp. 380, 387–88, 403–5; *Christian Hope*, March 7, 1902; *Truth*, September 9, 1905; *Birmingham Reporter*, November 13, 1915.

Throughout rural Alabama, the state, with the assistance of the Anna T. Jeanes Foundation, established industrial schools to teach young blacks skills they would need to meet the demands of employers in Birmingham and other industrial centers. See Alabama Department of Education, *Supervising Industrial Teachers*, p. 1; Anderson, *Education of Blacks*, p. 137; Grantham, *Southern Progressivism*, p. 261.

19. Rikard, "An Experiment in Welfare Capitalism," pp. 246–47; *Acipco News*, February, November 1916, May, October 1917.

20. U.S. Department of Commerce, Bureau of the Census, *Thirteenth Census of the United States*.

21. Registrants were between the ages of eighteen and forty. The age bias here undoubtedly produces some inflation of figures for semiskilled and unskilled workers. Still, the draft cards provide the only sources currently available for comparative analysis of racial hiring patterns at the firm level. None of the anecdotal evidence relevant to this issue or general statistics in the published census contradict these findings.

22. Manuscript Census, Jefferson County, 1900; U.S. Department of Commerce, Bureau of the Census, *Thirteenth Census of the United States*; *Birmingham Reporter*, June 23, 1917. On increased black movement into skilled positions during the early years of the twentieth century, see Worthman, "Working Class Mobility," p. 196; Greene and Woodson, *The Negro Wage Earner*, pp. 135–38; and Reich, *Racial Inequality*, pp. 244–50.

23. The best statement of this argument can be found in Gordon, Edwards, and Reich, *Segmented Work, Divided Workers*, chap. 4.

24. Fitch, *The Steel Workers*, p. 142; Stone, "Origins of Job Structures," p. 41; Norrell, "Caste in Steel." Several employees of the U.S. Steel Corporation, who will remain anonymous, contributed to my understanding of the workings of this system in Birmingham. They also helped me determine the skill level of a number of occupations.

Gavin Wright suggests that black representation in some skilled trades at TCI was "heavy." The evidence presented here gives cause for questioning that conclusion. He is correct in his assertion that blacks held a significant proportion of semiskilled jobs, but it bears repeating that few semiskilled blacks were found in the same jobs whites held. As Wright later states, northern-based steel firms tended to adopt the racial patterns of the locality. See Wright, *Old South, New South*, pp. 194, 265.

25. ACIPCO was the one company that granted me access to personnel records. Analysis

of a sample of employment cards for the period 1912 to 1920 reinforces the conclusions discussed here. I rely on the figures from the draft card analysis in my comments about ACIPCO, because I am comparing it to other companies whose personnel records are not available.

Will Prather described segregation at Sloss (p. 3) in an interview in "Like It Ain't Never Passed," a pamphlet available at the Sloss Furnaces National Historic Landmark. I am grateful to the late Randall Lawrence, director of the Sloss museum in Birmingham, for bringing this collection to my attention.

26. U.S. Immigration Commission, *Immigrants in Industries*, pp. 152, 191, 205.

27. There was clearly no dramatic transformation of race relations in industry, but workers perceived a trend away from past practice that was real. As Pierre L. van den Berghe has argued, while "racial criteria of selection" are not necessarily absent in a competitive racial order, the closing of the "status gap" between members of an "upper caste" and members of a "lower caste" generates anxiety among those who feel threatened ("Paternalistic versus Competitive Race Relations," pp. 27–28).

28. Some labor historians cite such strategies as evidence that workers, having recognized common class exploitation, began to bridge racial divisions. For an example, see Gordon, Edwards, and Reich, *Segmented Work, Divided Workers*, pp. 152–53. A much more subtle and sophisticated view can be found in Wright, *Old South, New South*, pp. 192–94.

29. *Labor Advocate*, June 29, 1895, April 13, 1901, May 9, 1903.

30. *Labor Advocate*, June 29, 1895; *Arbitrator*, January 4, 1900.

31. Worthman, "Black Workers and Labor Unions," pp. 72–73, 80–84; Stockton, "The Molders' Union and the Negro," p. 588; *Labor Advocate*, May 7, 1904; Philip S. Foner, *Organized Labor*, pp. 73–74, 87–88, 92–93.

32. *International Molders' Journal* 47 (May 1911): 379, and 51 (August 1915): 543–44; Stockton, "The Molders' Union and the Negro," p. 588; *Labor Advocate*, April 30, 1915; Washington, "Negro and the Labor Unions," pp. 765–66.

33. Harper, "Hobbies, Pets and Children," pp. 1–12, Southern Historical Collection.

34. *Labor Advocate*, April 30, 1915, July 8, 1916.

35. *Labor Advocate*, September 25, 1897.

36. *Birmingham News*, March 12, 22, 1918; *Ensley Industrial Record*, March 22, 1918. Stanley Greenberg argues that tactics such as these were unnecessary, because "artisans" in Birmingham perceived little threat from the unskilled (*Race and State*, pp. 341–42).

37. *Ensley Industrial Record*, March 22, 1918; *Birmingham News*, April 23, 1918; Spero and Harris, *The Black Worker*, p. 248; Taft, *Organizing Dixie*, pp. 49–50.

38. *Labor Advocate*, May 7, 1904; *Birmingham Hot Shots*, September 18, 1908; *Labor Advocate*, January 24, 1913; *Birmingham Workmen's Chronicle*, January 12, March 9, 1918; *Birmingham Reporter*, May 5, 12, June 2, 23, July 14, August 18, 1917, August 10, 16, 1918; Reich, *Racial Inequality*, pp. 244–50; Worthman, "Black Workers and Labor Unions," p. 73.

39. *Birmingham Reporter*, May 5, 12, June 2, 23, 1917; see *Labor Advocate*, July 1, 1916, for an example of its criticism of the *Reporter*.

40. *Acipco News*, July, August 1917; *Birmingham Reporter*, August 5, September 30, November 18, 1916. Carole Marks argues that blacks in the South were experiencing

declining opportunities in industry during this period (*Farewell—We're Good and Gone*, pp. 60–67). While this might have been the case when figures for the entire South are compiled, my data indicates that relative to the years before 1900 Birmingham's blacks were doing better.

41. *Acipco News*, June, November 1919, July 1920.

42. *Acipco News*, September 1920.

43. Silver to Dickinson, 1922, Welfare Department General File, American Cast Iron Pipe Company.

44. Notes, 1920–22, Eagan Papers, Atlanta Historical Society; draft of an unidentified and untitled speech, 1921, Eagan Papers, Atlanta Historical Society; Speer, *John J. Eagan*, pp. 142–43; Rebecca L. Thomas, "John J. Eagan and Industrial Democracy," pp. 279–83.

45. Speer, *John J. Eagan*, pp. 142–43; Zahavi, "Negotiated Loyalty," pp. 606–7.

46. Notes, 1920–22, Eagan Papers, Atlanta Historical Society; draft of an unidentified and untitled speech, 1921, Eagan Papers, Atlanta Historical Society; Speer, *John J. Eagan*, pp. 142–43; Myers, "Report and Recommendations," February 27, 1922, Eagan Papers, Atlanta Historical Society. In "John J. Eagan and Industrial Democracy," Rebecca Thomas fails to assess critically the implementation of Eagan's plan. She essentially repeats company-generated praise for Eagan's approach to management. Many workers saw matters differently.

47. Annual Report, Board of Operatives, April 2, 1923, Eagan Papers, Atlanta Historical Society; "Questionnaire concerning the best way to insure progress of the Plan," n.d., Eagan Papers, Atlanta Historical Society; Ware, "Field Experience," pp. 23–28.

48. Myers, "Report and Recommendations," February 27, 1922, pp. 4–5, Eagan Papers, Atlanta Historical Society; Ware, "Field Experience," p. 28. The latter is an account of Ware's experiences during several months of employment at ACIPCO. Although his report covered a period later than 1920, the men with whom he worked had been employed at the company for some time and "taught" him practices that appeared to have been common at the plant for some time.

CHAPTER 8

1. Norrell, *James Bowron*, pp. 186–87; Armes, *Story of Coal and Iron*, pp. 396–97.

2. White, *Village Creek*, pp. 45–46. Residences of workers in Ensley for the period before 1910–11 could not be plotted because there was no city directory available, and the Birmingham directories did not include Ensley. My conclusions about residential patterns there are based on data collected from World War I draft records.

3. U.S. Immigration Commission, *Immigrants in Industries*, pp. 187, 230–33; U.S. Bureau of Labor, *Iron and Steel Industry*, p. 435; Will Prather interview in "Like It Ain't Never Passed," p. 3; White, *Village Creek*, pp. 67–68.

4. U.S. Immigration Commission, *Immigrants in Industries*, pp. 187, 207–11, 229–33; U.S. Bureau of Labor, *Labor Conditions*, pp. 443–44; Frances Oddo interview, March 26, 1981, Birmingfind Collection, Birmingham Public Library; Fitch as quoted in Kulik, "Sloss Furnace Company," pp. 42–43.

5. "The Italians," Birmingfind Collection, Birmingham Public Library; U.S. Immi-

gration Commission, *Immigrants in Industries*, pp. 192, 229–32; Frances Oddo interview, March 26, 1981; Will Battle interview, May 21, 1981, both in Birmingfind Collection, Birmingham Public Library.

6. U.S. Immigration Commission, *Immigrants in Industries*, pp. 230–31.

7. Ibid., pp. 208, 229–32; U.S. Bureau of Labor, *Labor Conditions*, p. 443.

8. White, *Village Creek*, p. 62.

9. *Cost of Living*, p. 95; Will Battle interview, May 21, 1981, Birmingfind Collection, Birmingham Public Library; Will Prather interview in "Like It Ain't Never Passed," p. 3; Birmingham City Directories, 1883–84, 1888, 1903; World War I Draft Records, Jefferson County; White, *Village Creek*, pp. 58–60; Worthman, "Working Class Mobility," pp. 201, 204–5.

10. Rikard, "An Experiment in Welfare Capitalism," p. 113; Myers to Eagan, February 27, 1922, Eagan Papers, Atlanta Historical Society; American Cast Iron Pipe Company, *ACIPCO*, p. 19.

11. *Acipco News*, November 1915.

12. Originally the development was to be named Corey. A few years later the name of the town was changed to Fairfield. I have chosen to use Fairfield throughout to avoid confusion.

13. George H. Miller, "Corey—The Model Industrial City," p. 7; George H. Miller, "Corey—The Physical Plan," p. 27; *Ensley Industrial Record*, September 28, 1917; Wiebel, *Biography of a Business*, pp. 41–60; White, *Village Creek*, p. 67.

14. George H. Miller, "Corey—The Physical Plan," pp. 24–27; "Corey—The Model Industrial City," p. 6; George H. Miller, "The Wage-Earners' Home," pp. 37–38.

15. George H. Miller, "The Wage-Earners' Home," pp. 37–40.

16. Ibid., pp. 37–39, 41. For a suggestive discussion of the relationship between consumerism and the degradation of work, see Ewen, *Captains of Consciousness*, chap. 5. Aileen Kraditor argues that one reason working people during this period were not responsive to the appeals of radicals was their attitude that work was something to be endured if one hoped to build a comfortable life away from work. Her point is well taken, but her explanation of the origins of what we might call "instrumentalism" overlooks the role of employers and reformers in its promotion. The evidence here suggests that some employers did not assume that, as Kraditor argues, "John Q. Worker" saw work as "merely instrumental to the private-sphere relationships and activities that were of paramount significance to him" (*The Radical Persuasion*, p. 313).

17. Hart, *Social Problems of Alabama*, pp. 83–84.

18. Rikard, "An Experiment in Welfare Capitalism," pp. 139, 166–71, 249–50; *Acipco News*, December 1916, June 1918.

19. *Acipco News*, January, July, October 1916, June 1917, August 1918; Richard Gaines interview in Sloss Furnaces National Historic Landmark, "We've Come This Far by Faith," p. 18. For a discussion of team sports as a way to instill a spirit of cooperation, see Gelber, "Working at Playing," pp. 9–12. On sports in the rural South, see Ownby, *Subduing Satan*.

20. *Acipco News*, April 1918, July 1920.

21. U.S. Immigration Commission, *Immigrants in Industries*, pp. 207–11; Manuscript Census, Jefferson County, 1910.

22. "The Italians," Birmingfind Collection, Birmingham Public Library; Paul Lorino interview, April 2, 1981, Birmingfind Collection, Birmingham Public Library; *Labor Advocate*, March 5, 1898, August 2, 1902, August 12, 1910, February 24, 1917; *Weekly Voice*, July 15, 1916.

23. *Birmingham Reporter*, October 28, 1916; Bessie Sears Estell interview, May 22, 1981, Birmingfind Collection, Birmingham Public Library.

24. *Acipco News*, April 1920.

25. Lorino, Maenza, and Oddo interviews, Birmingfind Collection, Birmingham Public Library; "The Italians," Birmingfind Collection, Birmingham Public Library; U.S. Immigration Commission, *Immigrants in Industries*, p. 264.

26. Stanley, "Birmingham in 1901," p. 15.

27. *Independent*, October 15, 1898; *Birmingham News*, December 28, 1903, August 15, 1906; Carl Harris, *Political Power in Birmingham*, pp. 189–92.

28. *Birmingham News*, September 11, 18, October 1, 3, 23, 1907; Carl Harris, *Political Power in Birmingham*, pp. 193–94.

29. *Labor Advocate*, September 27, October 1, 11, 1907; *Bessemer Journal*, October 3, 1907; *Birmingham News*, October 4, 8, 14, 16, 17, 19, 23, 1907; *Birmingham Age-Herald*, October 12, 13, 1907; Sellers, *The Prohibition Movement in Alabama*, pp. 101–10; Carl Harris, *Political Power in Birmingham*, pp. 192–94.

30. *Birmingham News*, September 18, October 5, 14, 21, 1907; Norrell, *James Bowron*, pp. 177–78.

31. *Labor Advocate*, August 30, October 11, 1907; *Birmingham News*, October 8, 1907; *Birmingham Age-Herald*, October 12, 1907.

32. *Birmingham News*, October 29, 1907; Carl Harris, *Political Power in Birmingham*, p. 194.

33. *Birmingham News*, October 29, 1907.

34. *Cost of Living*, p. 96.

35. *Labor Advocate*, August 6, 1909; Sellers, *The Prohibition Movement in Alabama*, pp. 130–33.

36. *Labor Advocate*, September 24, 1909; Sellers, *The Prohibition Movement in Alabama*, pp. 135–36.

37. *Labor Advocate*, October 22, 1909.

38. *Labor Advocate*, October 29, 1909.

39. *Labor Advocate*, August 6, September 17, 24, October 22, 29, November 26, 1909; *Birmingham News*, July 29, August 6, September 6, 16, 17, November 26, 30, 1909; Sellers, *The Prohibition Movement in Alabama*, pp. 144–45; Grantham, *Southern Progressivism*, p. 167.

40. Sellers, *The Prohibition Movement in Alabama*, pp. 170–74.

41. The importance of the saloon as a center of working-class sociability waned across the nation during this period. See Powers, "Decay from Within," pp. 116–25; Duis, *The Saloon*, pp. 292–93.

42. *Birmingham News*, February 2, 5, 1915.

43. *Birmingham News*, February 7, 1915.

44. *Birmingham News*, February 9, 1915.

45. *Birmingham News*, February 9, March 10, 1915; *Birmingham Age-Herald*, February 10, 1918; *Labor Advocate*, February 12, March 5, July 23, 1915.

46. *Birmingham News*, December 1, 22, 23, 24, 1915; *Birmingham Age-Herald*, December 23, 24, 1915; *Labor Advocate*, December 3, 24, 1915.

47. *Birmingham News*, February 20, 1918; *Birmingham Age-Herald*, February 24, 1918; *Labor Advocate*, February 23, 1918.

48. *Birmingham Age-Herald*, May 6, 7, 8, 1918; *Labor Advocate*, May 11, 18, 1918.

CHAPTER 9

1. Edwards, *Contested Terrain*, pp. 65–67; Wiener, *Social Origins*, p. 223; C. Vann Woodward, *Origins of the New South*, pp. 382–87; Grantham, *Southern Progressivism*, pp. 150–57.

2. *Labor Advocate*, January 8, 22, 1898.

3. On the 1894 strike and Comer's role in it, see McKiven, "A Community in Crisis," pp. 10–35.

4. *Labor Advocate*, May 4, 1899; Flynt, *Mine, Mill, and Microchip*, pp. 94–104.

5. *Labor Advocate*, April 21, November 17, 1900, May 25, June 1, 1901.

6. *Labor Advocate*, October 1, 29, November 19, 26, 1898, March 4, September 30, October 28, 1899, February 2, 1902. Information on the early years of the child labor campaign, and the role of Birmingham labor organizations in it, can be found in correspondence between R. A. Mitchell, an agent for the Dwight Manufacturing Company of Boston, Massachusetts, and J. Howard Nichols, the treasurer of the company. Dwight operated a plant in Alabama City, Alabama. Mitchell had insisted upon the repeal of the child labor statute in 1894 before his company would agree to build in Alabama City. See Mitchell to Nichols, December 10 and 26, 1898, copy in possession of the author.

7. *Birmingham Daily News*, June 29, 1892; *Labor Advocate*, November 30, 1901; Murphy, *Problems of the Present South*, pp. 106–17, 114. For a suggestive discussion of opposition to child labor and compulsory education legislation in South Carolina, see Carlton, *Mill and Town*, pp. 232–35.

8. *Labor Advocate*, April 13, October 12, 26, 1901; *Birmingham News*, October 7, 12, 15, 18, November 12, 1901, June 2, 1902.

9. *Labor Advocate*, January 18, 19, March 3, April 7, 1900, January 26, 1901. On the AFL and politics, see Laurie, *Artisans into Workers*, p. 218.

10. *Labor Advocate*, February 28, March 15, April 5, 28, May 31, July 22, 26, 28, August 2, 16, 26, 30, 1902; Hackney, *Populism to Progressivism in Alabama*, p. 240. According to most accounts, organized labor joined the Comer coalition in an attack on corporate privilege. Clearly, though, labor organizations in Birmingham were ambivalent about the campaign to regulate freight rates and were always hostile toward Comer. There is little evidence that labor leaders considered Comer's crusade a general attack on the power of corporations. To them "Comerism" was synonymous with defense of corporate exploitation. See C. Vann Woodward, *Origins of the New South*, pp. 375–76, 382–84; Grantham, *Southern Progressivism*, pp. 48–49.

11. *Labor Advocate*, August 22, 1903.

12. See Chapter 4 on the Citizens' Alliance. *Labor Advocate*, February 4, 1905, April 6, 1906.

13. *Labor Advocate*, November 7, December 19, 1903, January 7, October 14, December 5, 9, 1905, February 10, April 6, August 18, 1906, November 15, 1907, February 28, April 24, 1908, June 25, July 16, 30, 1909.

14. *Birmingham News*, August 17, 25, 29, 1906; *Labor Advocate*, August 25, 1906.

15. *Labor Advocate*, October 1, 1907, May 27, 1910; *Birmingham News*, September 30, October 1, 1907; Mitchell, "Birmingham," pp. 90–93; Hays, "Politics of Reform," pp. 234–56.

16. *Birmingham News*, June 13, October 23, 24, 1907, December 7, 1908; *Labor Advocate*, December 11, 1908; Mitchell, "Birmingham," pp. 97–98; La Monte, *George B. Ward*, p. 34.

17. *Birmingham News*, January 8, 19, July 26, 1909.

18. *Labor Advocate*, January 8, 1909; *Birmingham News*, July 28, 1909.

19. *Labor Advocate*, March 25, 1910; Carl Harris, *Political Power in Birmingham*, pp. 83–84.

20. Alabama House of Representatives, *House Journal, 1911*, p. 1714; *Birmingham News*, January 13, 17, 24, 26, February 1, 7, 17, 24, March 3, 6, 12, 1911; *Labor Advocate*, March 25, 1910, January 27, February 17, 1911; Carl Harris, *Political Power in Birmingham*, pp. 83–84. Harris provides a more complete account of the debate over the commission, focusing on ethnocultural divisions.

21. *Labor Advocate*, May 23, June 6, 20, July 11, 1913.

22. *Labor Advocate*, June 20, August 29, 1913.

23. *Birmingham News*, June 18, 1913, July 6, 1913; *Labor Advocate*, June 20, 1913.

24. *Labor Advocate*, May 23, June 20, July 6, 1913.

25. *Labor Advocate*, June 6, 1913; *Birmingham News*, June 16, July 13, 1913.

26. *Labor Advocate*, September 5, August 8, 29, 1913; *Birmingham News*, July 13, 28, August 5, September 16, 1913.

27. *Birmingham News*, September 16, 1913.

28. *Birmingham Age-Herald*, October 16, 1915; *Birmingham News*, October 16, 17, 1915; *Labor Advocate*, November 5, December 10, 17, 1915.

29. *Labor Advocate*, January 20, February 3, 10, April 21, 1917.

30. On race relations in the workplace, see Chapter 4. For some enlightening observations concerning the relationship between increased economic competition and intensification of concern about political and social white supremacy, see Fredrickson, *White Supremacy*, pp. 225–27.

The author of a recent article about this election makes the assertion that white workers blamed their plight on blacks and immigrants. This was true, but his failure to explain the corporate policies that generated such anxieties leaves one with the impression that their fears were irrational. Indeed, as I have indicated in Chapter 4, white fears of losing privileges in the workplace to immigrants or blacks might have been exaggerated, but they certainly had a basis in reality. Their powers of analysis, in short, were not as poorly developed as some historians suggest. See Eskew, "Demagoguery in Birmingham," pp. 197–201.

31. *Labor Advocate*, January 20, February 3, 10, April 21, September 22, 1917.

32. *Birmingham News*, September 8, 9, 19, 25, 1917; *Birmingham Reporter*, October 13, 1917; Hamilton, *Hugo Black*, pp. 71–79.

33. *Labor Advocate*, August 14, 1914, October 13, 1917; Carl Harris, *Political Power in Birmingham*, p. 86.

34. *Labor Advocate*, October 13, 1917.

35. Carl Harris, *Political Power in Birmingham*, pp. 86–89.

36. *Labor Advocate*, April 26, May 10, 1919; Carl Harris, *Political Power in Birmingham*, p. 88.

37. Atkins, "Feuds, Factions, and Reform," p. 29; Tindall, *Emergence of the New South*, pp. 19–23, 246. On the Klan in Birmingham, see Snell, "Masked Men in the Magic City." For some perceptive remarks on why working people, particularly nonunion workers, found the Klan attractive, see Jackson, *The Ku Klux Klan in the City*, pp. 244–46.

38. Mangum to Underwood, January 28, 1920; Gunn to Hooper, January 17, 1920, both in Underwood Papers, Alabama Department of Archives and History; Hamilton, *Hugo Black*, pp. 74–75, 99; Tindall, *Emergence of the New South*, pp. 190–91, 242; Grantham, *Southern Progressivism*, pp. 414–16; Flynt, "Organized Labor."

39. As quoted in Flynt, "Organized Labor," pp. 178–79.

CONCLUSION

1. Roediger, *The Wages of Whiteness*. See also Walker, *Deromanticizing Black History*.

2. Stein, "Southern Workers in National Unions," pp. 183–222.

3. Norrell, "Caste in Steel." The policies of organized labor in Birmingham were not exceptional. On the larger context, see Hill, "Race, Ethnicity and Organized Labor."

4. King, *Why We Can't Wait*, pp. 48–49.

BIBLIOGRAPHY

NEWSPAPERS

Bessemer Journal
Bessemer Weekly
Bessemer Workman
Birmingham Advance
Birmingham Age
Birmingham Age-Herald
Birmingham Daily News
Birmingham Iron Age
Birmingham News
Birmingham Reporter
Birmingham State Herald
Birmingham Weekly Iron Age
Birmingham Weekly Review
Birmingham Workmen's Chronicle
Christian Hope
Ensley Industrial Record
Independent
People's Daily Tribune
Truth
Warrior Index

GOVERNMENT DOCUMENTS

United States

Bureau of Labor. *Labor Conditions in the Iron and Steel Industry.* Washington, D.C.:
    Government Printing Office, 1911–13.
——— . *Report on Conditions of Employment in the Iron and Steel Industry.* Washington,
    D.C.: Government Printing Office, 1911–13.
Department of Commerce, Bureau of the Census. *Fourteenth Census of the United States:
    Manufactures.* Washington, D.C.: Government Printing Office, 1923.
——— . *Religious Bodies: 1906.* Washington, D.C.: Government Printing Office, 1907.
——— . *Thirteenth Census of the United States, 1910.* Vol. 4, *Population Occupation Statis-
    tics.* Washington, D.C.: Government Printing Office, 1911.
Department of Commerce and Labor. *Sixth Annual Report.* Washington, D.C.: Govern-
    ment Printing Office, 1890.

Department of the Interior, Bureau of the Census. *Twelfth Census of the United States: Manufactures.* Washington, D.C.: Government Printing Office, 1902.

Department of the Interior, Census Office. *Statistics of Iron and Steel Production of the United States.* Washington, D.C.: Government Printing Office, 1883.

Immigration Commission. *Immigrants in Industries.* Vol. 2, pt. 2, *Iron and Steel Manufacturing.* Washington, D.C.: Government Printing Office, 1911.

Industrial Commission. *Hearings before the Industrial Commission: Conditions of Capital and Labor.* Washington, D.C.: Government Printing Office, 1901.

―――. *Report of the Industrial Commission on Agriculture and Agricultural Labor.* Washington, D.C.: Government Printing Office, 1901.

Senate. *Report of the Committee of the Senate upon Relations between Labor and Capital.* Washington, D.C.: Government Printing Office, 1885.

―――. *Report on Conditions of Employment in the Iron and Steel Industry in the United States.* 4 vols. Washington, D.C.: Government Printing Office, 1911–13.

Great Britain

Cost of Living in American Towns. London: His Majesty's Stationery Office, 1911.

Alabama

Acts of Alabama, 1880–90.

Department of Education. *The Work of the Jeanes Supervising Industrial Teachers.* Montgomery: Brown Printing, 1912.

General Laws of the Legislature Passed at the Session of 1903. Montgomery: Brown Printing, 1903.

House and Senate Journals, 1900–1920.

Milner, John T. *Alabama: As It Was, as It Is, and as It Will Be.* Montgomery: Barrett and Brown, 1876.

Tait, James L. *Report of the Commissioner of Industrial Resources to the Governor.* Montgomery: W. W. Screws, 1871.

MANUSCRIPTS

Alabama Department of Archives and History, Montgomery
   Thomas Goode Jones Papers
   Robert McKee Papers
   Milner Family Papers
   Minutes of the Birmingham Baptist Association, 1890–1910
   Minutes of the Birmingham Presbytery of the Cumberland Presbyterian Church, 1890–1910
   Minutes of the Presbyterian Church, U.S.A., 1890–1910
   Oscar W. Underwood Papers
American Cast Iron Pipe Company, Birmingham
   Personnel Records, 1903–20
   Welfare Department General File, 1915–25

Atlanta Historical Society
    John Eagan Papers
Birmingham Public Library
    Birmingfind Collection
    Birmingham City Directories, 1884–1920
    Diary of Julia Ward London
    Minutes of the Board of Directors Meetings, Sloss-Sheffield Steel and Iron Com-
        pany, 1905–19
    Personnel Cards, Woodward Iron Company, 1915–25
    Records of Knights of Pythias Lodge 85, 1896–98
    "Reminiscences of Julius C. Greene"
Livingston University, Livingston, Alabama
    Ruby Pickens Tartt Collection
National Archives, Southeastern Branch, East Point, Georgia
    Manuscript Census Schedules, Jefferson County, 1880, 1900, 1910, 1920
    World War I Draft Registration Cards, 1917–18, Record Group 147.
National Archives, Washington, D.C.
    Records of the Commissioner of Conciliation, 1918–19, Record Group 280.
Sloss Furnaces National Historic Landmark, Birmingham
    "Like It Ain't Never Passed: Remembering Life in Sloss Quarters"
    "We've Come This Far by Faith"
Southern Historical Collection, University of North Carolina, Chapel Hill
    Federal Writers' Project Papers
    Edward F. Harper, "Hobbies, Pets and Children"

COMPANY PUBLICATIONS

Acipco News, 1915–21
American Cast Iron Pipe Company. ACIPCO: *A Story of Modern Industrial Relations*.
    Birmingham: ACIPCO Publications, 1920.
——— . ACIPCO *Mutual Benefit Association Constitution and By-Laws*. Birmingham:
    ACIPCO Publications, 1923.
——— . *History of the American Cast Iron Pipe Company*. N.p., n.d.
——— . *People and Pipe*. Birmingham: ACIPCO Publications, 1955.
Caldwell, H. M. *History of the Elyton Land Company and Birmingham*. Birmingham:
    Elyton Land Company, 1892.
Miller, George H. "Corey—The Model Industrial City." *Jemison Magazine*, May 1910,
    pp. 6–7.
——— . "Corey—The Physical Plan." *Jemison Magazine*, March 1911, pp. 23–30.
——— . "The Wage-Earners' Home." *Jemison Magazine*, November 1911, pp. 37–41.
Speer, Robert E. *John J. Eagan: A Memoir of an Adventurer for the Kingdom of God on
    Earth*. Birmingham: ACIPCO Publications, 1939.
Tennessee Coal, Iron, and Railroad Company. *Annual Report*. Nashville: TCI, 1880,
    1888.

U.S. Steel. *Steel Making at Birmingham*. Fairfield, Ala.: TCI Division, U.S. Steel, 1954.

Wiebel, A. V. *Biography of a Business*. Birmingham: TCI Division, U.S. Steel, 1960.

LABOR PUBLICATIONS

Alabama Sentinel

Amalgamated Association of Iron and Steel Workers, *Journal of Proceedings*, 1889–1904

Arbitrator

Birmingham Labor Advocate

Iron Molders' Journal

Journal of United Labor

Labor Union

National Labor Tribune

Striking Machinist

Tariff and Labor Advocate

BOOKS

Anderson, James D. *The Education of Blacks in the South, 1860–1935*. Chapel Hill: University of North Carolina Press, 1988.

Armes, Ethel. *The Story of Coal and Iron in Alabama*. 1910. Reprint. Leeds, Ala.: Beechwood Books, 1987.

Arnesen, Eric. *Waterfront Workers of New Orleans: Race, Class, and Politics, 1863–1923*. New York: Oxford University Press, 1991.

Ayers, Edward L. *Vengeance and Justice: Crime and Punishment in the Nineteenth-Century American South*. New York: Oxford University Press, 1984.

Barefield, Marilyn Davis, ed. *Bessemer, Yesterday and Today, 1887–1888*. Birmingham: Southern University Press, 1986.

Barger, Harold, and Sam Schurr. *The Mining Industries, 1899–1939: A Study of Output, Employment and Productivity*. New York: Arno Press, 1975.

Bennett, James R. *Old Tannehill: A History of the Pioneer Iron Works in Roupes Valley*. Birmingham: Jefferson County Historical Commission, 1986.

Blassingame, John. *The Slave Community: Plantation Life in the Antebellum South*. New York: Oxford University Press, 1972.

Blumin, Stuart M. *The Emergence of the Middle Class: Social Experience in the American City, 1760–1900*. Cambridge: Cambridge University Press, 1989.

Bombhart, John Martin. *History of Walker County: Its Towns and Its People*. Thornton, Ark.: Cayce Publishing, 1937.

Bond, Horace Mann. *Negro Education in Alabama: A Study in Cotton and Steel*. Washington, D.C.: Associated Publishers, 1939.

Brandes, Stuart D. *American Welfare Capitalism, 1880–1940*. Chicago: University of Chicago Press, 1976.

Brody, David. *Labor in Crisis: The Steel Strike of 1919*. Philadelphia: J. B. Lippincott, 1965.

————. *Steelworkers in America: The Nonunion Era*. Cambridge: Harvard University Press, 1960.

Brooks, Charles H. *The Official History and Manual of the Grand United Order of Odd Fellows in America*. Philadelphia: Odd Fellows Journal, n.d.

Brown, James Seay. *Up before Daylight: Life Histories from the Alabama Writers' Project, 1938–1939*. Tuscaloosa: University of Alabama Press, 1982.

Carlton, David L. *Mill and Town in South Carolina, 1880–1920*. Baton Rouge: Louisiana State University Press, 1982.

Carnes, Mark C. *Secret Ritual and Manhood in Victorian America*. New Haven: Yale University Press, 1989.

Chapman, H. H. *The Iron and Steel Industries of the South*. Tuscaloosa: University of Alabama Press, 1953.

Clawson, Mary Ann. *Constructing Brotherhood: Class, Gender, and Fraternalism*. Princeton: Princeton University Press, 1989.

Cohen, Lizabeth. *Making a New Deal: Industrial Workers in Chicago, 1919–1939*. Cambridge: Cambridge University Press, 1990.

Cohen, William. *At Freedom's Edge: Black Mobility and the Southern White Quest for Racial Control*. Baton Rouge: Louisiana State University Press, 1991.

Conkin, Paul K. *Prophets of Prosperity: America's First Political Economists*. Bloomington: Indiana University Press, 1980.

Couvares, Francis. *The Remaking of Pittsburgh: Class and Culture in an Industrializing City, 1877–1917*. Albany: State University of New York Press, 1984.

Cruikshank, George M. *A History of Birmingham and Its Environs*. Chicago: Lewis Publishing, 1920.

Davis, James J. *The Iron Puddler: My Life in the Rolling Mills and What Came of It*. New York: Grossett, Dunlap, 1922.

Dawley, Alan. *Class and Community: The Industrial Revolution in Lynn*. Cambridge: Harvard University Press, 1976.

Dodd, Donald B., and Wynelle S. Dodd. *Winston: An Antebellum and Civil War History of a Hill County of North Alabama*. Birmingham: Oxmoor Press, 1972.

Donaldson, Paschal. *The Odd-Fellow's Text-Book*. Philadelphia: Moss and Brother, 1854.

Doster, James F. *Railroads in Alabama Politics, 1875–1914*. Tuscaloosa: University of Alabama Press, 1957.

Doyle, Don Harrison. *The Social Order of a Frontier Community: Jacksonville, Illinois, 1825–70*. Urbana: University of Illinois Press, 1976.

Dubofsky, Melvyn. *Industrialism and the American Worker, 1865–1920*. Arlington Heights, Ill.: AHM Publishing, 1975.

Dubose, John Witherspoon. *Jefferson County and Birmingham, Alabama: Historical and Biographical*. Birmingham: Teeple and Smith, Publications, 1887.

Duis, Perry. *The Saloon: Public Drinking in Chicago and Boston, 1880–1920*. Urbana: University of Illinois Press, 1983.

Edwards, Richard C. *Contested Terrain: The Transformation of the Workplace in the Twentieth Century*. New York: Basic Books, 1979.

Ewen, Stuart. *Captains of Consciousness: Advertising and the Social Roots of the Consumer Culture*. New York: McGraw-Hill, 1976.

Fitch, John A. *The Steel Workers*. 1911. Reprint. Pittsburgh: University of Pittsburgh Press, 1989.

Flamming, Douglas. *Creating the Modern South: Millhands and Managers in Dalton, Georgia, 1884–1984*. Chapel Hill: University of North Carolina Press, 1992.

Flynn, Charles L. *White Land, Black Labor: Caste and Class in Late Nineteenth-Century Georgia*. Baton Rouge: Louisiana State University Press, 1983.

Flynt, Wayne. *Mine, Mill, and Microchip: A Chronicle of Alabama Enterprise*. Northridge, Calif.: Windsor Publishing, 1987.

——— . *Poor but Proud: Alabama's Poor Whites*. Tuscaloosa: University of Alabama Press, 1989.

Foner, Eric. *Free Soil, Free Labor, Free Men: The Ideology of the Republican Party before the Civil War*. New York: Oxford University Press, 1970.

——— . *Reconstruction: America's Unfinished Revolution, 1863–1877*. New York: Harper and Row, 1988.

Foner, Philip S. *Organized Labor and the Black Worker, 1619–1981*. New York: International Publishers, 1981.

Fredrickson, George M. *The Arrogance of Race: Historical Perspectives on Slavery, Racism, and Social Inequality*. Middletown, Conn.: Wesleyan University Press, 1988.

——— . *The Black Image in the White Mind: The Debate on Afro-American Character and Destiny, 1877–1914*. New York: Harper and Row, 1971.

——— . *White Supremacy: A Comparative Study in American and South African History*. Oxford: Oxford University Press, 1981.

Gartman, David. *Auto Slavery: The Labor Process in the American Automobile Industry, 1897–1950*. New Brunswick: Rutgers University Press, 1986.

Genovese, Eugene. *Roll, Jordan, Roll: The World the Slaves Made*. New York: Vintage Books, 1976.

Gordon, David M., Richard Edwards, and Michael Reich. *Segmented Work, Divided Workers: The Historical Transformation of Labor in the United States*. Cambridge: Cambridge University Press, 1982.

Grantham, Dewey W. *The Life and Death of the Solid South: A Political History*. Lexington: University of Kentucky Press, 1988.

——— . *Southern Progressivism: The Reconciliation of Progress and Tradition*. Knoxville: University of Tennessee Press, 1983.

Greenberg, Brian. *Worker and Community: Response to Industrialization in a Nineteenth-Century American City, Albany, New York*. Albany: State University of New York Press, 1985.

Greenberg, Stanley. *Race and State in Capitalist Development*. New Haven: Yale University Press, 1980.

Greene, Lorenzo J., and Carter G. Woodson. *The Negro Wage Earner*. New York: Van Rees Press, 1930.

Gutman, Herbert. *The Black Family in Slavery and Freedom, 1750–1925*. New York: Pantheon Books, 1976.

——— . *Work, Culture, and Society in Industrializing America: Essays in American Working-Class and Social History*. New York: Vintage Books, 1977.

Guttmann, Allen. *A Whole New Ball Game: An Interpretation of American Sports*. Chapel Hill: University of North Carolina Press, 1988.

Hackney, Sheldon. *Populism to Progressivism in Alabama*. Princeton: Princeton University Press, 1969.

Hall, Jacquelyn Dowd, James Leloudis, Robert Korstad, Mary Murphy, Lu Ann Jones, and Christopher B. Daly. *Like a Family: The Making of a Southern Cotton Mill World*. Chapel Hill: University of North Carolina Press, 1987.

Hamilton, Virginia Van Der Veer. *Hugo Black: The Alabama Years*. Baton Rouge: Louisiana State University Press, 1972.

Hareven, Tamara K. *Family Time and Industrial Time: The Relationship between the Family and Work in a New England Industrial Community*. Cambridge: Cambridge University Press, 1982.

Harris, Carl. *Political Power in Birmingham, 1871–1921*. Knoxville: University of Tennessee Press, 1977.

Harris, Marvin. *The Problem of Race in the Americas*. New York: Walker, 1964.

Hart, Hastings N. *Social Problems of Alabama*. Montgomery: n.p., 1918.

Haydu, Jeffrey. *Between Craft and Class: Skilled Workers and Factory Politics in the United States, 1890–1922*. Berkeley: University of California Press, 1988.

Hill, Herbert. *Black Labor and the American Legal System: Race, Work, and the Law*. Madison: University of Wisconsin Press, 1985.

Hobsbawm, Eric. *Workers: Worlds of Labor*. New York: Pantheon Books, 1984.

Hogan, William T. *Economic History of the Iron and Steel Industry in the United States*. Vol. 2, pt. 3. Toronto: D. C. Heath, 1971.

Hyman, Michael R. *The Anti-Redeemers: Hill-Country Political Dissenters in the Lower South from Redemption to Populism*. Baton Rouge: Louisiana State University Press, 1990.

Jackson, Kenneth T. *The Ku Klux Klan in the City, 1915–1930*. New York: Oxford University Press, 1967.

Jacoby, Sanford M. *Employing Bureaucracy: Managers, Unions, and the Transformation of Work in American Industry, 1900–1945*. New York: Columbia University Press, 1985.

Jeans, J. Stephen, ed. *American Industrial Conditions and Competition*. London: Office of the British Iron Trade Association, 1902.

Katznelson, Ira. *City Trenches: Urban Politics and the Patterning of Class in the United States*. New York: Pantheon Books, 1981.

Kennedy, David. *Over Here: The First World War and American Society*. Oxford: Oxford University Press, 1980.

King, Martin Luther, Jr. *Why We Can't Wait*. New York: Mentor, 1963.

Kleppner, Paul. *The Third Electoral System, 1853–1892: Parties, Voters, and Political Cultures*. Chapel Hill: University of North Carolina Press, 1979.

Koditschek, Theodore. *Class Formation and Urban-Industrial Society: Bradford, 1750–1850*. Cambridge: Cambridge University Press, 1990.

Kraditor, Aileen S. *The Radical Persuasion: Aspects of the Intellectual History and Historiography of Three American Radical Organizations*. Baton Rouge: Louisiana State University Press, 1981.

La Monte, Edward S. *George B. Ward: Birmingham's Urban Statesman*. Birmingham: Birmingham Public Library, 1974.

Laurie, Bruce. *Artisans into Workers: Labor in Nineteenth-Century America*. New York: Noonday Press, 1989.

Luraghi, Raimondo. *The Rise and Fall of the Plantation South*. New York: New Viewpoints, 1978.

Marks, Carole. *Farewell—We're Good and Gone: The Great Black Migration*. Bloomington: Indiana University Press, 1989.

Mintz, Steven, and Susan Kellogg. *Domestic Revolutions: A Social History of American Family Life*. New York: Free Press, 1988.

Montgomery, David. *Beyond Equality: Labor and the Radical Republicans, 1862–1872*. New York: Alfred A. Knopf, 1967.

———. *The Fall of the House of Labor: The Workplace, the State, and American Labor Activism*. Cambridge: Cambridge University Press, 1987.

Murphy, Edgar Gardner. *Basis of Ascendancy*. New York: Longmans, Green, 1909.

———. *Problems of the Present South*. New York: Longmans, Green, 1909.

Nelson, Daniel. *Managers and Workers: Origins of the New Factory System in the United States, 1880–1920*. Madison: University of Wisconsin Press, 1975.

Newby, I. A. *Plain Folk in the New South: Social Change and Cultural Persistence, 1880–1915*. Baton Rouge: Louisiana State University Press, 1989.

Noble, Henry Jeffers. *History of the Cast Iron Pressure Pipe Industry in the United States of America*. New York: Newcomen Society, 1940.

Norrell, Robert J. *James Bowron: The Autobiography of a New South Industrialist*. Chapel Hill: University of North Carolina Press, 1991.

Ownby, Ted. *Subduing Satan: Religion, Recreation, and Manhood in the Rural South, 1865–1920*. Chapel Hill: University of North Carolina Press, 1990.

Painter, Nell Irvin. *Standing at Armageddon: The United States, 1877–1919*. New York: W. W. Norton, 1987.

Perkins, Crawford A. *The Industrial History of Ensley, Alabama*. Birmingham: Advance Publishing, n.d.

Perlman, Mark. *The Machinists: A Study in American Trade Unionism*. Cambridge: Harvard University Press, 1961.

Perman, Michael. *The Road to Redemption: Southern Politics, 1869–1879*. Chapel Hill: University of North Carolina Press, 1984.

Peterson, Joyce Shaw. *American Automobile Workers, 1900–1933*. Albany: State University of New York Press, 1987.

Phillips, William Battle. *Iron Making in Alabama*. Montgomery: Jas. P. Armstrong, 1896.

Rawick, George P. *The American Slave: A Composite Autobiography*. Westport, Conn.: Greenwood Press, 1972.

Reich, Michael. *Racial Inequality: A Political-Economic Analysis*. Princeton: Princeton University Press, 1981.

Richey, James. *Patternmaking*. Chicago: American School of Correspondence, 1908.

Riley, B. F. *The White Man's Burden*. Chicago: Regan House, 1910.

Robinson, Jesse S. *The Amalgamated Association of Iron, Steel, and Tin Workers*. Johns

Hopkins University Studies in History and Political Science, no. 38. Baltimore: Johns Hopkins University Press, 1920.

Rodgers, Daniel T. *The Work Ethic in Industrializing America, 1850–1920*. Chicago: University of Chicago Press, 1978.

Roediger, David. *The Wages of Whiteness: Race and the Making of the American Working Class*. London: Verso, 1991.

Rogers, William Warren. *The One-Gallused Rebellion: Agrarianism in Alabama, 1865–1896*. Baton Rouge: Louisiana State University Press, 1970.

Rosenzweig, Roy. *Eight Hours for What We Will: Workers and Leisure in an Industrial City, 1870–1920*. Cambridge: Cambridge University Press, 1983.

Ross, Stephen J. *Workers on the Edge: Work, Leisure, and Politics in an Industrial City, 1788–1890*. New York: Columbia University Press, 1983.

Rusinoff, S. E. *Foundry Practice*. Chicago: American Technical Society, 1925.

Sellers, James Benson. *The Prohibition Movement in Alabama, 1702 to 1943*. Chapel Hill: University of North Carolina Press, 1943.

Sennett, Richard. *Families against the City: Middle Class Homes of Industrial Chicago, 1872–1890*. Cambridge: Harvard University Press, 1970.

Shergold, Peter R. *Working-Class Life: The "American Standard" in Comparative Perspective, 1899–1913*. Pittsburgh: University of Pittsburgh Press, 1982.

Shifflett, Crandall A. *Patronage and Poverty in the Tobacco South: Louisa County, Virginia, 1860–1900*. Knoxville: University of Tennessee Press, 1982.

Shore, Laurence. *Southern Capitalists: The Ideological Leadership of an Elite, 1832–1885*. Chapel Hill: University of North Carolina Press, 1986.

Smith, J. Russell. *The Story of Iron and Steel*. New York: D. Appleton-Century, 1934.

Somers, Robert. *The Southern States since the War, 1870–71*. 1871. Reprint. New York: Arno Press, 1973.

Spero, Sterling D., and Abram L. Harris. *The Black Worker: The Negro and the Labor Movement*. Port Washington, N.Y.: Kennikat Press, 1931.

Stampp, Kenneth. *The Peculiar Institution: Slavery in the Antebellum South*. New York: Vintage Books, 1956.

Stott, Richard. *Workers in the Metropolis: Class, Ethnicity and Youth in Antebellum New York City*. Ithaca: Cornell University Press, 1990.

Taeuber, Karl E., and Alma F. Taeuber. *Negroes in Cities: Residential Segregation and Neighborhood Change*. Chicago: Aldine Publishing, 1965.

Taft, Philip. *Organizing Dixie: Alabama Workers in the Industrial Era*. Westport, Conn.: Greenwood Press, 1981.

Temin, Peter. *Iron and Steel in Nineteenth Century America: An Economic Inquiry*. Cambridge: Harvard University Press, 1964.

Thernstrom, Stephen. *Poverty and Progress: Social Mobility in a Nineteenth Century City*. Cambridge: Harvard University Press, 1964.

Thomas, Emory. *The Confederate Nation: 1861–1865*. New York: Harper and Row, 1979.

Thornton, J. Mills. *Politics and Power in a Slave Society: Alabama, 1800–1860*. Baton Rouge: Louisiana State University Press, 1978.

Tindall, George Brown. *The Emergence of the New South, 1913–1945*. Baton Rouge: Louisiana State University Press, 1967.

van den Berghe, Pierre L. *Race and Ethnicity: Essays in Comparative Sociology*. New York: Basic Books, 1970.

Voskuil, Walter H. *Minerals in Modern Industry*. New York: John Wiley and Sons, 1930.

Walker, Clarence. *Deromanticizing Black History: Critical Essays and Reappraisals*. Knoxville: University of Tennessee Press, 1991.

Walkowitz, Daniel J. *Worker City, Company Town: Iron and Cotton Worker Protest in Troy and Cohoes, New York, 1855–1884*. Urbana: University of Illinois Press, 1978.

Ward, Robert David, and William Warren Rogers. *Labor Revolt in Alabama: The Great Strike of 1894*. Tuscaloosa: University of Alabama Press, 1965.

Warren, Kenneth. *The American Steel Industry, 1850–1970: A Geographical Interpretation*. Oxford: Clarendon Press, 1973.

Welter, Rush. *The Mind of America, 1820–1860*. New York: Columbia University Press, 1975.

White, Marjorie L. *Village Creek: An Architectural and Historical Resources Survey of Ensley, East Birmingham, and East Lake, Three Village Creek Neighborhoods*. Birmingham: Birmingham Historical Society, 1985.

Wiebe, Robert H. *The Search for Order, 1877–1920*. New York: Hill and Wang, 1967.

Wiener, Jonathan. *Social Origins of the New South: Alabama, 1860–1885*. Baton Rouge: Louisiana State University Press, 1978.

Wilentz, Sean. *Chants Democratic: New York City and the Rise of the American Working Class, 1788–1850*. New York: Oxford University Press, 1984.

Wilson, William Julius. *The Declining Significance of Race: Blacks and Changing American Institutions*. Chicago: University of Chicago Press, 1978.

Woodward, C. Vann. *Origins of the New South, 1877–1913*. Baton Rouge: Louisiana State University Press, 1951.

Wright, Gavin. *Old South, New South: Revolutions in the Southern Economy since the Civil War*. New York: Basic Books, 1986.

Zunz, Olivier. *The Changing Face of Inequality: Urbanization, Industrial Development, and Immigrants in Detroit, 1880–1920*. Chicago: University of Chicago Press, 1982.

ARTICLES

Alexander, Magnus W. "Waste in Hiring and Discharging Men." *Iron Age* 94 (October 29, 1914): 1032–33.

Anderson, James D. "Education as a Vehicle for the Manipulation of Black Workers." In *Work, Technology and Education: Dissenting Essays in the Intellectual Foundations of American Education*, edited by Walter Feinberg and Henry Rosemont Jr. Urbana: University of Illinois Press, 1975.

Atkins, Leah Rawls. "Feuds, Factions, and Reform: Politics in Early Birmingham." *Alabama Heritage*, Summer 1986, pp. 22–33.

Barnard, William D. "George Huddleston, Sr. and the Political Tradition of Birmingham." *Alabama Review* 36 (October 1983): 243–58.

Berkner, Lutz K. "The Stem Family and the Developmental Cycle of the Peasant Household: An Eighteenth-Century Austrian Example." *American Historical Review* 77 (April 1972): 398–418.

Berlin, Isaiah, and Herbert Gutman. "Natives and Immigrants, Free Men and Slaves: Urban Workingmen in the Antebellum South." *American Historical Review* 88 (December 1983): 1175–1200.

Bigelow, Martha. "Birmingham's Carnival of Crime, 1871–1910." *Alabama Review* 3 (April 1950): 123–33.

Bonacich, Edna. "Abolition, the Extension of Slavery, and the Position of Free Blacks: A Study of Split Labor Markets in the United States, 1830–1863." *American Journal of Sociology* 81 (November 1975): 601–28.

——— . "Advanced Capitalism and Black/White Race Relations in the U.S.: A Split Labor Market Interpretation." *American Sociology Review* 41 (February 1976): 34–51.

——— "A Theory of Ethnic Antagonism: The Split Labor Market." *American Sociology Review* 37 (October 1972): 547–59.

Buttrick, John. "The Inside Contract System." *Journal of Economic History* 12 (Summer 1952): 205–21.

Carsten, Oliver. "Brotherhood and Conflict in Meriden and New Britain Connecticut, 1880–1920." In *Confrontation, Class Consciousness, and the Labor Process*, edited by Michael Hanagan and Charles Stephenson. Westport, Conn.: Greenwood Press, 1986.

Cassity, Michael J. "Modernization and Social Crisis: The Knights of Labor and Midwest Community, 1885–1886." *Journal of American History* 66 (June 1979): 41–61.

Chudacoff, Howard P. "New Branches on the Tree: Household Structure in the Early Stages of the Family Cycle in Worcester, Massachusetts, 1860–1880." In *Themes in the History of the Family*, edited by Tamara K. Hareven. Worcester: American Antiquarian Society, 1978.

Clark, Gregory. "Authority and Efficiency: The Labor Market and the Managerial Revolution of the Late Nineteenth Century." *Journal of Economic History* 44 (December 1984): 1069–83.

Cohen, William. "Negro Involuntary Servitude in the South, 1865–1940." *Journal of Southern History* 42 (February 1976): 31–60.

Couvares, Francis. "The Triumph of Commerce." In *Working-Class America: Essays on Labor, Community, and American Society*, edited by Daniel J. Walkowitz. Urbana: University of Illinois Press, 1983.

Doyle, Don Harrison. "The Social Functions of Voluntary Associations in a Nineteenth-Century American Town." *Social Science History* 1 (Spring 1977): 333–50.

Du Bois, W. E. B. "The Economic Revolution." In *The Negro in the South*, by Booker T. Washington and W. E. B. Du Bois. Philadelphia: George W. Jacobs, 1907.

——— . "The Negro in the Black Belt." *Bulletin of the Department of Labor* 22 (May 1899): 405–15.

Englander, Ernest J. "The Inside Contract System of Production and Organization: A Neglected Aspect of the History of the Firm." *Labor History* 28 (Fall 1987): 429–46.

Eskew, Glenn T. "Demagoguery in Birmingham and the Building of Vestavia." *Alabama Review* 42 (July 1989): 192–217.

Fields, Barbara J. "Ideology and Race in American History." In *Region, Race, and Reconstruction: Essays in Honor of C. Vann Woodward*, edited by J. Morgan Kousser and James M. McPherson. New York: Oxford University Press, 1982.

Fink, Leon. "The New Labor History and the Powers of Historical Pessimism: Consensus, Hegemony, and the Case of the Knights of Labor." *Journal of American History* 75 (June 1988): 115–36.

Fitch, John A. "The Human Side of Large Outputs: Steel and Steel Workers in Six American States." *Survey* 14 (January 6, 1912): 1527–40.

Flynt, Wayne. "Organized Labor, Reform, and Alabama Politics, 1920." *Alabama Review* 23 (July 1970): 163–80.

Ford, Lacy K. "Republican Ideology in a Slave Society: The Political Economy of John C. Calhoun." *Journal of Southern History* 54 (August 1988): 405–24.

Fuller, Justin. "Boom Towns and Blast Furnaces: Town Promotion in Alabama, 1885–1893." *Alabama Review* 29 (January 1976): 37–48.

Galloway, D. F. "Machine-Tools." In *A History of Technology*. Vol. 5, *The Late Nineteenth Century, 1850–1900*, edited by Charles Singer, E. J. Holmyard, A. R. Hall, and Trevor I. Williams. Oxford: Clarendon Press, 1958.

Gelber, Steven M. "Working at Playing: The Culture of the Workplace and the Rise of Baseball." *Journal of Social History* 16 (Summer 1983): 3–22.

Goldin, Claudia. "Family Strategies and the Family Economy in the Late Nineteenth Century: The Role of Secondary Workers." In *Philadelphia: Work, Space, Family, and Group Experience in the Nineteenth Century*, edited by Theodore Hershberg. New York: Oxford University Press, 1981.

———. "Female Labor Force Participation: The Origin of Black and White Differences, 1870 and 1880." *Journal of Economic History* 37 (1977): 87–108.

Gutman, Herbert. "The Negro and the United Mine Workers." In *Work, Culture, and Society in Industrializing America: Essays in American Working-Class and Social History*, by Herbert Gutman. New York: Vintage Books, 1977.

Hareven, Tamara, and John Modell. "Urbanization and the Malleable Household: An Examination of Boarding and Lodging in American Families." In *Family and Kin in Urban Communities, 1700–1930*, edited by Tamara K. Hareven. New York: New Viewpoints, 1977.

Harris, Carl V. "Stability and Change in Discrimination against Black Public Schools: Birmingham, Alabama, 1871–1931." *Journal of Southern History* 51 (August 1985): 379–416.

Haydu, Jeffrey. "Employers, Unions, and American Exceptionalism: Pre–World War I Open Shops in the Machine Trades in Comparative Perspective." *International Review of Social History* 18 (1988): 25–41.

Hays, Samuel P. "The Politics of Reform in Municipal Government in the Progressive Era." In *The American Past: Conflicting Interpretations of the Great Issues*. Vol. 2, edited by Sidney Fine and Gerald S. Brown. New York: Macmillan, 1976.

Hill, Herbert. "Myth-Making as Labor History: Herbert Gutman and the United Mine Workers of America." *International Journal of Politics, Culture and Society* 2 (Winter 1988): 132–200.

———. "Race, Ethnicity and Organized Labor: The Opposition to Affirmative Action." *New Politics* 5 (Winter 1987): 31–82.

Jensen, Richard J. "The Causes and Cures of Unemployment in the Great Depression." *Journal of Interdisciplinary History* 19 (Spring 1989): 553–83.

Katznelson, Ira. "Working-Class Formation: Constructing Cases and Comparisons."
In *Working-Class Formation: Nineteenth-Century Patterns in Western Europe and the
United States*, edited by Ira Katznelson and Aristide R. Zolberg. Princeton: Princeton
University Press, 1986.

Kazin, Michael, and Stephen J. Ross. "America's Labor Day: The Dilemma of a
Workers' Celebration." *Journal of American History* 78 (March 1992): 1294–1323.

Kelley, Robin D. G. "'We Are Not What We Seem': Rethinking Black Working-Class
Opposition in the Jim Crow South." *Journal of American History* 80 (June 1993):
75–112.

Kingsdale, John M. "The 'Poor Man's Club': Social Functions of the Urban Working-
Class Saloon." *American Quarterly* 25 (October 1973): 472–89.

Kleinberg, Susan J. "The Systematic Study of Urban Women." In *Class, Sex, and the
Woman Worker*, edited by Milton Cantor and Bruce Laurie. Westport, Conn.: Greenwood Press, 1977.

Knapp, Virginia. "William Phineas Brown, Business and Pioneer Mine Operator of
Alabama." *Alabama Review* 3 (April 1950): 108–22.

———. "William Phineas Brown, Business and Pioneer Mine Operator of Alabama,
Part II." *Alabama Review* 4 (July 1950): 193–99.

Kulik, Gary. "Black Workers and Technological Change in the Birmingham Iron Industry, 1881–1931." In *Southern Workers and Their Unions, 1880–1975: Selected Papers,
the Second Southern Labor History Conference, 1978*, edited by Merl E. Reed, Leslie S.
Hough, and Gary M. Fink. Westport, Conn.: Greenwood Press, 1978.

Licht, Walter. "Labor and Capital in the American Community." *Journal of Urban
History* 7 (February 1981): 219–38.

McCurry, Stephanie. "The Two Faces of Republicanism: Gender and Proslavery Politics in Antebellum South Carolina." *Journal of American History* 79 (March 1992):
1245–64.

McKenzie, Robert H. "Horace Ware: Alabama Iron Pioneer." *Alabama Review* 26 (July
1973): 157–72.

———. "Reconstruction of the Alabama Iron Industry, 1865–1880." *Alabama Review*
25 (July 1972): 178–91.

McLaughlin, Virginia Yans. "Patterns of Work and Family Organization: Buffalo's Italians." In *The Family in History*, edited by Theodore K. Rabb and Robert I. Rotberg.
New York: Harper and Row, 1971.

Miller, Randall M. "Daniel Pratt's Industrial Urbanism: The Cotton Mill Town in
Antebellum Alabama." *Alabama Historical Quarterly* 34 (Spring 1972): 5–35.

Modell, John. "Patterns of Consumption, Acculturation, and Family Income Strategies
in Late Nineteenth-Century America." In *Family and Population in Nineteenth Century
America*, edited by Tamara K. Hareven and Maris A. Vinovskis. Princeton: Princeton
University Press, 1978.

Montgomery, David. "Labor and the Republic in Industrial America: 1860–1920." *Le
Mouvement Social* 3 (April–June 1980): 201–15.

———. "Whose Standards? Workers and the Reorganization of Production in the
United States, 1900–20." In *Workers' Control in America: Studies in the History of*

Work, Technology, and Labor Struggles, by David Montgomery. Cambridge: Cambridge University Press, 1979.

Norrell, Robert J. "Caste in Steel: Jim Crow Careers in Birmingham, Alabama." *Journal of American History* 73 (December 1986): 669–94.

Nuwer, Michael. "From Batch to Flow: Production Technology and Work-Force Skills in the Steel Industry, 1880–1920." *Technology and Culture* 29 (October 1988): 808–38.

Oestreicher, Richard. "Urban Working-Class Political Behavior and Theories of American Electoral Politics, 1870–1940." *Journal of American History* 74 (March 1988): 1257–86.

Powers, Madelon. "Decay from Within: The Inevitable Doom of the American Saloon." In *Drinking: Behavior and Belief in Modern History*, edited by Susanna Barrows and Robin Room. Berkeley: University of California Press, 1981.

Rikard, Marlene. "George Gordon Crawford: Man of the New South." *Alabama Review* 31 (July 1978): 163–81.

Shefter, Martin. "Trade Unions and Political Machines: The Organization and Dis-organization of the American Working Class in the Late Nineteenth Century." In *Working-Class Formation: Nineteenth-Century Patterns in Western Europe and the United States*, edited by Ira Katznelson and Aristide R. Zolberg. Princeton: Princeton University Press, 1986.

Smith, Judith E. "The Transformation of Family and Community Culture in Immigrant Neighborhoods, 1900–1940." In *The New England Working Class and the New Labor History*, edited by Herbert G. Gutman and Donald Bell. Urbana: University of Illinois Press, 1987.

Smith, Merritt Roe. "Industry, Technology, and the 'Labor Question' in 19th-Century America: Seeking Synthesis." *Technology and Culture* 32 (July 1991): 555–70.

Snell, William R. "Masked Men in the Magic City: Activities of the Revised Klan in Birmingham, 1916–1940." *Alabama Historical Quarterly* 34 (Fall and Winter 1972): 206–27.

Speakes, J. W. "Southern Industry Spiritual Movement, Creating a New People." *Manufacturers' Record*, December 11, 1924, pp. 197–98.

Stanley, C. M. "Birmingham in 1901." *Journal of the Birmingham Historical Society* 2 (January 1961): 15–17.

Stecker, Mary Loomis. "The Founders, the Molders, and the Molding Machine." *Quarterly Journal of Economics* 32 (February 1918): 278–308.

Stein, Judith. "Southern Workers in National Unions: Birmingham Steelworkers, 1936–1951." In *Organized Labor in the Twentieth Century South*, edited by Robert H. Zieger. Knoxville: University of Tennessee Press, 1991.

Stockton, Frank T. "Membership in the Molders' Union." *International Molders' Journal* 52 (August 1916): 685–86.

———. "The Molders' Union and the Negro." *International Molders' Journal* 51 (August 1915): 588.

Stone, Katherine. "The Origins of Job Structures in the Steel Industry." In *Labor Market Segmentation*, edited by Richard C. Edwards, Michael Reich, and David M. Gordon. Lexington: D. C. Heath, 1973.

Stromquist, Shelton. "Enginemen and Shopmen: Technological Change and the Organization of Labor in an Era of Railroad Expansion." *Labor History* 24 (Fall 1983): 485–99.

Taylor, Graham Romeyn. "Birmingham's Civic Front." *Survey* 27 (January 6, 1912): 1464–70.

Thomas, Rebecca L. "John J. Eagan and Industrial Democracy at ACIPCO." *Alabama Review* 43 (October 1990): 270–89.

Vandiver, Frank. "The Shelby Iron Company in the Civil War: A Study of a Confederate Industry." *Alabama Review* 1 (January 1948): 12–26.

———. "The Shelby Iron Company in the Civil War: A Study of a Confederate Industry, Part II." *Alabama Review* 1 (April 1948): 110–27.

———. "The Shelby Iron Company in the Civil War: A Study of a Confederate Industry, Part III." *Alabama Review* 1 (July 1948): 203–17.

Washington, Booker T. "The Atlanta Exposition Address." In *Words That Made American History*. Vol. 2, edited by Richard N. Current, John A. Garraty, and Julius Weinberg. Boston: Little, Brown, 1978.

———. "The Economic Development of the Negro Race since Emancipation." In *The Negro in the South*, by Booker T. Washington and W. E. B. Du Bois. Philadelphia: George W. Jacobs, 1907.

———. "The Negro and the Labor Unions." *Atlantic Monthly*, June 1913, pp. 756–66.

White, Marjorie Longnecher. "Glen Iris Park and the Residence of Robert Jemison, Sr." *Journal of the Birmingham Historical Society* 6 (July 1979): 5–7.

Williams, Rhonda M. "Capital, Competition, and Discrimination: A Reconsideration of Racial Earnings Inequality." *Review of Radical Political Economics* 19 (Fall 1987): 1–13.

Woodward, Joseph H., II. "Alabama Iron Manufacturing, 1860–1865." *Alabama Review* 71 (July 1984): 199–207.

Worthman, Paul. "Black Workers and Labor Unions in Birmingham, 1897–1904." In *Black Labor in America*, edited by Milton Cantor. Westport, Conn.: Negro University Press, 1969.

———. "Working Class Mobility in Birmingham, Alabama, 1880–1914." In *Anonymous Americans: Explorations in Nineteenth Century Social History*, edited by Tamara K. Hareven. Englewood Cliffs, N.J.: Prentice Hall, 1971.

Zahavi, Gerald. "Negotiated Loyalty: Welfare Capitalism and the Shoeworkers of Endicott Johnson, 1920–1940." *Journal of American History* 70 (December 1983): 602–20.

THESES, DISSERTATIONS, AND UNPUBLISHED MANUSCRIPTS

Abernathy, John H. "The Knights of Labor in Alabama." Master's thesis, University of Alabama, 1960.

Bell, Robert K. "Reconstruction in Tuscaloosa, Alabama." Master's thesis, University of Alabama, 1933.

Clark, James Harold. "History of the North East and South West Alabama Railroad to 1872." Master's thesis, University of Alabama, 1949.

Flamming, Doug. "The Creation of an Industrial Community: The Crown Cotton Mills of Dalton, Georgia, 1884–1940." Ph.D. diss., Vanderbilt University, 1987.

Fuller, Justin. "History of the Tennessee Coal, Iron, and Railroad Company, 1852–1907." Ph.D. diss., University of North Carolina, 1966.

Gilmour, Robert Arthur. "The Other Emancipation: Studies in the Society and Economy of Alabama Whites during Reconstruction." Ph.D. diss., Johns Hopkins University, 1972.

Goldstein, Harold Joseph. "Labor Unrest in the Birmingham District, 1871–1899." Master's thesis, University of Alabama, 1951.

Head, Holman. "The Development of the Labor Movement in Alabama prior to 1900." Master's thesis, University of Alabama, 1955.

Kulik, Gary. "The Sloss Furnace Company, 1881–1931: Technological Change and Labor Supply in the Southern Pig Iron Industry." Birmingham, n.d. Typescript.

McKiven, Henry M., Jr. "A Community in Crisis: Birmingham during the Great Strike of 1894." Paper presented at the Citadel Conference on the History of the South, Charleston, S.C., April 1987.

Mitchell, Martha Carolyn. "Birmingham: Biography of a City of the New South." Ph.D. diss., University of Chicago, 1946.

Norrell, Robert J. "Steelworkers and Storekeepers: Social Mobility among Italian Immigrants in Birmingham." Birmingham, n.d. Typescript.

Rikard, Marlene. "An Experiment in Welfare Capitalism: The Health Care Services of the Tennessee Coal, Iron, and Railroad Company." Ph.D. diss., University of Alabama, 1983.

Rutledge, Sumner. "An Economic and Social History of Antebellum Jefferson County, Alabama." Master's thesis, University of Alabama, 1939.

Sisk, Glenn N. "Alabama Black Belt: A Social History, 1875–1917." Ph.D. diss., Duke University, 1950.

Sterne, Ellin. "Prostitution in Birmingham, 1890–1925." Master's thesis, Samford University, 1977.

Ware, Henry T. "Field Experience in the YMCA Graduate School for Spring Quarter, Beginning March 21 and Ending June 2, 1928." N.p., n.d. Typescript.

INDEX

Adams, Oscar W., 110
Alabama Federation of Labor: policy toward blacks, 50, 125
Aldrich, Truman: and creation of Pratt Coal and Coke Company, 12; on early labor problem, 16; on black labor, 29
Alexander, Magnus W., 117
Amalgamated Association of Iron and Steel Workers: recruiting of workers, 19; governance of shop floor, 27–29; and hiring of blacks, 29; conflict at Birmingham Rolling Mill, 31–36; recovery in the 1890s, 39
American Cast Iron Pipe Company: production innovations, 97; employee welfare program, 115–17, 128–31; education reform, 120–21; worker housing, 137; social work and recreational program, 139–41
American Federation of Labor: policy toward blacks, 50; strikes during World War I, 105; National Committee for the Organization of Iron and Steel Workers, 110
Antiboycott legislation, 103–4
Anti-Saloon League, 147
Avondale Iron Works, 19
Avondale Stove Foundry: strike at, 104

Bacon, Don, 98; and employee benefits, 116
Baldwin, W. H., 118–19
Barber, Arlie, 151; in 1915 city commission race, 161
Barrett, Nathaniel A.: in 1917 city election, 162; term as president of city commission, 162–63

Bascomb, L. B.: as principal of the Negro ACIPCO School, 121
Baxter, Nat: on shortage of unskilled labor in 1886, 50
Beggs, Hamilton T.: and Shelby Iron Company, 10; builder of Beggs Foundry, 17, 21
Beggs Pipe Foundry, 57
Bethel Baptist Church, 146
Birmingham Citizens' Alliance, 99–100, 156
Birmingham Civic Association, 161
Birmingham Machine and Foundry: 1918 strike, 105–7
Birmingham Metal Trades Council: 1918 strike, 106–8,
Birmingham Pastors Union, 147
Birmingham Rolling Mill Company: established, 12; labor problems in the 1880s, 31–36; worker housing, 56
Birmingham Trades Union Council: established, 39, 153–54; and child labor legislation, 155; opposition to city commission, 158–59
Boggan, M. M.: arrest of, 85
Bond, Horace Mann: on racial division of work, 4
Bowron, James, 108; on worker drinking, 148
Brotherhood of Boilermakers: racial policies, 29–30
Bush, T. G.: defense of open shop, 100

Caldwell, W. B.: finances Birmingham Rolling Mill Company, 12; and labor problems in the 1880s, 31–36

International Correspondence Schools, 120

International Iron Molders Union, 39: organization of blacks, 125

International Union of Mine, Mill, and Smelter Workers, 126–27

Iron breakers: work described, 47

Johnson, Randolph: on move to Birmingham, 46

King, B. W., 109

King, Henry, 109

Knights of Labor, 37–40; blacks and, 50, 52; and working-class housing, 60; politics of, 78–81

Ku Klux Klan, 44; political influence, 163–64

Labor forward movement, 125–26

Labor Party of Alabama, 80–81; and blacks, 81

Labor recruiters: in Black Belt, 43–44; 1879 law to restrict, 44

Lapsley, John W.: investor in Shelby Iron Company, 10; on black workers, 42, 48; and worker education, 117

Law and Order League, 74–75

Lesser, Emil: and building of Powderly and Trevillik, 61

Lewis, B. B.: vice president of Central Iron Works, 18

Lipscomb, J. A., 109

Lloyd, D. H.: migration to Birmingham, 19–20

Louisville and Nashville Railroad: interest in creation of Birmingham, 10; strike against, 104

Lowe, R. G., 81

McCrossin, W. P., 85

McElwain, W. S.: and Cahaba Iron Works, 9

Machinist: work described, 26–27, 96

McQueen, J. W., 105, 110

McWane, James R., 129

Majority Clubs, 155–56

Milner, John T.: survey for South and North Railroad, 8–9; and Red Mountain Iron and Coal Company; 14–15; on black workers, 42; campaign for state senate, 80–81

Molders: work described, 25–26

Moral reform, 72–75

Morgan, John: on shortage of agricultural labor, 44

Morris, Josiah: investment in Elyton Land Company, 10–11

Mt. Ararat Baptist Church, 146

Movies: movement to restrict, 150–52

Municipal Democratic Club, 154

Murphy, Edgar Gardner, 118–19

Musgrove, L. B., 164

Mutual Land and Improvement Company: creation of Powderly, 60

National Association of Machinists: racial policies, 30

National Metal Trades Association, 100

O'Connell, James: criticism of open shop movement, 101

Open hearth steel, 92–94; impact on structure of the workforce, 94–96

Ore mining: described, 47

Oxmoor, Alabama, 9

Parker, Arthur H., 121

Parry, D. M., 100

Patternmakers: work described, 25–26

Patternmakers League, 39; 1918 strike, 105

Percy, Walker: and campaign for creation of a city commission, 158–59

Pettiford, W. R.: on black work habits, 48–49; and education, 121

Pettyjohn, L. G.: and strike at Birmingham Rolling Mill Company, 32–33

Phillips, John Herbert, 120

Wadsworth, F. L.: on labor turnover at the Alice Furnace Company, 49

Ward, George: fight against political corruption, 157–58; in 1913 city commission race, 160–61

Ware, Horace: and Shelby Iron Company, 9–10

Ware, John: on black workers, 43

War Labor Board, 108

Warnock, Robert, 81, 85; campaign for mayor, 86–87

Welsh, Isaiah, 30

Williams, David U.: migration to Birmingham, 20; on organizing black workers, 125; as member of City Democratic Party Executive Committee, 157

Williamson, C. P.: manager of Linn Iron Works, 12–13; strike at his foundry, 38

Wilson, William B., 108–9

Wood, Clement: attacks on the city commission, 159–61

Wood, J. B., 151

Woodward Iron Company, 12, 98

Workingmen's Democratic Social Club, 82

Worthman, Paul, 2–3

Wright, Gavin, 3–4